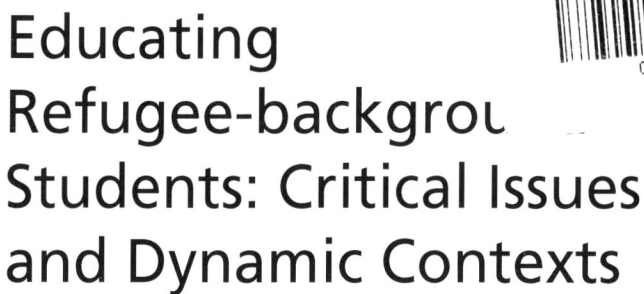

Educating Refugee-background Students: Critical Issues and Dynamic Contexts

NEW PERSPECTIVES ON LANGUAGE AND EDUCATION

Series Editor: Professor Viv Edwards, *University of Reading, UK* and Professor Phan Le Ha, *University of Hawaii at Manoa, USA*

Two decades of research and development in language and literacy education have yielded a broad, multidisciplinary focus. Yet education systems face constant economic and technological change, with attendant issues of identity and power, community and culture. This series will feature critical and interpretive, disciplinary and multidisciplinary perspectives on teaching and learning, language and literacy in new times.

All books in this series are externally peer-reviewed.

Full details of all the books in this series and of all our other publications can be found on http://www.multilingual-matters.com, or by writing to Multilingual Matters, St Nicholas House, 31-34 High Street, Bristol BS1 2AW, UK.

NEW PERSPECTIVES ON LANGUAGE AND EDUCATION: 59

Educating Refugee-background Students
Critical Issues and Dynamic Contexts

Edited by
Shawna Shapiro, Raichle Farrelly and Mary Jane Curry

MULTILINGUAL MATTERS
Bristol • Blue Ridge Summit

DOI https://doi.org/10.21832/SHAPIR9979
Library of Congress Cataloging in Publication Data
A catalog record for this book is available from the Library of Congress.
Names: Shapiro, Shawna, 1978- editor. | Farrelly, Raichle, editor. | Curry, Mary Jane, editor.
Title: Educating Refugee-background Students: Critical Issues and Dynamic Contexts/Edited by Shawna Shapiro, Raichle Farrelly and Mary Jane Curry.
Description: Bristol, UK; Blue Ridge Summit: Multilingual Matters, [2018] | Series: New Perspectives on Language and Education: 59 | Includes bibliographical references and index.
Identifiers: LCCN 2017060996| ISBN 9781783099962 (pbk : alk. paper) | ISBN 9781783099979 (hbk : alk. paper) | ISBN 9781788920001 (kindle) | ISBN 9781783099986 (pdf) | ISBN 9781783099993 (epub)
Subjects: LCSH: Refugees--Education--Case studies.
Classification: LCC LC3715 .E376 2018 | DDC 371.826/914--dc23 LC record available at https://lccn.loc.gov/2017060996

British Library Cataloguing in Publication Data
A catalogue entry for this book is available from the British Library.

ISBN-13: 978-1-78309-997-9 (hbk)
ISBN-13: 978-1-78309-996-2 (pbk)

Multilingual Matters
UK: St Nicholas House, 31-34 High Street, Bristol BS1 2AW, UK.
USA: NBN, Blue Ridge Summit, PA, USA.

Website: www.multilingual-matters.com
Twitter: Multi_Ling_Mat
Facebook: https://www.facebook.com/multilingualmatters
Blog: www.channelviewpublications.wordpress.com

Copyright © 2018 Shawna Shapiro, Raichle Farrelly, Mary Jane Curry and the authors of individual chapters.

All rights reserved. No part of this work may be reproduced in any form or by any means without permission in writing from the publisher.

The policy of Multilingual Matters/Channel View Publications is to use papers that are natural, renewable and recyclable products, made from wood grown in sustainable forests. In the manufacturing process of our books, and to further support our policy, preference is given to printers that have FSC and PEFC Chain of Custody certification. The FSC and/or PEFC logos will appear on those books where full certification has been granted to the printer concerned.

Typeset by Deanta Global Publishing Services Limited.
Printed and bound by CPI Group (UK) Ltd, Croydon, CR0 4YY

Contents

List of Tables vii

List of Figures viii

Acknowledgments ix

Contributors xi

   Introduction 1
   Shawna Shapiro

   Part 1: Language and Literacy

1 Recently Resettled Refugee Students Learning English in US High Schools: The Impact of Students' Educational Backgrounds 17
   Christopher T. Browder

2 'History Should Come First': Perspectives of Somali-born, Refugee-background Male Youth on Writing in and out of School 33
   Bryan Ripley Crandall

3 Translanguaging Pedagogy to Support the Language Learning of Older Nepali-Bhutanese Adults 49
   Koeun Park and Verónica E. Valdez

4 Girls with Refugee Backgrounds Creating Digital Landscapes of Knowing 66
   Delila Omerbašić

5 Sociocultural Literacy Practices of a Sudanese Mother and Son in Canada 82
   Katerina Nakutnyy and Andrea Sterzuk

6 Narratives of Trauma and Self-healing Processes in a Literacy Program for Adolescent Refugee Newcomers 92
   M. Kristiina Montero

7	The Role of English as a Foreign Language in Educating Refugees in Norway *Anne Dahl, Anna Krulatz and Eivind Nessa Torgersen*	107

Part 2: Access and Equity

8	Bridges and Barriers: Karen Refugee-background Students' Transition to High School in Australia *Amanda Hiorth and Paul Molyneux*	125
9	Educating Refugees through 'Citizenship Classes and Tests': Integration by Coercion or Autonomous Agency? *Amadu Khan*	144
10	Using Photovoice with Cambodian and Guatemalan Youth to Uncover Community Cultural Wealth and Influence Policy Change *Erin L. Papa*	159
11	Swedish Teachers' Understandings of Post-traumatic Stress Disorder among Adult Refugee-background Learners *Eva Holmkvist, Kirk P.H. Sullivan and Asbjørg Westum*	177
12	Education of Refugee-background Youth in Germany: Systemic Barriers to Equitable Participation in the Vocational Education System *Annette Korntheuer, Maren Gag, Phillip Anderson and Joachim Schroeder*	191
13	Iraqi Refugee-background Adolescents' Experiences in Schools: Using the Ecological Theory of Development to Understand Discrimination *Amy Pucino*	208
14	Besides a Degree, What Do Refugee-background Students Gain from College? *Eliana Hirano*	225
15	Conception Versus Reality: The Impact of Migration Experiences on Children's Educational Participation *Beatrix Bukus*	241
16	Afterword *Martha Bigelow*	256
	Index	260

List of Tables

Table 1.1	Differences between the educational backgrounds of the Chin and other EL students	25
Table 1.2	Bivariate relationships between students' educational backgrounds and English learning	27
Table 2.1	Summary of participants	36
Table 2.2	Summary of data sources	37
Table 10.1	Youth co-researchers' demographic information	163
Table 12.1	Research reports	196
Table 13.1	Interview participant characteristics	213
Table 14.1	The participants	228
Table 14.2	Major areas of growth in college	231
Table 14.3	Major accomplishments in college	233
Table 15.1	Coding tree	245

List of Figures

Figure 2.1	Participants' activity systems influencing perspectives on writing	35
Figure 3.1	Collaborative vocabulary building activity and language awareness	56
Figure 3.2	S4's drawing distinguishing between the terms 'rat' and 'mouse'	58
Figure 3.3	Students' writing illustrating their use of translanguaging	59
Figure 4.1	Elizabeth's use of Romanized Karen in a multimodal composition	73
Figure 4.2	Tait's request for feedback on her drawing	76
Figure 8.1	Lili imagines her social transition to high school	131
Figure 8.2	Hsar Hsar recalls his first day at his new school and his sadness at not having any friends.	132
Figure 8.3	Law Lu Eh depicts his unhappiness at not having any friends on his first day at his new school.	133
Figure 8.4	Moo Dar Eh at her new high school, without a known path to enter the building	135
Figure 8.5	Hsar Hsar imagines his first day at high school.	136
Figure 8.6	Mi Mi Moe depicts common happenings inside the classroom.	138
Figure 10.1	Sending clothes to family in Guatemala	166
Figure 10.2	Ace's attempt to write her name in Khmer	167
Figure 10.3	A multiservice Guatemalan bakery in Eagle City	170
Figure 10.4	The *ksai-see-ma*	172
Figure 15.1	Migration route of participants	246

Acknowledgments

The editors would first like to acknowledge Abla Laallam, Casey Lilley and Maddie Orcutt, who served as research assistants at various stages of this project. Shawna would also like to thank Garrett, Daniel and Mikey, for being a source of joy and inspiration every day. Raichle would like to thank her refugee-background students and colleagues at LESLLA who have inspired her and constantly reminded her why this project is important. Mary Jane wishes to thank Moritz Wagner for his continued support of her work. Thanks to Clare Zuraw for compiling the index.

Contributors

Phillip Anderson is a migration researcher of British origin based in Germany. He received a BA in history from the University of York. He holds a PhD in modern history from the University of Munich. He currently works as a professor of migration and intercultural social work in the Social and Health Sciences Faculty at the University of Applied Sciences in Regensburg, Germany. He provides lectures and seminars for professional practice in the social, educational and migration fields as well as supporting practitioners in an advisory capacity.

Martha Bigelow is a professor in second language education at the University of Minnesota. She has taught Spanish and English as a second language (ESL) and has been working as a teacher educator and consultant in the language education field for 18 years. Dr Bigelow's research focuses on linguistic and cultural processes, inclusive educational practices and policy advocacy for language minority K-12 children, particularly those with a refugee background who are from East Africa.

Christopher T. Browder is a teacher, professional developer and education researcher. He has been teaching English to speakers of other languages (ESOL) since 1993 and has taught in five different countries. He currently manages a US high school ESOL program with over 850 students in an area outside of Washington, DC. He is particularly interested in the role that English learners' educational backgrounds play in their educational achievement in US public schools. He has spoken at conferences and written articles about students with limited and/or interrupted formal education.

Beatrix Bukus (MA education and MA German as a second language) studied the migration–education nexus and trained teachers in Budapest, Bicske, Veszprém, Frankfurt am Main, München, Izmir and Washington, DC. Currently, she teaches a welcome class for migrant pupils at a high school in Leipzig. She also delivers seminars on migration and integration, transcultural learning and language proficiency assessment among learners of German as a second language at the in-service teacher training master program at the University of Leipzig. Her dissertation focuses on the educational careers of school-age children with multiple and multidirectional migration experience.

Bryan Ripley Crandall, PhD, is the director of the Connecticut Writing Project and an assistant professor of English education in the Graduate School of Education and Allied Professions at Fairfield University. He leads teacher institutes and young adult literacy labs, including Ubuntu Academy – a literacy camp for refugee and immigrant youth. His research interests include the teaching of writing, young adult literature, professional development, urban education and youth literacies. Crandall's scholarship-in-action received a 2017 Elizabeth M. Pfriem Civic Leadership Award from the Bridgeport Public Education Fund and a 2018 Divergent Award through the Initiative for Research in 21st Century Literacies.

Anne Dahl is an associate professor of English linguistics at the Department of Language and Literature at NTNU Norwegian University of Science and Technology in Trondheim, Norway. Her research focuses on second and third language acquisition from both theoretical and applied perspectives – in particular, she explores the acquisition of syntactic phenomena, the role of age in language acquisition and the relationship between implicit and explicit learning.

Maren Gag works as a staff member for passage gGmbH in the Department of Migration and International Cooperation in Hamburg, Germany. She has expertise in the management of local, national and transnational projects and networking activities, development studies and approaches in the area of vocational education training and guidance for migrants, refugees and asylum seekers.

Amanda Hiorth completed her doctorate at the University of Melbourne's Graduate School of Education. Her research focuses on educational transition and equitable outcomes for refugee-background English as an additional language (EAL) learners. She has a strong commitment to social justice in her professional and personal life, seeking to improve outcomes for marginalized, minority learners in the mainstream education system. Amanda has taught in the fields of EAL, languages other than English (LOTE) and teacher education at primary, secondary and tertiary levels across Japan and Australia.

Eliana Hirano is an assistant professor of teacher education at Berry College, where she coordinates the minor in teaching English as a foreign language. Her research interests include academic literacies in higher education and learner identity, with a focus on the refugee-background population. Her work can be found in journals such as *ELT Journal*, *Journal of Second Language Writing* and *English for Specific Purposes*.

Eva Holmkvist is a teacher of Swedish as a second language. She has been working with adult immigrants and refugees at different language levels since 2005. She uses a range of learning strategies, and an important source of inspiration for her is suggestopedia. She is particularly interested in language teaching and learning, and literacy development. Her latest teaching challenge is learning to teach blind students. This has made her particularly aware of the importance of how teachers use body language in the classroom. Eva is currently completing her postgraduate training in special education at Umeå University, Sweden.

Amadu Khan is an independent educational researcher and consultant. He has contributed to teaching and research at the University of Edinburgh and Njala University. In addition to conducting research with refugees and asylum seekers in Scotland and other parts of the United Kingdom, Khan is an award-winning human rights journalist and storyteller-performer artist. He is currently senior research fellow at the Nomoli Media Group.

Annette Korntheuer earned a PhD through the Faculty of Psychology and Educational Sciences, Ludwig Maximilian University, Munich, Germany. Her doctoral thesis focused on the educational participation of refugee youth in Munich and Toronto. Dr Korntheuer holds a degree in social work and has international experience working with youth and refugee populations in Germany, Spain, the Philippines and Canada. Currently, she is employed by the City of Munich as educational coordinator for newcomers. Dr Korntheuer collaborates as a lecturer with the Faculty of Social Work and is a member of the executive board of the German network for refugee studies.

Anna Krulatz is an associate professor of English at the Faculty of Teacher Education at the Norwegian University of Science and Technology in Trondheim, Norway, where she works with pre- and in-service English as a foreign language (EFL) teachers. Her research focuses on multilingualism with English, pragmatic development in adult language learners, content-based instruction and language teacher education.

Paul Molyneux is a senior lecturer in language and literacy education in the Graduate School of Education, University of Melbourne, Australia. He teaches pre-service and professional masters' courses and supervises at doctoral level. Paul's research centers on linguistically and culturally diverse students, particularly the transformative potential of bilingual and place-based education for immigrant, refugee and marginalized learners. His doctoral and postdoctoral research has been undertaken within Australia and internationally. He led a longitudinal study of Karen–English bilingual education among refugee-background students in Melbourne, and is currently on a team developing a literacy teaching resource for the Victorian Department of Education and Training.

M. Kristiina Montero, PhD, is an associate professor in the Faculty of Education at Wilfrid Laurier University, Waterloo, Canada. Her research and practice are framed in community-engaged scholarship that aims to use the space of research to engage with practical problems defined by community stakeholders. One of her overarching goals is to give voice to marginalized individuals and communities. Her recent work examines the impact of culturally responsive early literacy instructional practices on the language and literacy development of adolescent English language learners with limited prior schooling, and exploring the use of decolonizing pedagogies in teacher education.

Katerina Nakutnyy (MEd, curriculum and instruction, University of Regina) is an English as an additional language (EAL) high school teacher. She has also taught elementary school for 10 years, taught evening English classes to adult immigrants from Ukraine and tutored both adults and children learning English. In addition, for 11 years, Katerina taught Grades 5 and 6 in a Ukrainian culture and language program. Her MEd thesis was shortlisted for the 2014 Language and Literacy Researchers of Canada Master's Thesis Award.

Delila Omerbašić was born and raised in Sarajevo, Bosnia and Herzegovina, and resettled to the United States as a refugee in the mid-1990s. Her research focuses on language, literacies and education of youth with refugee and immigrant backgrounds in out-of-school contexts. She received her PhD in education, culture and society from the University of Utah and her bachelor's and master's degrees from the University of Pennsylvania.

Erin L. Papa is a dual language facilitator at the Pawtucket School Department. She earned her PhD in education at the University of Rhode Island (URI) and Rhode Island College (RIC) with a research focus on bilingual education access in language-minoritized communities. She holds a master's in teaching English as a second language (TESL) and has taught English to speakers of other languages in the United States, China and Australia. Erin is a past president of the Rhode Island Foreign Language Association (RIFLA) and an associate member of the National Council of State Supervisors for Languages (NCSSFL) in the absence of a language education official at the RI Department of Education.

Koeun Park is a doctoral student in the Department of Education, Culture and Society, a research assistant at the Urban Institute for Teacher Education and a Korean instructor in the Department of World Languages and Cultures within the University of Utah. Her experiences teaching English to students from refugee backgrounds and directing a Korean community heritage language school inform her research interests in the education of linguistically and culturally diverse students. Her areas of interest include bilingual education, heritage language education and teaching English to speakers of other languages (TESOL).

Amy Pucino is an assistant professor of sociology and coordinator of the service-learning program at the Community College of Baltimore County (CCBC). She received her doctorate from the University of Maryland, Baltimore County (UMBC) in the language, literacy and culture program. While completing her degree, she volunteered with the Refugee Youth Project and became committed to understanding schools' roles in the adjustment of migrant students, particularly exploring through research and community work how school policy and practices empower or disempower students. Her research centers on understanding how pedagogical relationships can build student and school agency toward equity for diverse student populations.

Joachim Schroeder is a professor of teaching and didactic methodology for learning impairments within the Faculty of Education at Hamburg University. His research focuses on education, schooling, vocational qualifications, social support and counseling under conditions of poverty and transnational migration. He is a speaker in the PhD program 'Ignored Topics of Refugee Research' coordinated by the University of Hamburg. He is also the co-founder of the German 'Working Group on Education and Flight': see http://fluechtlingsforschung.net/.

Andrea Sterzuk (PhD, second language education, McGill University) is an associate professor of education at the University of Regina. She is currently the president of the Canadian Association of Applied Linguistics. Her research examines issues of power, identity and language in education as they relate to settler colonialism. Her research projects have explored language variation in elementary schools, English-only ideology in higher education, language planning and policy in higher education and the development of language beliefs in pre-service teachers.

Kirk P.H. Sullivan is a professor of linguistics in the Department of Languages at Umeå University, Sweden. He holds a PhD from the University of Southampton, UK, and an EdD from the University of Bristol, UK. His research interests lie at the nexus of linguistics and education, and currently focus on the challenges of language teaching and learning, special educational needs, literacy development, academic writing, multilingualism, indigenous language literacies, doctoral training, distance education and forensic linguistics.

Eivind Nessa Torgersen is a professor of English at the Norwegian University of Science and Technology. He has worked on projects on Multicultural London English and language change in London. In particular, he worked on the modeling of phonological change and the use of spoken corpora in sociolinguistic research. Other research interests include experimental phonetics, multilingualism and second language acquisition.

Verónica E. Valdez is an associate professor at the University of Utah's Department of Education, Culture and Society. Her interdisciplinary research focuses on language learning efforts that foster multilingualism/biliteracy in school and out-of-school contexts; educational language policy and planning and its equity impacts for persons learning English as an additional language; and teacher education and practices that promote the values of multilingualism, multiculturalism and social justice across educational settings. Her work is published in the *Bilingual Research Journal*, *International Multilingual Research Journal*, *The Urban Review*, *International Journal of Qualitative Studies in Education* and *Educational Policy*, among others.

Asbjørg Westum, PhD, is senior lecturer in Scandinavian languages at Jönköping University, Sweden. Her research interests lie mainly in the field of language and culture, where she is currently investigating the emerging learned language in Swedish religious texts of the late Middle Ages. Her more recent interest in adult refugee-background education stems from a growing research interest in literacy development. In the research project Literacy in Sapmi: Multilingualism, revitalization and literacy development in the global north (project leader: Kirk P.H. Sullivan), she explored North Sámi schoolchildren's writing in Sami, English and the national majority languages (Finnish, Norwegian or Swedish).

Introduction

Shawna Shapiro

> While every refugee's story is different and their anguish personal, they all share a common thread of uncommon courage – the courage not only to survive, but to persevere and rebuild their shattered lives.
> António Guterres, United Nations High Commissioner for Refugees

In recent years, refugees and refugee resettlement have come to the forefront of public discourse worldwide. From the high numbers of unaccompanied minors from Latin America arriving in the United States to the mass exodus of Syrians seeking asylum in Europe, questions about the ethics and economics of refugee resettlement are frequently emerging in news reports. Anxieties about migration and resettlement have fueled a rise in anti-establishment and nationalist sentiment among voters in a number of countries. Often, public media employ a framing of 'crisis' in these discussions, rarely considering the question: What happens to former refugees and asylum seekers in the long run? Specifically, how do refugees build new lives after permanent resettlement? Education serves a crucial role in this process and is seen by many individuals and families as a means of cultural adjustment, social mobility and societal integration (Matthews, 2008). While research focused on the education of refugee-background students has been growing (cf. Feuerherm & Ramanathan, 2015; Rutter, 2006), there is still a dearth of scholarship in this area, as documented in reviews by McBrien (2005) and Pinson and Arnot (2007). Moreover, much of the existing research focuses on younger learners in primary grades, rather than on older children and adults (Feuerherm & Ramanathan, 2015; Hannah, 1999). This volume aims to address these gaps in the literature, focusing on the educational experiences of adolescents and adults with refugee backgrounds. To understand who these students are and what their stories might tell us, here we provide some background information about refugees and refugee resettlement.

A *refugee* is defined by international law as a person who

> owing to a well-founded fear of being persecuted for reasons of race, religion, nationality, membership of a particular social group or political opinion, is outside the country of his [or her] nationality, and is unable to, or owing to such fear, is unwilling to avail himself [or herself] of the protection of that country. (United Nations High Commissioner for Refugees, 2011)

While this definition emerged largely as a response to forced migration from Europe due to World War II, in keeping with other goals of the Geneva Convention, eligibility for this legal designation was eventually expanded to include individuals from other areas of the world, whose displacement was the result of other crises (United Nations High Commissioner for Refugees, 2017a).

Much of the coordination, administration and policymaking related to refugees is facilitated by the United Nations High Commissioner for Refugees (UNHCR). *Asylum seekers* – individuals who claim to have left their homes forcibly and are residing temporarily in a host country – must be evaluated by the UNHCR in order to receive the legal designation 'refugee'. While the number of refugees and asylum seekers worldwide fluctuates in parallel with the occurrence of civil unrest, natural disasters and other crises, there has been a sharp rise in recent years, with the number of forcibly displaced peoples currently totaling more than 65 million – the highest number ever recorded – and continuing to rise (United Nations High Commissioner for Refugees, 2017b). While political and military conflicts certainly play an important role in these rising numbers, climate change has also emerged as a major cause of forced migration – one which shows no sign of abating in the near future (Brown, 2008; United Nations High Commissioner for Refugees, 2015).

After receiving the official designation of 'refugee', which allows them to remain temporarily in the country of asylum (also known as a 'host country'), refugees begin the long wait for a more permanent solution. Individuals and families often remain in this 'temporary' state for many years, waiting for one of three possible outcomes: The first is voluntary repatriation, if the conditions in the country of origin have improved sufficiently for refugees to return home safely. A second option is local integration, in which refugees become more integrated into the host country. The final option is resettlement to a third country, with the possibility of obtaining a work visa in the short term, and eventual citizenship in some cases.

A fact little discussed in the popular media is that only a small fraction (around 8% annually) of refugees are determined to be in need of resettlement. To qualify for this option, refugees must belong to one of seven protected categories,[1] all of which preclude the option of repatriation to their country of origin. The number of refugees who are ultimately admitted by receiving countries is significantly lower than the number of those who qualify: less than 1% of all forcibly displaced people are given the opportunity for permanent resettlement. This discrepancy between the need for resettlement and the number of refugees actually resettled stems partly from the limits that most receiving countries place on the number of refugees they are willing to accept. Contrary to some popular beliefs, the application and vetting process for refugee resettlement is onerous and extensive. However, over the past decade, as the number of displaced persons has increased, so has the number of resettled refugees: In 2016, almost 150,000 refugees were resettled via the UNHCR, double the number from 2012 (United Nations High Commissioner for Refugees, 2016).

What happens to refugees after relocation to a third country? This question – particularly as it relates to the education of adolescents and adults – is at the center of this volume. We call this focal population *refugee-background students*, rather than 'refugee students', for several reasons. The first is that the latter term is inaccurate: Once they have relocated permanently – particularly within a resettlement community – these individuals are no longer legally considered refugees, as the term 'refugee' refers to a temporary state of asylum, rather than permanent residence. The label 'refugee students' is more applicable, therefore, to those who are living and studying in temporary host countries, often in refugee camps. The term 'refugee background', in contrast, acknowledges that the refugee condition is typically – and ideally – a short-term label rather than a permanent identity.

Moreover, as educational linguists, we recognize that the term 'refugee' carries a set of discursive connotations that many individuals wish to leave behind after they have relocated to a new community. For many people, the term 'refugee' invokes images of helplessness and victimization, rather than the resilience and agency shown by refugee-background students (MacDonald, 2015; Malkki, 1996; Shapiro, 2014). Not surprisingly, adolescent and adult students are often aware of these connotations and many actively resist labels that carry a deficit orientation (Bigelow, 2010; Roy & Roxas, 2011; Shapiro & MacDonald, 2017). At the same time, experiences of forced migration and resettlement form an important part of many students' stories. We therefore employ the label 'refugee-background' to allude to these experiences, while simultaneously highlighting that being a former 'refugee' is not the only aspect of identity that matters to students – or to us as researchers.

Why Focus on Refugee-background Students?

Much of the educational research in resettlement communities has tended to lump students with migrant backgrounds into one group – for example, 'immigrant and refugee students', 'linguistic minority students' or 'English learners'. We focus on refugee-background students for a few reasons: First, these students' educational backgrounds can vary widely. This variation is a crucial factor in understanding educational outcomes for certain populations (Bigelow & Vinogradov, 2011; DeCapua & Marshall, 2011; Feuerherm & Ramanathan, 2015). While some students may have had access to high-quality – even elite – education before leaving their country of birth, others have had few if any such opportunities and may not have developed print literacy in their home languages, if it exists (Hannah, 1999; McBrien, 2005; see also Browder, this volume). Moreover, the nature and availability of education in host countries (countries of first asylum) also vary a great deal: reports from the UNHCR show that resources for education in most refugee camps are scarce (e.g. Dryden-Peterson, 2011).

The psychological and social effects on students of experiencing civil conflict, forced migration and long-term residence in refugee camps can linger for decades after resettlement (Kanu, 2008; McBrien, 2005). While refugee-background students are not the only immigrant population that has experienced trauma, the prevalence of emotional stress within this group of students is often noted by teachers, counselors and administrators as well as the agencies involved in resettlement (McBrien, 2005; Taylor & Sidhu, 2012). However, in many cases, families, schools and communities respond to trauma by cultivating strategies and resources that promote resilience and high aspiration (e.g. Matthews, 2008; Shapiro & MacDonald, 2017). By focusing on refugee-background students in this volume, we aim to expand this line of inquiry to better understand the effects of trauma and the approaches used to resist these effects.

Finally, and perhaps most important, educational research has rarely engaged directly with the question: To what extent do the educational needs, experiences and assets of refugee-background students differ from those of other immigrant groups? By bringing together research from a variety of geographic and institutional contexts, this collection aims to answer that question.

This book grew out of a panel that Shawna and Mary Jane (editors one and three) convened for the convention of the American Association of Applied Linguistics (AAAL) in March 2015 (in Toronto, Ontario, Canada, entitled 'Current Research on Students with Refugee Backgrounds: Language, Literacy, Culture, and Education'). Both panelists and attendees noted the lack of research volumes on the topic of refugee-background students. We brought Raichle (editor two) on board to help us develop a call for proposals that was distributed widely to a variety of international listservs and organizations. We received dozens of proposals from around the world; from these, we selected proposals that were of the highest quality and that represented a diverse range of contexts and issues. This collection includes work from educational researchers in seven countries, three of which have traditionally been the 'top three' countries for resettlement – the United States, Australia and Canada. The other four are countries where the population of former refugees has been growing in recent years: Germany, Sweden, Norway and the United Kingdom (Scotland). The book also includes chapters presenting analyses from a variety of institutional settings, including public schools, community language/literacy programs and institutions of higher learning.

Our Assumptions

Undergirding the approach taken by the contributors to this volume are several key assumptions. First, that research on refugee-background students has sometimes promoted a deficit perspective, construing refugees as lacking in social, cultural, psychological and linguistic resources, as noted by scholars such as Feuerherm and Ramanathan (2015). Educational research often reinforces this perspective by focusing on themes such as trauma, poverty and illiteracy. While research must take into account these challenges – and indeed, we have referred to them here – this book includes studies that explicitly foreground concepts such as agency, resilience, social capital and other 'funds of knowledge' that refugee-background students, their families and community members bring to schools (Moll *et al.*, 1992; see also Keddie, 2012; Taylor & Sidhu, 2012).

A second key assumption is that education as an enterprise – particularly the education of refugee-background students – is shaped not just by what happens in classrooms, but also by the broader political context of school and society (Matthews, 2008; Pinson & Arnot, 2007; Rutter, 2006). Contributors to this collection therefore acknowledge the contextual factors that inform their analyses, including macro-level social, political and cultural dynamics, as well as local factors, such as school climate and family histories. A final key assumption is that researchers are not neutral observers. We have an ethical responsibility to make explicit our own positionality and to consider the impact of our scholarship on the educational communities within which we work (Ngo *et al.*, 2014). In this regard, when accepting proposals, we asked chapter authors to discuss their biases and assumptions in presenting their analyses. Keeping these assumptions in mind, the chapters collected here not only acknowledge the complexity of the issues at hand, but also present findings in ways that are accessible and relevant for practitioners working with refugee-background students.

Volume Overview

The chapters in this book are grouped under two themes: 'Language and Literacy' and 'Access and Equity'. Below, we discuss the rationale for each theme and the contribution the chapters make toward understandings of the experiences of refugee-background students in relation to that theme. While we hope this clustering allows readers to see threads that extend across chapters in each group, we recognize that there is also a great deal of overlap between the two themes. This overlap is evidenced in particular in the chapters by Dahl, Krulatz and Torgersen, which concludes the first part, and Hiorth and Molyneux, which begins the second part.

Language and Literacy

The umbrella of 'Language and Literacy' includes chapters examining students' development as language users as well as the pedagogical strategies employed in curriculum and instruction with refugee-background students in a variety of educational contexts. One theme running through the chapters in this section is that literacy cannot be studied outside of social and cultural contexts and is always connected to meaning-making. Hence, studying the literacy development of refugee-background students requires considering questions such as: How has forced migration and resettlement shaped students' values and practices in regard to literacy? How are language and literacy practices shaped by institutional, social and cultural contexts? What linguistic resources are often overlooked in traditional academic curricula (e.g. García & Wei, 2014)?

Another issue raised frequently in discussions of language and literacy development for refugee-background students is the variability in students' educational backgrounds (Curry, 2007). Some students may have had limited access to education – not only in countries of first asylum, but even prior to migration, since civil conflict often causes (and/or is caused by) societal marginalization of particular communities. Several chapters in this part therefore consider the impact of students' educational backgrounds prior to resettlement on their response to particular pedagogies and policies.

The first chapter, by Christopher Browder, presents a quantitative analysis of the role of educational background as a factor in the language development of high school English learners, focusing on students from the Chin ethnic group (originally from Burma [Myanmar]) living near Washington, DC. Browder's study both confirms and complicates some of the assumptions articulated in prior literature about students with limited or interrupted formal education (SLIFE). Perhaps his most noteworthy finding is that variance within the SLIFE population – even among those from the same ethnic background – may in fact be greater than the differences between SLIFE and other groups of English learners. Drawing on a rare quantitative study, Browder adds to the calls made by other researchers for more fine-grained assessments of newcomer students' first language (L1) literacy and content knowledge upon arrival; his findings also caution against 'one-size-fits-all' approaches to meeting newcomers' academic and linguistic needs.

In Chapter 2, Bryan Ripley Crandall shifts to a qualitative focus, considering the complex 'writing lives' of four Somali-born male students at a high school in the northeastern United States. Ripley Crandall employs activity theory to highlight the writing experiences that students find most meaningful, both inside and outside of the classroom. Participants in this study were particularly eager to share their personal stories and cultural/

historical understandings with peers and teachers from other backgrounds. Yet, the testing-dominated curriculum employed in their schools provided few opportunities for this sort of writing. The author concludes by discussing the teaching implications of his study, including the importance of authentic purposes, real-world audiences and multiphase processes in the writing lives of refugee-background youth.

In Chapter 3, Koeun Park and Verónica Valdez focus on meaning-making resources among another group of students: older adult learners of Nepali Bhutanese heritage in a US-based community language program. The authors link this approach to the concept of 'funds of knowledge' (Moll *et al.*, 1992), explaining that the translanguaging pedagogy they use 'recognizes and builds on students' existing linguistic abilities as strengths'. Drawing on excerpts from classroom dialogue as well as examples of student work, Park and Valdez show how a teacher and her students co-constructed a community where a variety of linguistic resources were employed in the construction of new knowledge.

Chapter 4, by Delila Omerbašić, traces similar themes, examining how two adolescent girls of Karen background in the intermountain west of the United States employ technology in their out-of-school lives to create multilingual multimodal texts. These 'digital landscapes', as Omerbašić calls them, foreground 'translocal knowledge' that is particularly prevalent within communities whose members have experienced forced migration and resettlement, and illustrate how students creatively use technology to express their multifaceted cultural and linguistic identities. The author, who herself went through the process of refugee resettlement as a child, sees her work as part of a larger conversation about how to foreground the 'strengths, resilience, and heterogeneity of people with refugee experiences'. She suggests ways that schools might draw on the assets that students bring as part of developing a '21st-century skills' curriculum.

In the fifth chapter, Katerina Nakutnyy and Andrea Sterzuk consider how literacy practices used by a Sudanese-background mother and son have changed during and since their resettlement in Canada. The authors highlight the social nature of participants' information-sharing networks prior to resettlement and consider how new social conditions in the country of resettlement create both challenges and opportunities for literacy mediation. In their conclusion, Nakytnyy and Sterzuk argue that language instruction must take into account the evolving sociocultural literacy practices in the lives of refugee-background students.

In Chapter 6, M. Kristiina Montero considers another asset that is often under-recognized in schools: expressions of self-healing among refugee-background students who have experienced trauma. Montero identifies these expressions in personal stories dictated by Rohingya young men, originally from Burma (Myanmar), who were living in Ontario, Canada.

Using narrative analysis, the author examines how students frame their personal stories in terms of aspiration, altruism and spirituality. Montero concludes that 'by welcoming students' trauma stories into the curriculum, educators might re-envision their academically oriented classrooms as spaces that support refugees' self-healing processes'.

The final chapter in this part, Chapter 7, by Anne Dahl, Anna Krulatz and Eivind Nessa Torgersen, examines the curricular goals and assumptions of refugee-background students in two small towns in Mid-Norway, comparing them with those held by their Norwegian language teachers. One key finding is that while both groups recognize that proficiency in Norwegian is important for employment and civic integration in their local community, students tend to view proficiency in English as equally important, while teachers tend to deemphasize the value of knowing English. The authors explain how this mismatch in beliefs is representative of larger language ideologies related to citizenship education, suggesting a nationalist and assimilationist hidden curriculum that is not usually articulated explicitly to students. This study highlights the tensions invoked when students' linguistic and economic realities clash with the assumptions made by gatekeepers involved in citizenship education – particularly in countries continually (re)defining themselves in relationship to the European Union.

Access and Adjustment

The theme of 'Access and Adjustment' includes a variety of issues related to educational policies and opportunities, as well as to students' educational aspirations and acculturation processes within a variety of educational settings. Prior research has suggested that educational programs and curricula for refugee-background students are often informed by a limited or inaccurate understanding of students' needs, goals and expectations (e.g. Kanu, 2008; McBrien, 2005; Pinson & Arnot, 2007). More research is needed, therefore, to examine the factors that inform educational decision-making on the part of teachers and students. Chapters in this part consider questions such as: What challenges do refugee-background students face in accessing appropriate and effective education in resettlement communities? Where are potential mismatches between the intent of educational policies and practices and the lived experience of students? What challenges and interventions have the greatest impact on students' cultural, emotional and social adjustment within educational institutions?

The first chapter in this section, Chapter 8, by Amanda Hiorth and Paul Molyneux, provides a segue from the previous theme, examining the experiences of Karen-background students as they transition from a newcomer program into a mainstream high school in Melbourne, Australia.

The authors' methodology includes student-generated drawings as a key data source, which participants reference in one-on-one interviews. These drawings offer insight into students' inner lives as they pursue social, academic and institutional integration at school. Hiorth and Molyneux conclude that transition is 'a highly complex, multifaceted, long-term, and non-linear process', in which students' social and academic experiences inform and often echo one another. They highlight the role of particular institutional spaces as well as of certain strands within the academic curriculum, in facilitating this complex process.

The theme of integration is central as well to Chapter 9, by Amadu Khan, which considers the perceptions by refugee-background students in Scotland of citizenship curricula and related policies. Khan's analysis shows how citizenship education in the United Kingdom is shaped by political tensions related to migration and national identity – tensions he has experienced first-hand as a former refugee. Khan finds that while participants recognize some benefits from the classes, such as the opportunity to interact with people from other language backgrounds and to gain knowledge that helps them advocate for themselves, they described a number of ways in which the curriculum and policies could better serve their function of social and cultural integration. Khan also highlights examples of participants' agency in pursuing other means of learning English beyond citizenship classes, even creating their own new, voluntary course offerings.

Chapter 10, by Erin Papa, reports on a youth participatory action research study, which employs a methodology known as 'photovoice', to engage the perspectives of refugee-background youth of Cambodian and Guatemalan heritage in an urban center in the northeastern United States. With this approach, students serve as co-researchers, submitting photographs that foreground important themes and issues in their lives. The student work presented in the chapter highlights various forms of social and cultural capital, including a commitment among participants to promoting community change. As with the chapters by Hiorth and Molyneux and by Omerbašić, Papa's study highlights the value of multimodal, student-generated texts as a source of insight into the lived experiences of refugee-background youth.

Next, in Chapter 11, Eva Holmkvist, Kirk Sullivan and Asbjørg Westum consider a topic often raised in the research literature about refugee-background students: the impact of their trauma history on students' classroom needs and behaviors. Specifically, this chapter examines knowledge and beliefs about post-traumatic stress disorder (PTSD) on the part of Swedish teachers working with adult refugee-background students in a mid-sized town near the Arctic Circle. The authors find that teachers' conceptions of PTSD are often limited, with many feeling unsure about how to recognize it. Nevertheless, these educators were able to articulate a variety of features of their pedagogical practice used to create a safe, comfortable and student-centered learning environment. One implication raised by this study is that educators who do not have extensive knowledge about the effects of trauma on adult learners can still support students by employing and expanding their repertoire of pedagogical practices known to effective with adult learners in general. The authors link this observation to the concept of Universal Design for Learning (Rose & Meyer, 2006), which has become widely used in K-12 settings, but has rarely been taken up in adult education.

Chapter 12, by Annette Korntheuer, Maren Gag, Phillip Anderson and Joachim Schroeder, examines the availability and quality of vocational education for refugees and asylum seekers in two urban centers in Germany – Munich and Hamburg – through a meta-analysis of previous reports as well as new analysis of their own data. The authors show how legal and institutional structures in both communities serve to exclude refugee-background students, and can be considered forms of discrimination – either directly or indirectly. Despite these concerns, students interviewed in both communities maintained high educational aspirations, which the authors see as a valuable 'coping strategy' for refugee-background students who must navigate these complex systemic challenges.

Amy Pucino, in Chapter 13, considers discrimination from another vantage point, studying how Muslim, Iraqi-born adolescents in a mid-Atlantic community in the United States respond to racist and/or xenophobic interactions with classmates and teachers. Students reported a variety of strategies, including avoidance, the use of humor, confrontation and attempts to educate others. Each student's choice of strategy was influenced by his or her personality as well as by the context in which the interaction occurred. Pucino employs ecological theory (e.g. Bronfenbrenner, 1995) in her analysis in order to link student experiences to broader, macro-level ideologies perpetuated in particular by media discourse.

In Chapter 14, Eliana Hirano addresses a question often overlooked in educational research: What do refugee-background students gain from higher education? Hirano focuses holistically on students' personal growth – particularly on their membership in non-academic 'communities of practice' – at a small, liberal arts college in the southeastern United States. Hirano highlights how experiences such as extracurricular involvement, campus leadership activities and employment contributed to students' identities beyond the classroom. The author finds, in fact, that some students saw these 'non-academic' accomplishments as even more valuable than grades or other markers of academic achievement, in terms of their sense of belonging and legitimacy in higher education. This study suggests that researchers in post-secondary settings may need to broaden their conceptions of educational success – particularly for refugee-background students.

Finally, Chapter 15, by Beatrix Bukus, complicates some of the assumptions underlying this collection – particularly the dichotomy of 'voluntary' versus 'forced' migration. Drawing on interviews with 10 students ages 11–18 in Leipzig, Germany, about their educational expectations and experiences as they migrated through other European Union countries, Bukus highlights the ways that students' individual goals and expectations can play a much greater role than their legal citizenship status (e.g. economic migrant or refugee/asylum seeker) in shaping their attitudes toward education. Ultimately, Bukus's work suggests that educators should exercise caution in making assumptions about students' educational goals based solely on the voluntary–forced migration dichotomy, and that holding deeper conversations with students about their lived experience of multifaceted, multidirectional migration can offer valuable insights to both teachers and researchers.

Conclusion

Taken as a whole, this collection elucidates a range of issues critical to the education of refugee-background youth and adults. The chapters discuss a number of significant barriers to educational access and achievement for refugee-background students. However, they also reveal a robust array of assets and strategies that students and teachers employ in reducing those barriers. We hope that this book offers readers not only a nuanced understanding of educational challenges, but also insights on how to address such challenges. Studies included in this volume were conducted in a variety of geographic contexts in North America, Europe and Australia, as well as from a range of institutional settings. While none of these chapters can capture the nuances of its geographical and institutional settings, we hope the collection helps readers see how the dynamics of a particular context can both constrain and enable certain educational experiences for refugee-background students. Finally, we hope that the range of disciplinary perspectives, conceptual frameworks and research methodologies presented in this collection will offer a multidimensional snapshot of current trends in educational research with refugee-background students, and provide inspiration for research and practice among our readers.

Note

(1) The seven categories are: Legal and/or Physical Protection Needs, Survivors of Torture and/or Violence, Medical Needs, Women and Girls at Risk, Family Reunification, Children and Adolescents at Risk and Lack of Foreseeable Alternative Durable Solutions. More at http://www.unhcr.org/3d464c842.html.

References

Bigelow, M. (2010) *Mogadishu on the Mississippi: Language, Racialized Identity, and Education in a New Land*. New York: Wiley-Blackwell.

Bigelow, M. and Vinogradov, P. (2011) Teaching adult second language learners who are emergent readers. *Annual Review of Applied Linguistics* 31, 120–136.

Bronfenbrenner, U. (1995) Developmental ecology through space and time: A future perspective. In P. Moen, G. Elder Jr. and K. Lüscher (eds) *Examining Lives in Context: Perspectives on the Ecology of Human Development* (pp. 619–647). Washington, DC: American Psychological Association.

Brown, O. (2008) *Migration and Climate Change* (IOM Migration Research Series No. 32). Geneva: International Organization for Migration (IOM).

Curry, M.J. (2007) A 'head start and a credit': Analyzing cultural capital in the basic writing/ESOL classroom. In J. Albright and A. Luke (eds) *Pierre Bourdieu and Literacy Education* (pp. 275–295). Mahwah, NJ: Lawrence Erlbaum.

DeCapua, A. and Marshall, H. (2011) *Breaking New Ground: Teaching Students with Limited or Interrupted Formal Schooling in Secondary Schools*. Ann Arbor, MI: University of Michigan Press.

Dryden-Peterson, S. (2011) *Refugee Education: A Global Review*. United Nations High Commissioner for Refugees. See http://www.unhcr.org/4fe317589.html (accessed 4 January 2018).

Feuerherm, E. and Ramanathan, V. (eds) (2015) *Refugee Resettlement in the United States: Language, Policies, Pedagogies*. Bristol: Multilingual Matters.

García, O. and Wei, L. (2014) (eds) *Translanguaging: Language, Bilingualism and Education*. London: Palgrave Macmillan.

Hannah, J. (1999) Refugee students at college and university: Improving access and support. *International Review of Education* 45 (2), 151–164.

Kanu, Y. (2008) Educational needs and barriers for African refugee students in Manitoba. *Canadian Journal of Education* 31 (4), 915–940.

Keddie, A. (2012) Pursuing justice for refugee students: Addressing issues of cultural (mis)recognition. *International Journal of Inclusive Education* 16, 1295–1310.

MacDonald, M.T. (2015) Emerging voices: Emissaries of literacy: Representations of sponsorship and refugee experience in the stories of the lost boys of Sudan. *College English* 77 (5), 408–428.

Malkki, L.H. (1996) Speechless emissaries: Refugees, humanitarianism, and dehistoricization. *Cultural Anthropology* 11 (3), 377–404.

Matthews, J. (2008) Schooling and settlement: Refugee education in Australia. *International Studies in Sociology of Education* 18 (1), 31–45.

McBrien, J.L. (2005) Educational needs and barriers for refugee students in the United States: A review of the literature. *Review of Educational Research* 75 (3), 329–364.

Moll, L.C., Amanti, C., Neff, D. and Gonzalez, N. (1992) Funds of knowledge for teaching: Using a qualitative approach to connect homes and classrooms. *Theory into Practice* 31 (2), 132–141.

Ngo, B., Bigelow, M. and Lee, S.J. (2014) Introduction to the special issue: What does it mean to do ethical and engaged research with immigrant communities? *Diaspora, Indigenous, and Minority Education* 8 (1), 1–6.

Pinson, H. and Arnot, M. (2007) Sociology of education and the wasteland of refugee education research. *British Journal of Sociology of Education* 28 (3), 399–407.

Rose, D.H. and Meyer, A. (2006) *A Practical Reader in Universal Design for Learning*. Cambridge, MA: Harvard Education Publishing Group.

Roy, L.A. and Roxas, K.C. (2011) Whose deficit is this anyhow? Exploring counter-stories of Somali Bantu refugees' experiences in 'doing school'. *Harvard Educational Review* 81 (3), 521–542.

Rutter, J. (2006) *Refugee Children in the UK*. Maidenhead: Open University Press.

Shapiro, S. (2014) 'Words that you said got bigger': English language learners' lived experiences of deficit discourse. *Research in the Teaching of English* 48 (4), 386–406.

Shapiro, S. and MacDonald, M. (2017) From deficit to asset: Locating discursive resistance in a refugee-background student's written and oral narrative. *Journal of Language, Identity & Education* 16 (2), 80–93.

Taylor, S. and Sidhu, R.K. (2012) Supporting refugee students in schools: What constitutes inclusive education? *International Journal of Inclusive Education* 16 (1), 39–56.

United Nations High Commissioner for Refugees (2011) Protecting refugees: Questions and answers. See http://unhcr.org.ua/en/who-we-help/2011-08-26-06-55-36 (accessed 4 January 2018).

United Nations High Commissioner for Refugees (2015) In photos: Climate change, disasters and displacement. See http://www.unhcr.org/en-us/climate-change-and-disasters.html (accessed 4 January 2018).

United Nations High Commissioner for Refugees (2016) Information on UNHCR resettlement. See http://www.unhcr.org/en-us/information-on-unhcr-resettlement.html (accessed 4 January 2018).

United Nations High Commissioner for Refugees (2017a) Figures at a glance. See http://www.unhcr.org/en-us/figures-at-a-glance.html (accessed 4 January 2018).

United Nations High Commissioner for Refugees (2017b) What is a refugee? See http://www.unrefugees.org/what-is-a-refugee/ (accessed 4 January 2018).

Part 1
Language and Literacy

1 Recently Resettled Refugee Students Learning English in US High Schools: The Impact of Students' Educational Backgrounds

Christopher T. Browder

This chapter reports on a quantitative study that examined the English learning of 146 US high school English learner (EL)[1] students with a focus on 35 recently resettled ethnic Chin refugees from Myanmar. The goals were to understand how students' educational backgrounds influenced their learning of English and to identify the most useful variables for understanding the challenges facing recently resettled refugees and students with limited or interrupted formal education (SLIFE). The study had three main findings: (1) the Chin students learned English much more slowly than other groups; (2) most of the Chin students could be identified as SLIFE, but very few had low first language (L1) literacy; (3) some of the variables used to identify students as SLIFE were associated with slower English learning, but were not very strong or reliable predictors, due to high variability. These findings suggest that there must be other, important reasons why some students learn English more slowly than others, and that students characterized as SLIFE may not have all the same characteristics and needs. This study broadens our understanding of SLIFE and provides insights for school systems considering how to best serve recently resettled refugees.

Introduction

In recent years, there has been a movement to fill a gap in research on second language acquisition that is particularly relevant to refugee-background students (Bigelow & Watson, 2012) – namely, our lack of understanding of how EL students' educational backgrounds impact their learning of English. A number of researchers have shown that prior schooling, literacy or other educational experiences in students' first languages influence their learning of English as an additional language in high school settings (e.g. Brown *et al.*, 2006; Klein & Martohardjono, 2015; Thomas & Collier, 2002).

In 2014, I conducted a study to build on this research, examining the relationship between high school EL students' educational backgrounds before emigrating and their rates of English learning once in the United States. Specifically, I wanted to know whether SLIFE learned English more slowly than other EL students. In the course of this study, I had to determine the best way to categorize students as SLIFE. Based on definitions of SLIFE drawn from the existing literature, I began to look at a group of EL students and identify variables related to their educational backgrounds. As a result of that study, I encountered a group of students whom most people would consider to be SLIFE based on how the data had set them apart: recently resettled ethnic Chin refugees from Myanmar. Most of them had experienced interruptions in their schooling, and on average, they were learning English more slowly than the other EL students in their school system. This study delves further into the trends among the Chin students in my study in order to better understand the impact that refugee-background students' educational backgrounds have on their English learning.

Literature Review: Recently Resettled Refugee Students and SLIFE

At present, the educational literature has a tendency to conflate recently resettled refugee students and SLIFE. For example, some studies on recently resettled refugees refer to them as students with 'truncated formal education' (cf. Gahungu *et al.*, 2011) or 'limited formal schooling' (cf. Walsh, 1999), but do not disaggregate the data for those with more previous formal education from those with less. Similarly, some of the educational literature on SLIFE is based on the experiences of teachers working with groups of recently resettled refugees, but it is not clear from this literature whether all of those students actually had documented interrupted education or verified low L1 education and literacy (cf. DeCapua *et al.*, 2010).

Admittedly, most US school systems still do not collect enough information on EL students' educational backgrounds to systematically or accurately identify students as SLIFE (Advocates for Children of New York, 2010). In fact, one study found that students identified as having 'interrupted formal education' by their school system often did not have such interruptions (Klein & Martohardjono, 2006). At present, US school systems generally conduct interviews and collect transcripts during the federally mandated Home Language Survey to determine which newly arrived EL students have experienced interruptions in their education (Zacarian & Haynes, 2012), but very few administer objective tests to determine which have low L1 literacy or limited academic content knowledge, as such tests are only now being developed (Klein & Martohardjono, 2015; Silverstein, 2016; Zehr, 2009).

Given the circumstances of most refugees, it is understandable why researchers might conflate recently resettled refugee students with SLIFE: It is well documented that many refugees have limited access to education in their homeland due to injustice, conflict and physical hardships (Flaitz, 2006; United Nations International Children's Emergency Fund [UNICEF], 2014). We also know that this educational deprivation often continues during forced migration, in intermediary nations and in refugee camps (Dryden-Peterson, 2015).

There are also limits to the literature on immigrant and refugee students who do have documented gaps in their educational backgrounds. Research is still quite limited on how L1 education and literacy influence second language learning (Tarone, 2010; Zehr, 2009). Much of the research that specifically investigates SLIFE generally relies on case studies (cf. Bigelow, 2007), or otherwise small samples (cf. Brown *et al.*, 2006), rather than using quantitative data with larger samples. Some of the studies related to SLIFE do not include sufficient data to determine whether the students in the sample are actually SLIFE (cf. Thomas & Collier, 2002). Finally, some of the research related to SLIFE involves participants with no formal literacy or education (cf. Brucki & Rocha, 2004; Castro-Caldas, 2004), but those participants may be dissimilar to the typical SLIFE in US schools and quite different from most recently resettled refugees, who often have at least some experience with formal schooling (Mace-Matluck *et al.*, 1998).

In both research and educational policy, the criteria used to identify SLIFE vary widely (Advocates for Children of New York, 2010). The New York State Department of Education (2011: 2), for example, expects students to have 'at least two years less formal schooling than their peers' in order to be classified as 'students with interrupted formal education', while the State of Maryland expects students to have been out of school for only six months to be classified as having 'interrupted schooling' (COMAR 13A.05.07, 2016). Other researchers point out that a person can have uninterrupted formal schooling yet be undereducated due to inadequate schooling (DeCapua *et al.*, 2010), which suggests that policymakers should consider students' content knowledge and academic skills (e.g. math, literacy) instead of just their schooling history. This view is supported by research showing that time spent in school does not correspond as closely with literacy and content learning as one might assume (Browder, 2015; Tarone & Bigelow, 2005).

These lingering concerns with the SLIFE label have an impact on decision-making in US school districts. When a large number of refugees are resettled into an area, the local school system must decide what educational services are appropriate. If a school system's decision-making is not informed by quality research, students may in some places be denied the support they need, or in other places, forced into inappropriate support programs (Feinberg, 2000), which has even led to civil rights lawsuits (cf. Issa v. the School District of Lancaster, 2016).

This study aims therefore to broaden our understandings of SLIFE and provide insights for school systems considering how to best serve recently resettled refugees. It focuses on the following questions:

(1) To what extent does limited or interrupted formal education affect the rate of English learning for EL students – particularly those with refugee backgrounds?
(2) What independent variables are most useful for understanding the challenges that SLIFE have with learning English in formal educational settings?

Chin refugees

The recently resettled refugees in this study were ethnic Chin from Myanmar (formerly known as Burma). For some time now, Myanmar has been one of the leading countries of origin for refugees accepted into the United States (Martin & Yankay, 2014). In 2014, about 23% of all refugees admitted into the United States originated from Myanmar. About a third of those were from the Chin ethnic group (Burmese American Community Institute, 2015). The Chin have been fleeing religious and ethnic discrimination from the military in Myanmar for many decades (Human Rights Watch, 2009). Because the neighboring countries of India, Malaysia and Thailand are not parties to the 1951 UN Convention on Refugees (United Nations High Commissioner on Refugees, 2010), Chin refugees fleeing Myanmar have to wander in search of a safe place to live while applying for asylum elsewhere and often wind up involuntarily placed in jails, detention centers and refugee camps. Chin refugees often spend many years or even decades living without stability or security in Malaysia, Indonesia and/or Thailand before eventually coming to the United States (Burma Link, 2015).

Over 40% of the Chin refugees accepted into the United States have been of school age (Martin & Yankay, 2014), but often they were unable to attend school consistently prior to resettlement. In Myanmar, less than 60% of the general population has attended secondary school, and only 9% has received any preschool education (UNICEF, 2014). When Chin youth leave Myanmar, they usually spend many years in refugee camps where they receive little if any formal schooling before emigrating to their new home (World Relief, 2015). In Malaysia, for instance, only 41% of the children in refugee camps attend primary school, and fewer than 2%

attend secondary school (Dryden-Peterson, 2015). To make matters worse, Chin are generally not allowed to attend local schools when outside of the camps. For all these reasons, school-age Chin refugees are likely to arrive in the United States with limited or interrupted formal education. Therefore, one could assume that recently resettled Chin refugees fit into the SLIFE category and would have the same disadvantages when learning English in US schools.

The Setting for this Study

The county school system for this study is located in central Maryland, near Washington, DC. Although it is one of the nation's most affluent and educated counties, it is also one of its most diverse and well integrated in terms of race, socioeconomic status and ethnicity (US Census Bureau, 2016). Although it is more suburban than urban, it is an immigrant gateway community with very large populations of first-generation Korean and Latin American immigrants. A few years ago, it also rather suddenly became home to about 1,500 recently resettled ethnic Chin refugee-background persons from Myanmar (Lee, 2012).

The participating school system has a reputation for excellence (US News and World Report, 2013). The EL students in this study were as well supported, if not better supported, than other EL students typically in US high schools (cf. Gandara et al., 2003). In this district, high school EL students arriving with very low or no English were placed in a special program, called a newcomer program, for a year or more. After about a year, they transferred to their neighborhood schools where their schedules included some classes from a program of English for speakers of other languages (ESOL).[2]

Methodology

To answer the above research questions, I undertook the following methods:

Sampling and data collection

In 2012, with the permission of the school district and the help of its teachers in the ESOL program, I recruited high school EL students to participate in the original study. All 12 of the county high schools with EL students agreed to participate in the study. The ESOL program teachers in those schools met with students to obtain informed consent from them and their legal guardians. In total, 199 of the 352 high school EL students in the county assented with their parents' consent to participate in the study. Admittedly, students who were not frequently working with ESOL program teachers were less likely to participate because it was more difficult to establish and maintain contact with them. About 40 (20%) of those students were taking no classes offered by the ESOL program. On average, students took about two ESOL classes, but some took as many as five. The analyses for this study only include the 146 students who were in the system long enough to collect two sets of mid-year English proficiency test scores one full year apart. Some analyses include as few as 134 students because of incomplete data on students' educational backgrounds. The school system data had been collected during the enrollment process and supplemented with English proficiency test scores to measure the students' rate of English learning.

This study augmented district data with the results of a literacy survey that I developed and administered to the students, with help from teachers and bilingual assistants. The survey was used to collect information on the students' self-reported L1 reading and writing ability. It was necessary to collect these data using self-report, since there were too many different first languages among the students in the sample to have one objective test of L1 literacy. Admittedly, self-reported L1 literacy could be measuring educational self-efficacy instead of actual proficiency (Fox *et al.*, 2008), but studies show that self-reported L1 literacy corresponds well with L1 literacy measured by objective tests (Marian *et al.*, 2007; Ross, 1998; Shameem, 1998).

The sample

Within the sample of 146 high school EL students, 35 (24%) were recently arrived ethnic Chin refugee-background adolescents from Myanmar. The other students were mainly Hispanics (29%) and Koreans (15%) but otherwise were a diverse group that included students from Haiti, India, China and many other countries. The Chin were of special interest to me in this study because they were recently resettled refugees. In addition, their data set them apart in two ways: (a) most had some indicators of limited or interrupted formal education; and (b) as a group they were learning English more slowly on average than the other EL students.

Preliminary analyses of the sample showed that the Chin refugee-background students were in many other ways like most of the other EL students in the sample. Most had recently emigrated to the United States and were relatively new to the country, the English language and US schooling. Chin students generally took the same number of ESOL classes as the other students in the study (two on average). There was no evidence that the quality or quantity of their ESOL services was different from that of other EL students. Nor was there any evidence that the schools the Chin attended were inferior to other schools. All of the schools in the county had high graduation rates and high scores on the major state-mandated tests. However, as mentioned earlier, the

Chin students tended to progress more slowly in their English language development. I therefore examined a range of variables that might have impacted English gains.

Variables

The dependent variable in this study was created to measure students' progress in learning English over the course of a year. The independent variables were measures of students' educational backgrounds.

Dependent variable: English gains

This variable measures how much an individual student's English proficiency test score increased over the course of a year. During the study, the state education agency changed the test used to measure students' English proficiency. In the first year of the study, the state used the LAS links (CTB/McGraw-Hill LLC, 2007), and in the second year it used the WIDA ACCESS (WIDA Consortium, 2007). However, the two tests used the same metrics and were relatively well calibrated (Kenyon, 2006). In order to make findings more accessible, I used the change in the students' overall proficiency scores to measure progress in English learning, as is done by teachers and school systems. To ensure that these estimates were accurate, I confirmed them using standardized coefficients (β)[3] and tests of significance (p values) using scale scores converted into z scores.[4]

Independent variables for educational background

The five independent variables used in this study were all measures taken of the students when they first enrolled in a US school, except for self-reported L1 literacy, which was collected later. These variables were used to identify students as SLIFE. The first two were measures of schooling, or time spent in school. The last two were measures of education, or the actual academic learning the student possessed prior to schooling in the United States.

Interrupted schooling indicates an interruption in the continuity of the students' formal schooling of six months or more in the past six years not including sanctioned vacation time (COMAR 13A.05.07, 2016). Students who never experienced an interruption in schooling were identified with a zero for this variable; students who had experienced an interruption were identified with a one. This variable did not take into account the length of an interruption, the last grade of schooling completed or what the student had learned in school.

Missing years of schooling is based on the last grade that students completed compared to the grade that they were placed in when they enrolled in a US school. Thus, a student who completed sixth grade before emigrating to the United States but was placed in ninth grade instead of seventh would have two years of missing schooling (i.e. $9 - 7 = 2$ missing years). Unlike interrupted schooling, the missing schooling variable takes into account the variation in the number of years of missing schooling.

Although missing schooling and interrupted schooling seem similar, it is possible for a student to have one and not have the other as these cases illustrate:

- Case 1: A student stopped attending school in eighth grade, then did not attend school for two years before enrolling in ninth grade in the United States. This student has a one for interrupted schooling but a zero for missing schooling.
- Case 2: A student attended school consistently for six years, but started school at a later age and repeated seventh grade. After completing seventh grade, the student emigrated to the United States and enrolled in ninth grade. This student has a zero for interrupted schooling, but a one for missing years of schooling.

English proficiency on arrival is based on the scores from the LAS links ESOL placement test that students took when they first enrolled in a US school. This test gave students an overall proficiency score ranging from one to five.

L1 literacy is a measure of students' self-reported L1 reading and writing ability on arrival. These data came from the aforementioned survey (see Browder, 2014). Scores ranged from one to four, with lower scores indicating lower L1 literacy. Survey items asked about both reading and writing and were worded as in this example: 'When I first came to the US, I could *read* as well in [*student's first language*] as most American kids my age could read in English'. Students agreed or disagreed to each statement using a Likert-scale response (i.e. 1 = strongly disagree, 2 = disagree, 3 = agree, 4 = strongly agree). Bilingual assistants showed students how to complete the survey items and read the survey aloud in the students' first language when students had low English, low literacy and/or low previous education.

Methods of analysis

First, I conducted preliminary analyses to test whether the data would work well for my chosen methods of statistical analysis.[5] I analyzed the data for the whole sample and subgroups in the sample. Second, I conducted bivariate regression analyses (Agresti & Finlay, 2009), using the whole sample to see which of the independent variables related to students' educational backgrounds had significant associations with English gains.

While conducting the preliminary analyses using T tests (Agresti & Finlay, 2009), I began to notice that the results for the Chin students in my sample were different from the others. First, I noticed that their rate of English learning was slower on average. Second, analyses showed significant differences in their educational backgrounds compared to other groups, indicating that many might be SLIFE.

Findings

In the course of my study, I identified several findings related to the Chin refugee-background students, as indicated in the section subtitles below.

Slower English learning

On average, the Chin students learned English significantly more slowly than the other EL students in the sample. The progress for the Chin students was on average 0.84 levels per year, while the non-Chin EL students progressed at a rate of 1.34. The difference between the two averages, or mean difference, was −0.49, which amounts to a 37% difference in their rates of English learning. This estimate suggests that, if all students started at proficiency Level 1, most would take fewer than four years to reach the state proficiency standard (Level 5), while the Chin students would take nearly six years. The Pearson coefficient, or 'p value', for the mean difference was 0.003, indicating that this finding was statistically significant. It is important to note, however, that the standard deviations were rather large (0.70 for non-Chin and 0.74 for Chin), indicating that the rate of English learning for all students was extremely variable.

Limited or interrupted schooling and formal education

As Table 1.1 shows, the Chin students had less formal schooling than the other EL students. For example, about 67% of the Chin students reported such interruptions in their schooling, compared to 26% for other students. The Chin students were also more likely to have missing years of schooling, as described above. The average for this variable was 1.19

Table 1.1 Differences between the educational backgrounds of the Chin and other EL students

	Non-Chin	Chin	Mean difference
Interrupted schooling (0 = no, 1 = yes)	0.26 (0.04)	0.67 (0.08)	+0.40 (0.08)***
Missing years of schooling (years)	0.28 (0.06)	1.19 (0.23)	+0.91 (0.23)***
English proficiency on arrival (1–5)	2.40 (0.10)	1.61 (0.13)	−0.79 (0.17)***
L1 literacy (1–4)	3.50 (0.06)	3.27 (0.15)	−0.23 (0.16)

Note: Numbers in parentheses are the standard errors for the estimates.
***$p < 0.001$.

for the Chin, compared to 0.28 for non-Chin. For this reason, most of the Chin students in this study could be called SLIFE. It is important to note, however, that not all Chin had interrupted or missing schooling. Indeed, 33% of the Chin reported no interruption in their schooling history and 62% had no missing schooling relative to their US grade placement. Table 1.1 also suggests that the Chin arrived in the United States with lower English proficiency. The Chin also had a lower average score for self-reported L1 literacy than the other EL students, but this difference was not statistically significant. Overall, the Chin did not report having low L1 literacy (i.e. a score of 1 or 2 out of 4); in fact, they generally reported being literate in their own language.

In short, based on these data, one *cannot* conclude that the Chin typically arrived with low literacy, despite having fewer years of schooling prior to arrival. This is an important finding because researchers (e.g. DeCapua *et al.*, 2010) and policymakers (e.g. New York State Department of Education, 2011) often assume that the two are closely connected. It is well documented, however, that young people in Myanmar are usually literate (UNICEF, 2014). The Chin, in particular, have been using the Roman alphabet to read and write for over 100 years (Bawi, 2001). Thus, this finding complicates assumptions often made about SLIFE and students with refugee backgrounds.

Association between educational backgrounds and English learning

As Table 1.2 shows, there was a weak but statistically significant relationship between interrupted schooling and English gains. Students with interrupted schooling had lower English gains than those of the other EL students by 0.12 proficiency levels. In other words, in one year, the overall English proficiency for students with interrupted schooling increased by 1.15 proficiency levels, while the English proficiency for other students increased by 1.27 (the y intercept). However, the standard deviation of 0.13 shows that the English gains for students with interrupted schooling were quite variable. The standardized coefficient (β) was −0.12, indicating that the actual 'strength' of the relationship between interrupted schooling and

Table 1.2 Bivariate relationships between students' educational backgrounds and English learning

	b	*β*	*p*
Interrupted schooling (0 = no/1 = yes)	−0.12 (0.13)	−0.12	0.033*
Missing years of schooling (years)	−0.02 (0.06)	−0.10	0.084
English proficiency on arrival (1–5)	0.01 (0.05)	0.14	0.099
L1 literacy (1–4)	0.12 (0.07)	0.11	0.046*

Note: Numbers in parentheses are the standard errors for the estimates.
*p < 0.05.

English gains was weak despite being statistically significant ($p = 0.003$). Thus, interrupted schooling seemed to be a predictor of slower English learning but not a particularly strong or reliable one.

Table 1.2 also shows that missing years of schooling did not have a statistically significant relationship with English gains. One may wonder why interrupted schooling had a statistically significant relationship to English gains, but missing years of schooling did not. As noted in the section titled 'Methodology', interrupted schooling is determined based on time spent out of school while missing schooling is determined based on the last grade that students completed relative to the grade that they were placed in once enrolled in a US school. The p value of 0.084 for missing schooling was above but close to the level of 0.05 used to determine significance, while the p value of 0.033 for interrupted schooling was statistically significant but not much lower. It is possible that missing schooling might have passed the test of significance if the sample size had been larger (Agresti & Finlay, 2009). Both variables had standardized coefficients (β) that indicated weak relationships to English gains.

Table 1.2 also shows that students' English proficiency on arrival did not have a significant relationship to their English gains, although again, the relationship might have been significant if there had been a larger sample. It is important to point out, however, that the standardized coefficient for this relationship was the highest of all ($\beta = 0.14$), indicating that it may have had a larger impact than the other independent variables. There was, however, a significant relationship between self-reported L1 literacy and English gains. Each level of L1 literacy corresponded to English gains that were 0.12 points higher per year. Thus, a student with an L1 literacy level of 4 would increase his/her overall proficiency 0.36 levels higher per year than a student with an L1 literacy level of 1. The p value of 0.046 showed that this finding was statistically significant.

In summary, interrupted schooling and L1 literacy showed significant but weak relationships to English gains, while missing years of schooling and English proficiency on arrival did not show a statistically significant association. The high standard deviations indicate a high degree of variability. We may therefore conclude that these variables for students' educational backgrounds explain some of the variability among students in the sample but leave much of the variability unexplained. Besides educational background, there must be other important reasons why some EL students such as the Chin, in this case, learn English more slowly than others.

Discussion

The findings from this study challenge some of the generalities found in the literature on recently resettled refugees and SLIFE. First, some of the students within this group possibly characterized as SLIFE did not present all of the characteristics one might expect to find in SLIFE. In particular, students with interrupted schooling did not necessarily have lower L1 literacy. Second, the rate of English learning for the students in this study was extremely variable – even when they had similar educational backgrounds. In other words, differences in students' educational backgrounds did not explain the variability in their rates of English learning sufficiently to qualify as a reliable predictor.

It is possible that the lack of strength and reliability of these variables resulted from their inaccuracy as instruments for measuring the quality or quantity of students' previous formal education. Interrupted schooling, for example, was a dichotomous or 'dummy' variable that placed students in two different groups – students with interruptions and students without – and therefore did not take into account differences in the lengths and nature of the interruptions to formal schooling. The other variables used in this study have similar limitations. However, the data on these variables were collected by a public school district in a manner that was consistent with that of most other US public schools, as per federal mandates (Zacarian & Haynes, 2012). Hence, researchers seeking to address these limitations in future studies may find it difficult to do so, given the limits in the type of data available. This study therefore illustrates the need for more thorough data-gathering about students' educational histories at the time of entry into US schools.

Conclusion

The findings of this study are relevant to communities charged with providing appropriate educational services for recently resettled refugees, many of whom may be SLIFE. Schools need to know how to determine which of those new EL students are likely to need more help learning English and might benefit from special programs for SLIFE. This study suggests variables that school systems might attend to in making these determinations. Findings also illustrate that, while recently resettled refugee students in this study learned English more slowly on average as a group, such students should not necessarily be lumped together into a one-size-fits-all program, since there may be high variability in both their educational backgrounds and English learning outcomes.

This study also contributes to the evolving construct of SLIFE. It shows that there are multiple variables encompassed by the SLIFE label, each with its own effect on learning. Among the measures of schooling (e.g. time spent in school), only interrupted schooling predicted slower English learning, but its actual impact on English learning was relatively weak. Among the measures of learning, only self-reported L1 literacy predicted slower English learning, but its actual impact on English learning was also weak. There is an abundance of research, however, that confirms a strong relationship between low L1 literacy and slower English learning when that literacy is measured using an objective test instead of self-report data (Curringa & Garrison-Fletcher, 2015; Klein & Martohardjono, 2015; Tarone & Bigelow, 2005). This body of research, along with my findings, supports the argument from some educational advocates that we cannot rely on transcripts or self-reports of previous schooling and literacy to determine a newly arrived refugee-background student's educational needs; we need to have other measures for making such determinations (Advocates for Children of New York, 2010).

Ultimately, this research tells us that the current construct of SLIFE may be useful in some ways, but it may also lead to ineffective placement decisions if misapplied. We need tests of L1 literacy, mathematics and other subject areas to determine how much help each student will need. Fortunately, there are new developments in this area, such as the Academic Language and Literacy Diagnostic (ALLD) in New York (Zehr, 2009) and the Native Language Literacy Assessment (NLLA) in Minnesota (Silverstein, 2016). Communities receiving large numbers of recently resettled refugees may use the findings of this study to explore better ways to determine the needs of newcomer EL students, and should be wary of making decisions based solely on assumptions or limited information about students' educational backgrounds.

Notes

(1) This study uses the acronym 'EL' to refer to US public school students learning English as a second language. This is the term currently being promoted by the US Department of Education (Every Student Succeeds Act of 2015).
(2) ESOL is the term used in US public schools to refer to academic departments or programs that serve EL students (Zacarian & Haynes, 2012).
(3) Presently, there is a movement among researchers to include standardized coefficients in their findings, in addition to p values (Plonsky, 2014).
(4) WIDA recommends that researchers use students' scale scores instead of their overall proficiency scores when calculating progress. Converting those scale scores into z scores standardized both tests in a manner that compensated for differences between the two and provided more accurate estimates (Abdi, 2007).
(5) As is expected for studies of this type, these analyses include tests for sample bias, scale reliability, multicollinearity and kurtosis (Agresti & Finlay, 2009; Allison, 1999). These tests did not find anything too alarming. They can be found in Browder (2014).

References

Abdi, H. (2007) Z-scores. In N. Salkind (ed.) *Encyclopedia of Measurement and Statistics* (pp. 1–4). Thousand Oaks, CA: Sage.
Advocates for Children of New York (2010) Students with interrupted formal education: A challenge for the New York City Public Schools. See http://www.advocatesforchildren.org/SIFE%20Paper%20final.pdf?pt=1 (accessed 4 January 2018).

Agresti, A. and Finlay, B. (2009) *Statistical Methods for the Social Sciences* (4th edn). Upper Saddle River, NJ: Pearson Prentice Hall.
Allison, P. (1999) *Multiple Regression: A Primer*. Thousand Oaks, CA: Pine Forge Press.
Bawi, H. (2001) Literacy and Language Maintenance in Chin State, Myanmar. Adult Literacy Project: Chin Association for Christian Communication. See http://www.burmalibrary.org/docs22/Bawi-Hu_Literacy-and-Language-Maintenance-in-Chin-State_2001.pdf.
Bigelow, M. (2007) Social and cultural capital at school: The case of a Somali teenage girl with limited formal schooling. In N. Faux (ed.) *Low-Educated Adult Second Language Literacy Acquisition Proceedings of Symposium* (pp. 7–22). Richmond, VA: Literacy Institute at Virginia Commonwealth University.
Bigelow, M. and Watson, J. (2012) The role of educational level, literacy, and orality in L2 learning. In S. Gass and A. Mackey (eds) *Handbook of Second Language Acquisition* (pp. 461–475). New York: Routledge/Taylor & Francis.
Browder, C. (2014) English learners with limited or interrupted formal education: Risk and resilience in educational outcomes (Doctoral Dissertation) (Order No. 3637307). Available from ProQuest Dissertations & Theses Full Text (1617448282).
Browder, C. (2015) The educational outcomes of English learner students with limited or interrupted formal education. In M. Santos and A. Whiteside (eds) *Proceedings of the Ninth LESLLA Symposium, 2013* (pp. 150–172). San Francisco, CA: Lulu Publishing Services.
Brown, J., Miller, J. and Mitchell, J. (2006) Interrupted schooling and the acquisition of literacy: Experiences of Sudanese refugees in Victorian schools. *Australian Journal of Language and Literacy* 29 (2), 150–162.
Brucki, S. and Rocha, M. (2004) Category fluency test: Effects of age, gender, and education on total scores, clustering and switching in Brazilian Portuguese-speaking subjects. *Brazilian Journal of Medical and Biological Research* 7 (12), 1771–1777.
Burma Link (2015) Refugee camps. See http://www.burmalink.org/background/thailand-burma-border/displaced-in-thailand/refugee-camps/ (accessed 4 January 2018).
Burmese American Community Institute (2015, Aug. 1) Burmese population in the U.S. See http://www.baci-indy.org/resources/burmese-refugee-population-in-the-us (accessed 4 January 2018).
Castro-Caldas, A. (2004) Targeting regions of interest for the study of the illiterate brain. *International Journal of Psychology* 39 (1), 5–17.
COMAR 13A.05.07. (2016) Programs for English Learners. Code of Maryland Regulations.
CTB/McGraw-Hill LLC (2007) *LAS Links: Connecting Assessment, Language, and Learning*. Monterey, CA: McGraw-Hill.
Curringa, R. and Garrison-Fletcher, L. (2015) The importance of first-language reading skills in English reading comprehension for adolescent newcomers. In M. Santos and A. Whiteside (eds) *Proceedings of the Ninth LESLLA Symposium, 2013* (pp. 196–215). San Francisco, CA: Lulu Publishing Services.
DeCapua, A., Smathers, W. and Tang, L. (2010) *Meeting the Needs of Students with Limited or Interrupted Schooling*. Ann Arbor, MI: The University of Michigan Press.
Dryden-Peterson, S. (2015) *The Educational Experiences of Refugee Children in Countries of First Asylum*. Washington, DC: Migration Policy Institute.
Every Student Succeeds Act (2015) S.1177, U.S.C. US Government Publishing Office. See https://www.gpo.gov/fdsys/pkg/BILLS-114s1177enr/pdf/BILLS-114s1177enr.pdf.
Feinberg, R. (2000) Newcomer schools: Salvation or segregated oblivion for immigrant students? *Theory into Practice* 39 (4), 220–227.
Flaitz, J. (2006) *Understanding Your Refugee and Immigrant Students: An Educational, Cultural, and Linguistic Guide*. Ann Arbor, MI: University of Michigan Press.

Fox, R., Kitsantas, A. and Flowers, G. (2008) English language learners with interrupted schooling: Do self-efficacy beliefs in native language proficiency and acculturation matter? *AccEllerate* 1 (1), 14–16.

Gahungu, A., Gahungu, O. and Luseno, F. (2011) Educating culturally displaced students with truncated formal education (CDS-TFE): The case of refugee students and challenges for administrators, teachers, and counselors. *International Journal of Educational Leadership Preparation* 6 (2), 1–19.

Gandara, P., Rumberger, R., Maxwell-Jolly, J. and Callahan, R. (2003) English learners in California schools: Unequal resources, unequal outcomes. *Education Policy Analysis Archives* 11 (36), 1–19.

Human Rights Watch (2009, Jan. 27) We are like forgotten people: The Chin people of Burma: Unsafe in Burma, unprotected in India. Human Rights Watch. See https://www.hrw.org/report/2009/01/27/we-are-forgotten-people/chin-people-burma-unsafe-burma-unprotected-india (accessed 4 January 2018).

Issa v. the School District of Lancaster, 5-16-cv-03881-EGS (The United States District Court for the Eastern District of Pennsylvania August 26, 2016).

Kenyon, D. (2006) *The Bridge Study between Tests of English Language Proficiency and ACCESS for ELLs (R): Part II B: LAS Results*. Washington, DC: Center for Applied Linguistics. See https://www.wida.us/get.aspx?id=134 (accessed 4 January 2018).

Klein, E. and Martohardjono, G. (2006) Understanding the Student with Interrupted Formal Education (SIFE): A Study of SIFE Skills, Needs and Achievement. Report by the Research Institute for the Study of Language in Urban Society, CUNY Grad Center (RISLUS) to the Office of English Language Learners, New York City Department of Education.

Klein, E. and Martohardjono, G. (2015) English language learners with low native language literacy: A profile and intervention in New York City. In M. Santos and A. Whiteside (eds) *Proceedings of the Ninth LESLLA Symposium, 2013* (pp. 174–195). San Francisco, CA: Lulu Publishing Services.

Lee, A. (2012, Dec. 13) County Home to Growing Number of Chin Refugees. *Baltimore Sun*. See http://www.baltimoresun.com/news/maryland/howard/columbia/ph-ho-vw-chin-20121213-story.html (accessed 4 January 2018).

Mace-Matluck, B., Alexander-Kasparik, R. and Queen, R. (1998) *Through the Golden Door: Educational Approaches for Immigrant Children with Limited Formal Schooling*. Washington, DC: Center for Applied Linguistics and Delta Systems.

Marian, V., Blumenfeld, H. and Kaushanskaya, M. (2007) The language experience and proficiency questionnaire (LEAP-Q): Assessing language proficiencies in bilinguals and multilinguals. *Journal of Speech, Language, and Hearing Research* 50 (4), 940–967.

Martin, D. and Yankay, J. (2014) Annual Flow Report: Refugees and Asylees: 2013. Department of Homeland Security, Office of Immigration Statistics. See https://www.dhs.gov/sites/default/files/publications/ois_rfa_fr_2013.pdf (accessed 4 January 2018).

New York State Department of Education (2011) Guidelines for educating limited English proficient students with interrupted formal education. See http://www.p12.nysed.gov/biling/docs/NYSEDSIFEGuidelines.pdf.

Plonsky, L. (2014) Study quality in quantitative L2 research (1990–2010): A methodological synthesis and call to reform. *The Modern Language Journal* 98 (1), 450–470.

Ross, S. (1998) Self-assessment in second language testing: A meta-analysis and analysis of experiential factors. *Language Testing* 15 (1), 1–20.

Shameem, N. (1998) Validating self-reported language proficiency by testing performance in an immigrant community: The Wellington Indo-Fijians. *Language Testing* 15 (1), 86–108.

Silverstein, K. (2016, Oct. 10) Native language literacy assessment promises better outcomes for immigrant students. CE+ED News. See http://news.cehd.umn.edu/

native-language-literacy-assessment-promises-better-outcomes-for-immigrant-students/ (accessed 4 January 2018).

Tarone, E. (2010) Second language acquisition by low-literate learners: An under-studied population. *Language Teaching* 43 (1), 75–83.

Tarone, E. and Bigelow, M. (2005) Impact of literacy on oral language processing: Implications for second language acquisition research. *Annual Review of Applied Linguistics* 25, 77–97.

Thomas, W. and Collier, V. (2002) *A National Study of School Effectiveness for Language Minority Students' Long-Term Academic Achievement*. Santa Cruz, CA: Center for Research on Education, Diversity & Excellence.

US Census Bureau (2016) Selected economic characteristics: 2014 American community survey 1-year estimates. See https://factfinder.census.gov/faces/nav/jsf/pages/community_facts.xhtml (accessed 4 January 2018).

US News and World Report (2013) Education: High schools. US News and World Report. See http://www.usnews.com/education/best-high-schools/maryland/districts/howard-county-public-schools.

United Nations High Commissioner on Refugees (2010) States Parties to the 1951 Convention Relating to the Status of Refugees and the 1961 Protocol. See http://www.unhcr.org/3b73b0d63.html.

United Nations International Children's Emergency Fund (2014) *State of the World's Children 2015*. New York: United Nations Children's Fund. See http://www.unicef.org/publications/files/SOWC_2015_Summary_and_Tables.pdf.

Walsh, C. (1999) *Enabling Academic Success for Secondary Students with Limited Formal Schooling: A Study of the Haitian Literacy Program at Hyde Park High School in Boston*. Providence, RI: Brown University.

World-Class Instructional Design and Assessment (WIDA) Consortium (2007) *Understanding the WIDA English Language Proficiency Standards: A Resource Guide*. Madison, WI: University of Wisconsin System.

World Relief (nd) Burma (Myanmar) Chin Cultural Profile. See https://worldreliefmoline.org/burma-myanmar-chin-cultural-profile/ (accessed 4 January 2018).

Zacarian, D. and Haynes, J. (2012) *The Essential Guide for Educating Beginner English Learners*. Thousand Oaks, CA: Corwin.

Zehr, M. (2009, Mar. 2) N.Y.C. test sizes up ELLs with little formal schooling. *Education Week* 28 (23), 13.

2 'History Should Come First': Perspectives of Somali-born, Refugee-background Male Youth on Writing in and out of School

Bryan Ripley Crandall

This chapter presents ethnographic case studies of four male, Somali-background youth, highlighting perspectives on writing in and out of a high school in the northeastern United States. The four young men were enrolled in mainstream English classrooms while preparing to exit advanced English for speakers of other languages (ESOL) classes. Using writing activity genre research (e.g. Russell, 2009), this study finds that culture and history are central to how these participants see themselves as writers and that they benefit from opportunities to develop their thinking through multiple writing processes. The young men were particularly invested in writing for authentic audiences, sharing their history and lived experiences and promoting respect for their larger communities. Such writing was rare in school, however, where instruction tended to focus on literary analysis and writing for standardized tests. Hence, students' out-of-school writing experiences tended to be more meaningful. The implications of these findings for writing pedagogy and program design with other refugee-background youth are discussed.

This chapter builds on research about refugee-background youth by engaging the perspectives and experiences of four Somali-born young men with writing inside and outside of secondary English classrooms in the United States. According to Alvermann (2009: 25), listening to and observing youth offers insights 'that might otherwise be lost or taken for granted in the rush to categorize literacy practices as either in-school or out-of-school, adolescents as either struggling or competent, and thereby either worthy of our attention or not'. The four young men in this study, who arrived with limited and interrupted formal education (DeCapua

& Marshall, 2010), discussed their purposes for writing and offered a window to the writing experiences they had in and out of school. Here, I build on prior work with refugee-background youth (Crandall, 2012, 2014) by focusing on writing experiences described by participants as most meaningful. I draw on these young men's perspectives to discuss implications for teaching writing in secondary schools.

Research shows that writing instruction in school is often decontextualized and disengaging and that in-school assessment fails to account for the out-of-school spaces where youth write in meaningful ways (Hull & Schultz, 2002). This is especially true for immigrant and refugee youth (Black, 2009; Campano, 2007; Fu, 1995; Sarroub, 2002). According to Fu (1995: 202), English language learners are often 'bombarded' in school with 'endless worksheets' and 'surrounded by meaningless mechanical skills and decontextualized spelling words, and suffocated with frequent quizzes and tests'. Research suggests, in contrast, that student writing benefits from acknowledgment of out-of-school experiences and a teacher's deliberate attention to what Campano (2007: 40) calls the 'second classroom' – i.e. spaces that exist between the academic English of school and literacies enacted out of school. Campano (2007: 40) posits that those teachers who follow 'leads, interests, desires, forms of cultural expression, and especially stories' of immigrant students beyond school are better prepared to help in-school achievement. This includes 21st-century 'technologically mediated environments' (Black, 2009: 689) where refugee-background youth often choose to communicate after relocation.

Although studies examining the literacy practices of African refugee-background adults exist (e.g. Perry, 2008, 2009; Perry & Purcelle-Gates, 2005), few are specific to the writing development of youth. Additionally, Roxas (2010: 72) called for more collaboration between teachers and community members to reach 'the great and sometimes unfulfilled promise that public education often holds for many refugee students and their families'. For these reasons, this study focuses on listening to African-born refugee-background male youth as experts on their writing lives in and out of mainstream English classrooms.

Methodology

For this project, I drew from activity theory (Engeström, 1998) and writing activity genre research (Russell, 2009, 2010). As Russell (2010: 355) wrote, 'To understand the various ways participants interpret and use the tools, object, motive, rules/norms, etc. of an activity system, it is often necessary to analyse the relations among various contexts'. I saw each young man as an agentive writer (*subject*) and analyzed his writing (*outcome*) in relation to the motives he had for composing, the tools he named as useful, the rules he followed, the community influences he discussed and the roles he chose to inhabit. I located participants at the center of the activity systems named as influential to his writing, including relocation histories and memories before arriving to the United States (see Figure 2.1).

As the young men shared with me their writing from mainstream English classes, they also discussed the importance of cultural centers, afterschool programs, sports teams, content area classrooms (including advanced English as a second language [ESL] classes) and digital spaces on who they were as writers. As a result, I expanded my data collection to include these other activity systems, many of which were out of school.

I used a qualitative case study design to help highlight the perspective of each participant (Dyson & Genishi, 2005; Heath & Street, 2008), and also assumed a critical ethnographic stance (Trueba & McLaren, 2000: 61) to 'discover the rich cultural and linguistic capital of the immigrant family'. These frameworks were in keeping with my view of writing as social and cultural acts that are shaped by environments, experiences and histories (Englert *et al.*, 2006).

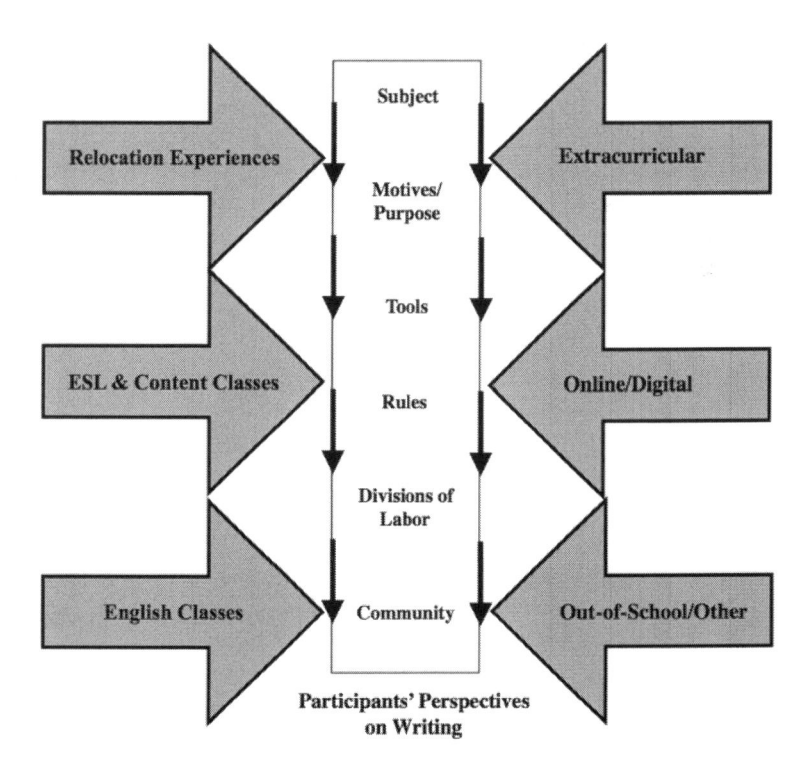

Figure 2.1 Participants' activity systems influencing perspectives on writing

Table 2.1 Summary of participants

Participant	Country of origin	Refugee services	Age	Arrival to United States	Years in United States	Years in mainstream English
Ali (9th grade)	Kenya Somalia (Bantu)	Dadaab Dahley, Kakuma, Kenya	16	2004	6	3
Najm (10th grade)	Somalia (Benadiri)	Maadi, Nasir City, Egypt	17	2006	4	1
Shafac (11th grade)	Somalia (Bantu)	Kakuma, Kenya	19	2004	6	1
Ade (12th grade)	Somalia (Bantu)	Tanzania to Kakuma	20	2004	6	2

Setting and participants

Data were collected during a six-month period in the northeastern United States. School demographics were 63% Black or African American, 25% White, 8% Hispanic or Latino, 3% Asian/Native Hawaiian/Other Pacific Islander and 1% American Indian. The school did not differentiate between African American-born and African-born youth, yet ESL teachers approximated that 200 African-born, refugee-background youth were enrolled in a school of 1200 students. Male participants were chosen to honor the request of elders in the community who suggested it would be inappropriate for a male researcher to work closely with female students. I chose participants to represent a ninth- through twelfth-grade spectrum; all names are pseudonyms. Enrollment at a grade level, however, did not necessarily align with the participant's class level. At times, English language learners were placed in lower levels of mainstream English classrooms at the school before exiting ESL classrooms (Table 2.1).

Data sources and analysis

Data sources for this study included audiotaped, semi-structured interviews (Rubin & Rubin, 1995), participant observations (Bogdan & Biklen, 2007), student work, informal conversations, lesson plans, artistic creations/projects and research memos (Heath & Street, 2008), as seen in Table 2.2. During observations, I wrote descriptive portraits of activities, captured dialogue, detailed settings, accounted for events and made observational comments (Bogdan & Biklen, 2007). I used guided conversation protocols (Rubin & Rubin, 1995) for interviews and qualitative procedures to locate emerging themes (Bogdan & Biklen, 2007).

Role of researcher

Since 1998, I have volunteered with refugee programs, and because of my position as a White, Western-educated male and teacher, I consulted postcolonial theories and literature (Eastmond, 2007; Windance-Twine & Warren, 2000) to become more critical of my subjectivities. I read

Table 2.2 Summary of data sources

Interviews	Field observations	Other
Two semi-structured, 60-minute interviews with each participant	84 participant-observations in mainstream English classrooms	Programs, school newspapers, district documents, sample state assessments, handouts, emails, Facebook posts, etc.
One semi-structured, 60-minute interview with each participant's English teacher	36 participant-observations in non-mainstream English classrooms (e.g. history, ESL, science)	158 pages of written work
One semi-structured, 60-minute interview with other individuals named by participants	60 observations out-of-school (e.g. athletic facilities, parks, malls, tutoring programs, community centers)	Totals: 16 interviews 180 observations Approximately 1430 pages of data

historical texts to help me advocate participants as 'active agents of their own history, rather than passive victims' (Windance-Twine & Warren, 2000: 208). Participants helped edit my writings, making suggestions to clarify how I represented them.

Findings

Students and teachers reported that writing in English classrooms centered on passing state examinations. Lessons typically required students to fill out packets of questions designed to help students read canonical texts (e.g. *Lord of the Flies*). Writing in English class was rare, except for on-demand assessments given to prepare students for state tests. All four participants reported, though, that writing was important in their lives. They highlighted their cultural histories, alluded to African colonization and 20th-century globalization, and discussed the civil wars (Besteman, 1999; Grady, 2015; Harrell-Bond & Voutira, 2007) that had uprooted their families. For these reasons, I have chosen to present a partial history of each participant in relation to the perspective on writing in and out of school being offered.

Ali: Writing with a purpose – 'The future wasn't always open.'

Ali, born in 1994 after his parents fled Somalia, spent the first 10 years of his life in refugee camps, and attended school in Kakuma for only three months:

> It was like living in hell. They had nothing there. We organized everything when we came. The Somali Bantus. The Somalians. The Sudanese. I didn't learn nothing to tell you the truth. I didn't hardly do any writing.

Ali viewed education, though, as an opportunity to advance himself and he remembered hearing elders' discussions in the camp: 'In America, they have shoes that help you ride the world and help you find your place in everything. You just have to put them on'.

Ali relocated to the United States in 2004 and entered fifth grade. By ninth grade, he was simultaneously enrolled in advanced ESL and a mainstream English class. He worked diligently, but grew frustrated with American-born students who 'fooled around too much and never listen to teachers'. Teachers spent a majority of the class time controlling the behavior of classmates. 'We don't write that much in English', he lamented. Instead, he was given worksheets to invoke literary analysis in preparation for state assessments. The work, he speculated, was given to keep students 'quiet and in their seats. We only write for the tests, really'.

Ali sought writing opportunities, however, to teach American audiences about his family's story. As a ninth grader, he recruited classmates, an ESL teacher and a school librarian to create a student publication. 'The magazine', Ali reflected, 'was designed to show everyone we [ESL students] have a social life, too'. He and 20 students worked on weekends, after school and through holiday breaks to publish *Hope for New Life*, a magazine that included articles, photographs, poetry and biographies. As editor, Ali divided work responsibilities among members of his team. Each writer drafted and revised stories until they were ready for publication and distribution around the school.

One article written by Ali featured the community center he attended outside of school, where he received academic support. He interviewed the director and researched the center's history. The six-paragraph article was the lengthiest writing he composed during data collection and the only piece of writing he revised (an expectation he placed on himself). The article began, 'American students are taught everything is possible. For many students arriving to America, however, the future wasn't always open'.

Ali was motivated to create *Hope for New Life* to educate others about ESL students at the school. His team looked at newspapers for models and taught themselves how to conduct interviews. Through Ali's leadership, *Hope for New Life* was distributed to school mailboxes and displayed proudly outside the principal's office. In sum, Ali demonstrated himself as a writer with intent to share his lived experiences with others. He initiated his own writing opportunities, recruited others and took charge of communicating the histories of ESL students.

Shafac: Writing creatively about lived experiences – 'I wrote about Africa.'

Shafac was two years old in 1991 when war came to his home and his father was killed. He learned at an early age that his people were discriminated against, explaining:

> They were killing Somali Bantus so we had to escape. Bantus were slaves. They farm and are not rich. Every time the Bantus had a farm, gangs take it from them. We didn't have life so we left.

Shafac helped his mother escape with their family at night, and from 1993 to 2001 they lived in Hagadera refugee camp. They reached Kakuma three years later. By age 14, he realized he was 'the man of the family' and this meant he needed to contribute his labor to help his mother.

While in Kakuma, Shafac chose not to attend schools because 'The schools only teach grammar. I didn't like it'. He stayed at home with his mother and collected bags left by the United Nations. Together, they sewed them into walls that protected families from the Kenyan winds. Supporting his family economically was a high priority. He realized that they did not have clothing like others in the camp, which embarrassed him. He did not like the way he and other Bantus were treated by their non-Bantu Somali peers, a discrimination documented throughout Somali's history (Besteman, 1999). This discrimination was another reason for not attending schools in the camp.

In 2004, at age 13, Shafac came to the United States with no formal education. The first priority was to learn 'how to hold a pencil'.

> I already knew the alphabet, so I just need to start writing my mind. When I used to write paragraphs I had to number it, like put number one, number two, each paragraph, so I knew where to write words. I wrote about Africa.

Writing about his childhood was easy because he had 'pictures in my head' that he could 'find English words for'. Numbering words to match these pictures helped him to sequence sentences.

Shafac received ESL services from seventh to twelfth grade and, as a senior, was enrolled in a tenth-grade English class. During an interview, his mother conveyed that Shafac 'needed to finish school' so he could get a job, to 'get money' to support their relatives in Africa. Shafac lamented, however, 'My mother doesn't understand how I get an A in gym, but don't do well in other classes. She thinks I'm not working hard enough'. During the study, Shafac failed the state English examinations twice and struggled with its emphasis on literary analysis. He admitted, 'I little bit hate it. I could do it, but I don't know how. I'm trying to know the big words, make it a big deal, but it couldn't work'. He knew that passing the state exams was a doorway to his future, even if writing about literature didn't make sense to him.

The only time that Shafac felt successful with writing was during a short-lived unit that was presented to him in his mainstream English class. The teacher used Walter Dean Myer's *Monster* as a mentor text and guided students to co-construct characteristics of the screenplay genre. Shafac wrote about Kakuma, and a time when he was bullied in the camps. In his script, Muhammad Ali arrives in his dreams and teaches a boy to fight. Part of the script reads:

Boy: I don't want to fight you, Muhammad. I want to be you, to be strong, to achieve, to dream and keep the faith. Cut to: inside of a bus. Camera moves to boy, age eleven, traveling across Africa.
Mother: (wiping off sweat) You were fighting again.

Shafac found an unusual break from literary analysis through scriptwriting. The creative exercise prompted him to learn new tools that tapped into his personal experiences, and in his writing, he demonstrated that he could implement genre conventions and literary devices that he was unable to recognize when analyzing literature on demand.

As was the case with Ali, writing from personal experience benefited Shafac's language acquisition and confidence. His teacher, too, recognized that creative and personal writing was useful for developing beginning writers, yet reported being under pressure by administration to provide test-only instruction. Shafac's teacher reflected, 'At the end, will the superintendent ask me what writing I've done outside the box or outside the state test? No. The tests speak'.

Test-centered instruction in school limited Shafac's opportunities to develop his writing skills. The screenwriting instruction that had engaged Shafac was cut short and replaced with worksheets typically offered by English teachers, asking students to locate literary devices in the texts they were assigned to read. Shafac needed to pass the state exams to graduate, and was unsuccessful. This made him doubt himself as a writer. Even so, Shafac became engaged intellectually when given an opportunity to write about his past. Whereas state assessments positioned Shafac as an unsuccessful writer, a freedom to write creatively and personally motivated him to take more risks.

Ade: Writing as self-empowerment – 'When African pride was still shining...'

Ade, the eldest of eight children, was born in 1990 in Hamar, Somalia. His Bantu mother and father fled with him to Haridari, Kenya, when he was two years old. In 1997, Ade's family moved to Kakuma where he began school for the first time. He spoke Somali, Swahili, Arlie Af Maay, Bemal, Zuer, Mai Mai and a little Dinka – languages he needed to survive. He also recalled that his earliest education was tied to his religion.

When you go to Muslim school you've got to read your assignment in the Qur'an. They teach me to be a very good brother. Then the teacher will stand up and tell everybody 'Don't do this. Be a nice brother'.

Ade reported that his religion was his foundation for reading and writing, and elders expected him to memorize passages of the Qur'an, a practice he credited to his academic success in US schools. Learning the complicated teachings of the Qur'an, he felt, prepared him for the hard work it would take to be successful in an American high school.

Ade attended classes with Sudanese students in Kakuma and felt that Sudanese teachers weren't as strict as those in the Somali school.

> The teacher gives a lot of notes in Swahili. They don't have pen or paper like that. You come up with the paper and pen. The teacher writes in English. You copy what they write. They teach in English, but explain in Swahili. Most kids can't read, so teacher reads everything for us. You copy. I couldn't write my own words so I copy theirs.

Ade knew that education would advance his future and he described learning best by following rules. He appreciated when teachers modeled what they wanted students to do, and also enjoyed playing school when he returned home. He practiced writing in a book, 'Today is a nice day. Today the sky is blue. Today I will get water for my family'. Thus, writing what he knew and lived helped him to learn language.

Ade and his family relocated to the US in 2004 and, a senior in high school, he continued to value when teachers provided models for what they expected. Unlike in other English classes I observed, Ade's teacher encouraged a writing workshop where students wrote every day. Ade boasted, 'I'm not afraid to write. They say you read and write all the time in college'. He was already accepted into a four-year program for nursing and, driven to succeed, enrolled in AP psychology where he was excited to learn research skills. He loved reading articles in the AP course and reflected that 'they help me to make sense of what I lived in refugee camps'. Although unsuccessful at passing the AP psychology exam, he appreciated that the class helped him to learn more about himself and to prepare for college-level writing.

Ade took the most pride in writing an essay entitled 'Daah' for which he estimated that he wrote 'seven to nine drafts'. The essay described an heirloom carried by his mother 'for over ten years' when 'no one knew she had it'. In Ade's essay, he explained, 'The Daah is a white square with colorful strings and yarn that shines like a white scarf. Since it was made it has traveled from Somalia to Kenya to America and survived two generations'.

When he returned from school one day, Ade saw the Daah hanging in the living room and 'couldn't believe' his 'eyes'. He knew the importance of the heirloom to his family's history, and wrote his essay to share his family's story of relocation. On reading August Wilson's *The Piano Lesson*, his English teacher assigned an heirloom essay, offering students one-on-one writing conferences and encouraging students to peer review one another's work. Ade appreciated the collaborative community created by his teacher and reflected, 'Because my other English classes, we just do one draft and the teacher marks it with pen. But in this class, I write it over and over and learn my mistakes. Each time I read it I find another mistake. It's never correct'.

Similar to Ali and Shafac, one of Ade's goals was to share Bantu culture with American-born readers. He talked often about his writing and personal heirloom in his English class, and was the only participant who claimed to write more in English than in other subject areas. The teacher's writing community helped Ade and his classmates to see themselves as writers and to communicate lived experiences with each other.

Najm: Writing for cultural pride – 'History should come first.'

Najm was born in Mogadishu, Somalia, in 1992 and, proud of his Benadiri ancestry, described himself as a 'mix of Somali and Arab blood'. He left Qur'an school in 2001 after civil conflict came close to his home. He reported during an interview, 'I was walking at first, running. I saw fire, guns and bullets. I hid in the bushes until the war was over. Then they left and I went home. It was the worst thing I see in my life'.

Soon after, Najm's mother fled with him to Cairo, Egypt, and they remained there for five years, first living in an aunt's small apartment and then settling in a refugee camp. Najm attended an Arabic school for third through sixth grade, where he had much respect for his teachers, most of whom were Palestinian. Similar to Ade's reports, Najm said these teachers wrote information on the board for students to copy: 'What the teachers wrote was important. They gave us lists to write down. There were 16 boys in class. If you didn't do your homework, you'd get beat up. Like, you know, with the stick'. At this school, Najm took special interest in the United States, 'especially about how slavery came to America from Europe'. Colonial histories, oppression and discrimination became central to his thinking.

In 2006, Najm's family was relocated to the United States, where he immediately enrolled in an eighth-grade ESL class. Najm, a member of the Reer Xamar ethnic group and non-Bantu, was a minority within the school's Somali community. He read on his own about African and African American history, subjects he felt teachers ignored. Najm showed little patience for American teachers who, he claimed, 'never discuss issues of race besides slavery and civil rights'. He reported that American teachers were 'ignorant' when it came to African history, and wished they knew more. He felt he had much to contribute, but often restrained himself in his classes.

As a junior, Najm was enrolled in a tenth-grade English class with 5 American-born students and 27 English language learners, a demographic his teacher felt untrained to work with: 'I wish college [teacher education] classes exposed us to the diversity of American classrooms', she explained in an interview, a frustration that Najm also shared. Although he completed assignments, he would not turn them in because he had an altercation with the teacher over missing work earlier in the year. He discussed, 'I'm not supposed to argue with her. I know the facts. I just ignore her'. He claimed in an interview that his teacher's lack of 'historical knowledge on global issues', made any work he did for her 'pointless'. While reading *Lord of the Flies*, for instance, he told a friend, 'Conflict is still alive, but people don't see it. The boys on the island, they see it, though'. In class and out of school, he discussed the parallels of the young men on the island with the experiences of fleeing Somalia and living in a refugee camp. When asked why he didn't share his insight with the teacher he responded, 'She don't care'.

Najm desired to share what he knew about African history in class, but had few opportunities to do so. The worksheets given didn't encourage students to discuss what they read with one another. Few opportunities were provided for developing their writing. Even so, Najm reported:

> Writing is the best thing to do in life, but not that much in school. I write on my own. My own imagination. Writing brings my happiest moments. Like, I write at home about how Africa used to be nice. I search the news about Somalia.

Like the other participants, Najm wrote more on his own time. He debated history incessantly and even created a Facebook page where he and his friends discussed African history. He posted:

> When I graduate, I want to be historian. I want to study about those old Africans, east Africans, that mixed with my family, especially where my mom is from... I want to be a journalist and report the truth about the world.

Najm envisioned a future where he wanted to write. He composed mini-editorials on Facebook about events in Somalia, Palestine and Egypt, and often posted what he called 'quotes', poetic thoughts about the world that rhymed and followed lyrical patterns. In one, 'History should come first', he wrote:

> I wish I can take you back, time,
> when African pride was still shining.
> African king was more than a dream.

> Consider it supreme and heart of the lion,
> before children suffer and are dieing,
> before bullet was already flying
> before leaders was already lying
> killing wrong people so.
> They know we would fight them,
> before streets filled with blood,
> before our hearts turn cold, then filled again with love.

Although his writing demonstrates critical thinking, poetic talents, political commentary and historical insight, Najm was unsuccessful at passing his tenth-grade English class. Ultimately, he was unmotivated to write for the teacher. Outside of school, though, he received feedback from readers around the world who connected with his thinking, left commentary and encouraged him to keep writing.

Najm, like Ali, Shafac and Ade, was invested in writing about personal history, and he resented teachers who failed to understand Africa, especially the experiences of refugees. On Facebook, Najm purposely wrote for audiences that mattered to him and engaged his friends in intellectual discussion. In English class, however, he chose to do the worksheets given to him, but not to submit them for a grade, as both a commitment to his education and an act of protest.

Discussion and Implications

The intent of this research has been to honor the voices, perspectives and experiences of four Somali-born, refugee-background youth who might otherwise be ignored in what Kinloch (2010: 64) refers to as 'larger sociopolitical debates'. Such views cannot be separated from the immense histories and experiences that these young men lived as postcolonial subjects (Duncan, 2003; Gilroy, 1987). I chose to include historical snapshots in these case studies (Dyson & Genishi, 2005; Eastmond, 2007) to validate the perspectives on writing that the young men offered. These findings suggest several useful pedagogical directions for secondary school educators:

Provide authentic writing opportunities. One implication echoed elsewhere (e.g. Campano, 2007; Fisher, 2007; Kinloch, 2010) is that an exam-focused writing curriculum more often than not inhibits meaningful writing experiences for young people. The primary purpose for school writing reported by Ali, Najm, Shafac and Ade was to prepare for state examinations, rather than to develop as individual writers (cf. Applebee & Langer, 2009, 2013; Hillocks, 2002). Participants suggested that mainstream classroom teachers might find more success if they provided more opportunities to write about lived experiences rather than having students fill out worksheets. Written outcomes such as Ade's heirloom essay or Shafac's screenplay resulted when teachers pushed against test-only instruction and provided opportunities for storytelling (cf. Perry, 2008). Findings suggest that these students would have responded well to a theme-based curriculum that built vocabulary through the integration of reading, writing and speaking, and offered opportunities to explore themes through personal writing that connects to their out-of-school experiences. Teachers should therefore encourage authentic, personal writing in relation to the content they deliver, as a way to help refugee-background youth develop language around their improvised (Grady, 2015) and in-between (Ibrahim, 2008; Sarroub, 2002) experiences.

Establish legitimate audiences. A second implication derived from participants' perspectives is that the writing lives of youth are more robust than schools might assume. These young men were motivated to connect with audiences beyond teachers. All four were eager to share their writing, to teach about Somalia and to put their migration histories within the context of the American dream – Ali through his journalistic advocacy of ESL students; Shafac through a screenplay seeking advice from Muhammad Ali; Ade through a celebration of a cultural heirloom; and Najm through poetic quotes on Facebook. Communicating to larger audiences helped each writer to feel validated as an immigrant and global citizen (cf. Campano, 2007; Fu, 1995) through use of their personal funds of knowledge (Moll *et al.*, 1992). Teachers should therefore encourage writing that requires students to communicate with audiences important to them that transcend school, including those in digital spaces (Black, 2009).

Attend to multiple writing processes. A third implication of this study is that fostering meaningful writing processes matters more than pre-formulated written outcomes. These case studies – especially Ali's article, Shafac's screenplay and Ade's heirloom essay – highlight that better writing resulted when teachers encouraged brainstorming, planning, drafting, editing, revising and sharing. Shafac's screenplay emerged from discussions and modeling in class that helped him understand the genre of a screenplay. Ade's heirloom essay, too, resulted from a writer's workshop and a teacher's emphasis on mini-lessons, models and peer conferencing. Similarly, Ali, in his leadership role with *Hope for New Life*, advocated for brainstorming, drafting, sharing and revision with his team, before they submitted the magazine for publication. These examples suggest that teachers should spend time developing the many writing processes that young people use to achieve personal goals, and they should be intentional with naming those writing processes as they occur.

Recognize community memberships. A fourth implication emerging from participants' perspectives is that written outcomes are better achieved when young people feel that they belong to a writing community.

An in-school writing community should recognize the out-of-school communities to which each student belongs. Teachers who encourage young people to explore their out-of-school lives in school may better assist the writing proficiency expected of students in school, as has been indicated by research in similar urban contexts (e.g. Fisher, 2007; Kinloch, 2010). Sadly, few classrooms had a mission to develop such a writing community in school. Najm faulted his teacher, in fact, for failing to recognize the communities and experiences that he and his classmates lived outside of the classroom, while Ade celebrated a teacher who promoted cultural histories through his heirloom writing assignment. Teachers should explore the multiple ways that students write in out-of-school communities and highlight the ways that these communities communicate with one another.

Respect personal history. The fifth, and perhaps most important, implication resulting from participants' perspectives on writing is the importance of history as part of the context for how each writer viewed who he was in the United States. Youth like those in this chapter desire respect from teachers and recognition of their lived histories. In all four cases, a desire to share history and identities was central to achieving written outcomes. Ali wanted an American audience to know the struggles of his relocation. Shafac wanted to share the influence of a boxing icon from his childhood who helped him as a Bantu youth in a refugee camp. Ade recognized his historical place in the world through admiration of an heirloom that his mother carried with her to the United States. Najm wanted Facebook readers to know that 'History should come first', by establishing an online space (cf. Black, 2009) to promote African history. As they help refugee-background youth to develop as writers, teachers benefit from listening to the cultures, histories and traditions of students as valuable resources to inform curriculum, instruction and scholarship (cf. Alvermann, 2009; Moje, 2002).

The four Somali-born participants presented in this chapter reported the importance that writing has in their lives. They desired to write more in school, especially about their communities and histories, yet were frustrated with how state assessments limited their opportunities for authentic writing (cf. Roy & Roxas, 2011). Each young man in this study wanted to write about his Somali culture and lived experiences, what Ibrahim (2008: 247) calls a 'negotiated product' of being African and Black in the Western world. Despite the lack of writing instruction received in school, all four participants described themselves as writers. In the words of Najm:

> When I write, I'm not just writing for myself. I am speaking for others. That's what I do. I tell others what's going on. I speak for me. I speak for them, too. The background where I'm from. I speak globally.

It is our responsibility as educators, researchers and citizens of the world to understand the complexity of the refugee experience and the obstacles that refugee-background youth face in our schools. We need to speak globally with instruction, too, as we promote writing to recognize history, to celebrate the power of storytelling and to emphasize the importance of speaking within and across communities.

References

Alvermann, D.E. (2009) Sociocultural constructions of adolescence and youth people's literacies. In L. Christenbury, R. Bomer and P. Smagorinksy (eds) *Handbook of Adolescent Literacy Research* (pp. 14–28). New York: Guilford Press.

Applebee, A.N. and Langer, J.A. (2009) What is happening in the teaching of writing. *English Journal* 98 (5), 18–28.

Applebee, A.N. and Langer, J. (2013) *Writing Instruction that Works: Proven Methods for Middle and High School Classrooms*. New York: Teachers College Press.

Besteman, C. (1999) *Unraveling Somalia: Race, Violence, and the Legacy of Slavery*. Philadelphia, PA: University of Pennsylvania Press.

Black, R.W. (2009) English language learners, fan communities, and 21st-century skills. *Journal of Adolescent & Adult Literacy* 52 (8), 688–697.

Bogdan, B. and Biklen, S. (2007) *Qualitative Research for Education: An Introduction to Theories and Methods*. New York: Allyn & Bacon.

Campano, G. (2007) *Immigrant Students and Literacy: Reading, Writing, and Remembering*. New York: Teachers College Press.

Crandall, B.R. (2012) 'A responsibility to speak out': Perspectives on writing from black African-born males with limited and disrupted formal education. Unpublished doctoral dissertation, Syracuse University.

Crandall, B.R. (2014) Lost voices in an American high school: Sudanese male English-language learners' perspectives on writing. In C. Compton-Lilly and E. Halverson (eds) *Time and Space in Literacy Research* (pp. 107–121). New York: Routledge.

Decapua, A. and Marshall, H.W. (2010) Students with limited or interrupted formal education in US classrooms. *The Urban Review* 42 (2), 159–173.

Duncan, D. (2003) A flexible foundation. In D.T. Goldberg and A. Quayson (eds) *Relocating Postcolonialism* (pp. 320–333). Oxford: Blackwell.

Dyson, A.H. and Genishi, C. (2005) *On the Case: Approaches to Language and Literacy research*. New York: Teachers College Press.

Eastmond, M. (2007) Stories as lived experience: Narratives in forced migration research. *Journal of Refugee Studies* 20 (2), 248–264.

Engeström, Y. (1998) Activity theory and individual and social transformation. In Y. Engeström, R. Miettinen and R.-L. Punamäki (eds) *Perspectives on Activity Theory* (pp. 1–38). Cambridge: Cambridge University Press.

Englert, C.S., Mariage, T.V. and Dunsmore, K. (2006) Tenets of sociocultural theory in writing instruction research. In C.A. MacArthur, S. Graham and J. Fitzgerald (eds) *Handbook of Writing Research* (pp. 208–221). New York: The Guilford Press.

Fisher, M.T. (2007) *Writing in Rhythm; Spoken Word Poetry in Urban Classrooms*. New York: Teachers College Press.

Fu, D. (1995) *'My Trouble is My English': Asian Students and the American Dream*. Portsmouth, NH: Heinemann Press.

Gilroy, P. (1987) *'There Ain't No Black in the Union Jack': The Cultural Politics of Race and Nation*. Chicago, IL: University of Chicago Press.

Grady, S. (2015) *Improvised Adolescence: Somali Bantu Teenage Refugees in America*. Madison, WI: University of Wisconsin Press.

Harrell-Bond, B. and Voutira, E. (2007) In search of 'invisible' actors: Barriers to access in refugee research. *Journal of Refugee Studies* 20 (2), 281–298.

Heath, S.B. and Street, B.V. (2008) *On Ethnography: Approaches to Language and Literacy*. New York: Teachers College Press.

Hillocks, G. (2002) *The Testing Trap: How State Writing Assessments Control Learning*. New York: Teachers College Press.

Hull, B. and Schultz, K. (2002) *School's Out! Bridging Out-of-School Literacies with Classroom Practice*. New York: Teachers College Press.

Ibrahim, A. (2008) The new flâneur: Subaltern cultural studies, African youth in Canada and the semiology of in-betweenness. *Cultural Studies* 22 (2), 234–253.

Kinloch, V. (2010) *Harlem on Our Minds: Place, Race, and the Literacies of Urban Youth*. New York: Teachers College Press.

Moje, E. (2002) But where are the youth? On the value of integrating youth culture into literacy theory. *Educational Theory* 52 (1), 97–120.

Moll, L.C., Amanti, C., Neff, D. and Gonzalez, N. (1992) Funds of knowledge for teaching: Using a qualitative approach to connect homes and classrooms. *Theory into Practice* 31 (2), 132–141.

Perry, K. (2008) From storytelling to writing: Transforming literacy among Sudanese refugees. *Journal of Literacy Research* 40 (3), 317–388.

Perry, K. (2009) Genres, contexts, and literacy practices: Literary brokering among Sudanese refugee families. *Reading Research Quarterly* 44 (3), 256–276.

Perry, K. and Purcell-Gates, V. (2005) Resistance and appropriation: Literacy practices as agency within hegemonic contexts. In B. Maloch, J. Hoffman, D.L. Schallert, C.M. Fairbanks and J. Worthy (eds) *54th Yearbook of the National Reading Conference* (pp. 272–285). Oak Creek, WI: National Reading Conference.

Roxas, K. (2010) Who really wants 'the tired, the poor, and the huddled masses' anyway?: Teachers' use of cultural scripts with refugee students in public schools. *Multicultural Perspectives* 12 (2), 65–73.

Roy, L.A. and Roxas, K.C. (2011) Whose deficit is this anyhow? Exploring counter-stories of Somali Bantu refugees' experiences in 'doing school'. *Harvard Educational Review* 81 (3), 521–541.

Rubin, H.J. and Rubin, I.S. (1995) *Qualitative Interviewing: The Art of Hearing Data*. Thousand Oaks, CA: Sage.

Russell, D. (2009) Uses of activity theory in written communication research. In A. Sannino, H. Daniels and K.D. Gutiérrez (eds) *Learning and Expanding with Activity Theory* (pp. 40–52). New York: Cambridge University Press.

Russell, D.R. (2010) Writing multiple contexts: Vygotskian CHAT meets the phenomenology of genre. In C. Baserman, R. Krut, K. Lunsford, S. Mcleod, S. Null, P. Rogers and A. Stansell (eds) *Traditions of Writing Research* (pp. 353–364). New York: Routledge.

Sarroub, L.K. (2002) In-betweenness: Religion and conflicting visions of literacy. *Reading Research Quarterly* 37 (2), 130–148.

Trueba, E.T. and McLaren, P. (2000) Critical ethnography for the study of immigrants. In E.T. Trueba and L.I. Bartolomé (eds) *Immigrant Voices: In Search of Educational Equity* (pp. 37–74). New York: Rowman & Littlefield Publishers Inc.

Windance-Twine, F. and Warren, J. (2000) *Racing Research, Researching Race: Methodological Dilemmas in Critical Race Studies*. New York: New York University Press.

3 Translanguaging Pedagogy to Support the Language Learning of Older Nepali-Bhutanese Adults

Koeun Park and Verónica E. Valdez

In many English for speakers of other languages (ESOL) classrooms, instruction does not recognize or make use of students' linguistic resources other than English. Identifying this language compartmentalization as having negative effects on students' English learning, particularly for older adults from refugee backgrounds, this chapter investigates how a translanguaging pedagogy, which recognizes students' funds of knowledge as valuable assets, can be an effective means of facilitating English learning and disrupting the deficit views of students and their home languages and cultures. Findings from a study of an ESOL classroom for older Nepali-Bhutanese adults from refugee backgrounds showcase how student meaning-making and metalinguistic and crosslinguistic awareness emerged as a result of the teacher's strategically enacted translanguaging pedagogy. Students engaged in a variety of translanguaging practices to learn English and to convey their understandings of themselves and their world. The authors conclude that by valuing the existing linguistic abilities and rich linguistic repertoires that older adults from refugee backgrounds bring into classrooms, educators increase students' English gains in affirming ways.

A person unexpectedly visited my classroom [of older Nepali-Bhutanese students] to see [them]. She introduced herself as their former English teacher. She was very excited to see them and wanted to engage them. However, I was a bit puzzled because the students seemed indifferent, enough for me to think that they might not know her. The class atmosphere became awkward all of a sudden. Soon after she became aware of the mood, she left. Right when the door closed after her, the students started to express their discomfort towards her. One of the students mocked her by raising his voice 'English! English! No Nepali!' I had never seen them displaying such strong anger until that day. (Field notes)

During refugee resettlement, learning a new language in the destination country is thought to be crucial because of its association with access to educational, social and economic opportunities (Warriner, 2007b). Thus, in the United States, focus is put on providing individuals from refugee backgrounds with access to ESOL instruction. Studies on the language and literacy learning of individuals with refugee backgrounds have argued for the importance of providing student-centered, academically challenging language learning experiences that respond to their specific needs, reflect their sociopolitical lived experiences and set high educational expectations (Hirano, 2015; Ortmeier-Hooper, 2013; Warriner, 2007a, 2007b). However, much ESOL instruction continues to promote strict language compartmentalization in the classroom, despite research that has long shown the value of using students' home languages to support English language and literacy instruction (e.g. Wright, 2015).

As the opening vignette (see previous page) illustrates, being reprimanded by a teacher for speaking their home language in an English classroom in the United States can produce strong emotional responses from students. These responses can disengage students from the teacher and hinder their language learning (Krashen, 1981). As Auerbach (1993: 16) argues, 'Prohibiting the native language within the context of ESL instruction may impede language acquisition precisely because it mirrors disempowering relations'. This seems particularly problematic when it occurs in classrooms with older adults who have undergone many hardships prior to and during resettlement and who may interpret this policy as an additional impediment to successful engagement in language learning. Older adults from refugee backgrounds comprise 3% of the total refugee population (60 years or older) (United Nations High Commissioner for Refugees, 2015) and currently make up 3% of resettlement cases (65 years or older) in the United States (Capps *et al.*, 2015). They are often depicted as poor language learners and labeled as 'preliterate' or 'non-literate'. These misconceptions stem from generalizations that older adults' linguistic abilities are diminished (Grognet, 1997; Weinstein-Shr, 1993) as well as from dominant literacy approaches that 'impose Western, urban or class-based conceptions of literacy' (Prinsloo & Street, 2014: 67) to determine who is considered literate. We argue that such students' funds of knowledge (González *et al.*, 2005), particularly their home languages and literacies, are the most readily available and effective tools for fostering meaning-making during language learning and need to be taken up as pedagogical resources in ESOL classrooms.

In this chapter, we offer a theoretical overview of the key concepts and studies that ground our study: the funds of knowledge framework (González *et al.*, 2005) as well as translanguaging and translanguaging pedagogy (García & Kleyn, 2016; García & Wei, 2014). We then discuss the methods used to investigate our central research question: 'How do non-traditional, older students from refugee backgrounds enact translanguaging practices to learn English in a classroom where translanguaging pedagogy is implemented in the curriculum?' We include a description of the context and student-centered, asset-based translanguaging pedagogy we implemented. Our findings illustrate how older Nepali-Bhutanese adults with refugee backgrounds learn English through translanguaging pedagogy. We conclude by discussing the implications of our findings.

Theoretical Framework

The term 'funds of knowledge' refers to 'the historically accumulated and culturally developed bodies of knowledge and skills essential for household or individual functioning and well-being' (Moll *et al.*, 1992: 133). This body of knowledge and skills includes students' full repertoire of linguistic practices that can be utilized when learning English. 'Translanguaging', a term introduced by the Welsh educator Cen Williams (1996), was first conceptualized as a pedagogical practice employing two languages in a lesson to develop students' productive and receptive language skills. We view translanguaging pedagogy as a funds of knowledge-based approach focused on the linguistic dimension. García (2009) expanded on Williams' ideas to conceptualize a translanguaging theory, deriving from the linguistic concept of *languaging* advanced by Swain (2006), which describes the dynamic process of producing and using language to understand, problem-solve and make meaning. Moving away from the monoglossic view that perceives bilinguals as having two separate linguistic systems, translanguaging posits bilinguals as engaging in multiple discursive practices using one linguistic repertoire from which they strategically select features to communicate effectively and make sense of their bilingual worlds (García, 2009, 2011). In other words, translanguaging rejects the idea of bilingualism as the sum of two separate monolingual codes – a premise that distinguishes it from the concept of code-switching, in which languages are perceived as 'autonomous, closed systems with their own linguistic structures' (García & Kleyn, 2016: 14). Therefore, translanguaging centers on language practices, not on the languages themselves.

Within the field of education, translanguaging has been gaining attention as a pedagogical tool. García and Kano point to translanguaging as:

> a process by which students and teachers engage in complex discursive practices that include ALL the language practices of ALL students in a class in order to develop new language practices and sustain old ones, communicate and appropriate knowledge, and give voice to new sociopolitical realities by interrogating linguistic inequality. (García & Kano, 2014: 261, emphasis original)

In articulating a translanguaging pedagogy, García and Wei (2014) point to several key principles: (a) adapt instruction to different types of students and multilingual classrooms; (b) build background knowledge so that students can make meaning of the content being taught and the languaging used in the lesson; (c) deepen understandings of linguistic inequality, disrupt linguistic hierarchies and increase social political engagement; (d) develop critical thinking and critical consciousness, and extend new knowledge; (e) raise learners' crosslinguistic and metalinguistic awareness to strengthen their ability to meet the communicative contingencies of the socioeducational situation; (f) allow crosslinguistic flexibility so that learners use language practices competently; and (g) increase learners' identity investments.

Educators need to take an active role in laying the groundwork necessary to accomplish these goals. García *et al.* (2016) offer three important elements that an educator needs to consider when adopting translanguaging pedagogy: the teacher's stance, the teacher's design and the teacher's shifts. First, educators must develop a philosophical stance in which they recognize bilingualism as a resource for class activities, position students at the center and believe in the transformative capability that translanguaging holds to disrupt the linguistic hierarchies of schools. Next, when designing and planning instruction, educators need to create collaborative and student-centered structures, incorporate various and appropriate multilingual and multimodal resources and strategically facilitate students' full language repertoires. The final element is the need to be flexible and to shift instruction and planning as needed, to respond quickly to an individual student's linguistic needs.

The significance of translanguaging as a pedagogy is that it does not view students' home languages as simply a scaffolding resource for acquiring another language, as do many traditional ESOL pedagogies; rather, it focuses on sustaining and legitimizing home language practices (García & Kleyn, 2016). Thus, multilingual voices and experiences that may have been silenced, unsupported and marginalized in some traditional language classrooms are directly engaged during instruction through a translanguaging pedagogy. Research on translanguaging pedagogy has tended to focus on children and adolescents (e.g. García *et al.*, 2016; García & Wei, 2014, 2015), rather than older adults. This same gap is present in the larger body of language and literacy research on students from refugee backgrounds. Hence, this study makes important contributions to existing research by including the experiences of older adults from refugee backgrounds.

Investigating a Translanguaging Curriculum

The qualitative interpretive research (Denzin & Lincoln, 2011) reported in this chapter is based on 18 months of classroom data. In this section, we describe our research approach, the classroom setting and participants, and the translanguaging curriculum that was employed in the class. We begin with a discussion of our positionality as researchers. Park's positionality as a Korean, multilingual immigrant, teacher and researcher for this study offered challenges and opportunities. Park's existing relationships with the students helped her to recognize the students' funds of knowledge and implement that knowledge within the translanguaging pedagogy in her classroom. Many of the opportunities for deep engagement with students came from her multilingualism, including her efforts to learn Nepali from students and through self-study, allowing her to have basic conversations in Nepali with students. These efforts and linguistic ability communicated to students that the classroom was a space where their languages were appreciated and promoted. The challenges mostly centered on the balancing of her perspectives as a teacher with her interpretations as a researcher. To counter the possibility of bias and provide another point of view, Valdez was asked to join this study as a co-researcher. As a Latina, Spanish–English bilingual researcher with expertise in ESOL and bilingual pedagogies and research, Valdez lent her experiences working with immigrant and refugee-background communities by helping to develop the translanguaging curriculum and in the research design and analysis of this study.

Park's ESOL class and students

The local county's aging and adult services department offered nine free, government-funded ESOL classes at seven senior centers taught by five instructors and three volunteers. Each class was held twice weekly for two hours. Among the nine classes, three were offered to older adults with refugee backgrounds – two classes for Nepali-Bhutanese students and one for Sudanese students. Local refugee resettlement agencies refer older adults with refugee backgrounds who are in need of English instruction to this ESOL program. This study examined the translanguaging experiences of 13 students, ranging from 61 to 76 years old, who entered the Nepali-Bhutanese ESOL class taught by Park as a cohort. Although they were the largest population attending these classes, other students could join regardless of their ethnic or immigrant backgrounds. However, only one to three students who were not from refugee backgrounds attended the class. Students attending Park's classroom were informed that two to three classroom activities (20–30 minute segments) a month were being recorded as a regular part of the course. All 13 students gave consent through use of an interpreter.

The Nepali-Bhutanese students in this ESOL class were resettled in the United States as refugees between two and five years before they started attending the class in 2014. Their ancestors migrated from Nepal to Bhutan in the late 19th and early 20th centuries. In the late 1980s, the Bhutanese government enacted policies that discriminated against and oppressed the Nepali-speaking Southern Bhutanese; the resulting political tensions led them to flee Bhutan for refugee camps in Nepal (Evans, 2010). The United States started to accept Nepali-Bhutanese refugees in 2008 (Shrestha, 2008). Although the Nepali-Bhutanese students represented five ethnic groups, they spoke Nepali as a common language. According to the students, they spoke their ethnic languages to various extents, as most of them were more fluent in Nepali than in their ethnic languages. Only a few students spoke their ethnic languages at home, and only with their partners. Their children and grandchildren could only speak Nepali. Most participating students were farmers before moving to the United States and none had formal education prior to resettlement. In spite of this, a few had learned the Nepali script *Devanagari* informally, through their own efforts.

Park's translanguaging curriculum

For its curriculum, the ESOL program used the state's Adult Education Curriculum Framework for English for Speakers of Other Languages and for English Language/Civics Education (EL/Civics). For each level (ESOL 1 through 6), the state's framework suggests functional level descriptors for each strand (listening, speaking, reading and writing), curriculum materials and possible topics such as public and community service, health, transportation, etc. Within this framework, teachers could design lessons based on their students' needs and interests as well as their English proficiency levels, which were generally assessed by the program to be very low. Park, with the assistance of Valdez, drew on the translanguaging pedagogy literature to augment the state's curriculum for her classroom. The curriculum drew on unit topics from the state's curriculum framework as well as from topics that students expressed as being of interest to them, such as health literacy. Park also enhanced the state curriculum with a strategically designed routine of instructional activities that allowed translanguaging practices by her and her students.

The typical classroom routine started with a collaborative vocabulary building activity, since contextualizing the meaning of terms through translanguaging is an integral part of translanguaging pedagogy (e.g. García *et al.*, 2012). At the beginning of class, key vocabulary words for the day's lesson were presented to students. Any related words that students shared or wanted to know were also added to the list. The students and teacher worked collaboratively to negotiate and identify the meaning, form and pronunciation of the words and their equivalents (or closest possible) in the students' home language. Once the meanings of the vocabulary words were identified, the students wrote the key words on the board in both English and their home language (Romanized form, Devanagari script and adding pictures when possible). This information was used throughout the day's lesson to make connections between the students' home language and the new English vocabulary words. The next instructional activity was engaging students in a translanguaging writing task. Park presented the main topic of the lesson and brainstormed ideas with students on what to write about at the end of each unit. The students worked individually on writing drafts using their full linguistic repertories and visuals to convey their messages at their own pace. This also meant that they were encouraged to use grammar and vocabulary that they had previously learned in class. Once finished, students were assigned to small groups to support each other in filling any gaps in knowledge. The students then revised their writing based on their peers' feedback. Finally, the teacher reviewed and gave additional feedback before students completed their final draft. Through the translanguaging opportunities offered in this curriculum, we hoped that Park's students would make meaning together, recognize the value of using their full linguistic repertoire and understand how these English additions fit into their linguistic repertoire, thus increasing their crosslinguistic and metalinguistic awareness.

Data for this research study included: (a) forty-four 20–30 minute audio recordings (later transcribed) of classroom interactions recorded during the collaborative vocabulary building activity and the writing activity/discussion of class sessions; (b) digital copies of students' work (notebooks and worksheets); and (c) teacher field/reflection notes. Data were analyzed through a systematic coding process that identified patterns and themes (Miles *et al.*, 2013) related to language and literacy translanguaging events and their connection to students' linguistic funds of knowledge. We identified *meaning-making* and *crosslinguistic and metalinguistic awareness* as themes that emerged across students' language and literacy translanguaging events. Selected data excerpts are presented below to illustrate how students enacted and learned English through translanguaging. Although data from all 13 students in the classroom was analyzed, we selected the data excerpts based on three students' use of translanguaging to represent our findings. Pseudonyms were assigned to the three students (Padma, Bhim and Himal) whose writings were selected, with identifiable personal information removed or replaced with alternative equivalents.

Findings

This section showcases how meaning-making and crosslinguistic and metalinguistic awareness emerged for older Nepali-Bhutanese adults through their use of the translanguaging practices enacted in Park's pedagogy. We present these findings in the context of the two instructional activity routines implemented in her classroom: (1) a collaborative vocabulary building activity and (2) a translanguaging writing activity (see Figure 3.1).

1	Teacher:	(Pointing to the computer mouse) We call it mouse. Mouse, Nepali
2		*keho*, mouse?
3	S1:	Same, same.
4	S2:	(Pointing to mouth) *Mook*.
5	S1:	*Mook haina!*
6	Teacher:	(Pointing to mouth) Oh, that's a mouTH. *Mook* is a mouth. MouSE is
7		an animal. What's mouse in Nepali? Mouse *keho*?
8	Students:	XXX
9	Teacher:	*Jjik, jjik, jjik, jjik, biralo, ha-ak!*
10	S2, S3:	*Musa!*
11	Teacher:	Oh, *musa*! Mouse has *dui-ta* meanings (showing two fingers). One
12		*musa*, another one computer mouse. Because this (pointing to the
13		computer mouse), looks like *musa*.
14	S3:	Teacher, English, rat *keho*?
15	Teacher:	Rat is a big mouse. *Thulo musa* is a rat. *Sano musa* is a mouse.[1]

Figure 3.1 Collaborative vocabulary building activity and language awareness

Note: Transcription conventions: ( ) = non-verbal activities; *italics* = languages spoken other than English; CAPITALS = emphasized sound; XXX = unintelligible sound.

The classroom conversation we focus on in this section took place during a collaborative vocabulary building activity as part of a lesson about working with computers. Park tried to help the students understand why a computer mouse was named after the animal by shifting her questions and statements in response to the students. When she first asked the students what 'mouse' was in Nepali, S1 answered 'same, same' in Line 3, indicating that a computer mouse is also called a 'mouse' in Nepali. Failing to differentiate between the sound of 'mouse' and 'mouth', S2 mistakenly answered that 'mouse' is *mook*, which is 'mouth' in Nepali. In Line 5, S1 interrupted and said that it was not a mouth. This offered Park an opportunity to raise students' metalinguistic awareness as she shifted her instruction toward comparing the words 'mouth' and 'mouse' by modeling the sound differences between these two similar words (Lines 6–7). She then positioned students as experts by asking what 'mouse' was in Nepali in Line 7. The students, in pairs or small groups, then collaboratively discussed these different words to figure out the meaning of the English word 'mouse' (Line 8). Park then modeled for students how one can draw on one's full linguistic repertoire to make or convey the meaning of a word by using Korean onomatopoeia to mimic the sound of a mouse (*jjik jjik*) and a cat's hissing (*ha-ak*) in Line 9. After hearing the sound of animals and the word 'cat' in Nepali (*biralo*), S2 and S3 exhibited their crosslinguistic awareness by saying *musa*, which is a Nepali equivalent for the word 'mouse' (Line 10). Park then explicitly explained that mouse has two meanings in English, and that the computer mouse was named after the animal because it looks similar (Lines 11–13). Student S3 asked what the word 'rat' was in English (Line 14). Using translanguaging, Park explained to the students that a big *musa* is a rat and a small *musa* is a mouse (Line 15), extending their metalinguistic understandings of the difference between rat and mouse.

This excerpt illustrates the potential of translanguaging to include students in the meaning-making process, regardless of their proficiency in English. While S1 had been learning English for a few years and was at a higher level of English proficiency than the other students, S2 and S3 only knew basic words in English and had not yet mastered the English alphabet when the conversation took place. However, as this example shows, translanguaging enabled all of these students to participate in the activity. This excerpt also shows collaborative meaning-making among the students and teacher when S2 answered the teacher's question despite the risk that her answer could be wrong, and S3 raised the difference between a mouse and a rat.

Through participating in this translanguaging vocabulary activity in each class, students could focus on meaning-making and build on what they already knew. Sometimes it was easy for the students to express their crosslinguistic awareness by finding equivalent terms in their language, but as this excerpt illustrates, the activity also promoted students' metalinguistic awareness by providing opportunities for nuanced distinctions between vocabulary concepts, such as that between 'mouse' and 'rat'. The collaborative translanguaging process also often involved corrective feedback, conflicts, arguments and negotiations, providing students with an opportunity to use multiple languages. For example, during this activity, S1 pointed out to S2 that her answer was wrong (Line 5), and the students had discussions to figure out the definition of the word 'mouse' in their language (Line 8). As the discussion in the excerpt shows, when the students could not reach a conclusion for what 'mouse' meant in their language, Park modeled crosslinguistic strategies by using Korean onomatopoeia to mimic the sound of a mouse and said the word 'cat' in Nepali to help students understand the meaning. The questions raised by the students also benefited other students by providing learning opportunities. Therefore, the collaborative nature of the translanguaging activity supported what Collins and Cioè-Peña (2016: 133) refer to as the 'deepen[ing] of the thinking of students, while also enabling students to gain different perspectives'.

This classroom conversation also shows that translanguaging stimulated and developed metalinguistic and crosslinguistic awareness, similar to García *et al.*'s (2012) findings. When S2 misunderstood 'mouse' to mean *mook* (mouth in Nepali) and S1 pointed out the error, instead of ignoring the mistake, the teacher elaborated on the student's negative transfer by comparing the sound of 'mouse' and 'mouth'. After noticing

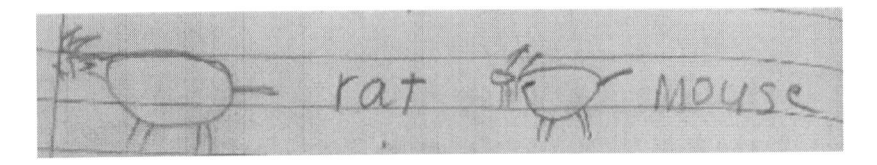

Figure 3.2 S4's drawing distinguishing between the terms 'rat' and 'mouse'

that the voiceless dental fricative /θ/ is missing in Nepali consonants, as it is in her home language Korean, through learning Nepali and interacting with the students, Park was able to recognize why her students had trouble differentiating between these two words and the need for an explanation to the students that emphasized the differences in sound and meanings of the words (Line 6).

Another example of crosslinguistic awareness was shown when S3 asked what a 'rat' was because he knew that 'rat' meant *musa* in Nepali. Having learned that 'mouse' means *musa* in Nepali, he wanted to validate his existing knowledge. Instead of asking for a translation of 'rat' in Nepali from the students, the teacher explained that a 'rat' was a big mouse (Line 15). Understanding that Nepali does not have a distinct vocabulary to distinguish a mouse from a rat, similar to other Asian languages, she was able to communicate the difference in the two English terms using size as a distinction. These examples suggest that a teacher's efforts to learn the student's language can also make a contribution to the collaborative process by facilitating students' meaning-making and bridging their crosslinguistic and metalinguistic awareness across their full linguistic repertoire as well. Reflecting on this conversation, S4, who was not a central participant during this classroom interaction, displayed his crosslinguistic and metalinguistic awareness in written form. In his notebook, he drew the pictures shown in Figure 3.2 of a rat and mouse based on the information he received from the teacher: *Thulo musa* (big mouse) is a rat; *sano musa* (small mouse) is a mouse (Line 15). He attempted to differentiate the two English terms by drawing pictures of mice of different sizes based upon what he knew as *musa*. His notebook became a voluntarily created translanguaging space for him where he controlled his own learning and meaning-making of the content without the teacher's direction.

Building meaning and linguistic awareness through a translanguaging writing activity

In one writing activity, students were asked to use any linguistic code they preferred to write their stories and to draw a picture of themselves. The following section focuses on the writing artifacts of three students: Padma, Bhim and Himal (Figure 3.3), captured during the drafting phase of the writing process. These texts were selected to illustrate how students used different aspects of their linguistic repertoires to work through problems, make meaning and showcase their crosslinguistic and metalinguistic abilities.

Drawing on numeracy to make and express meaning in English

Padma was a 69-year-old male student who first attended Park's ESOL class two years before the study and knew how to write some letters and

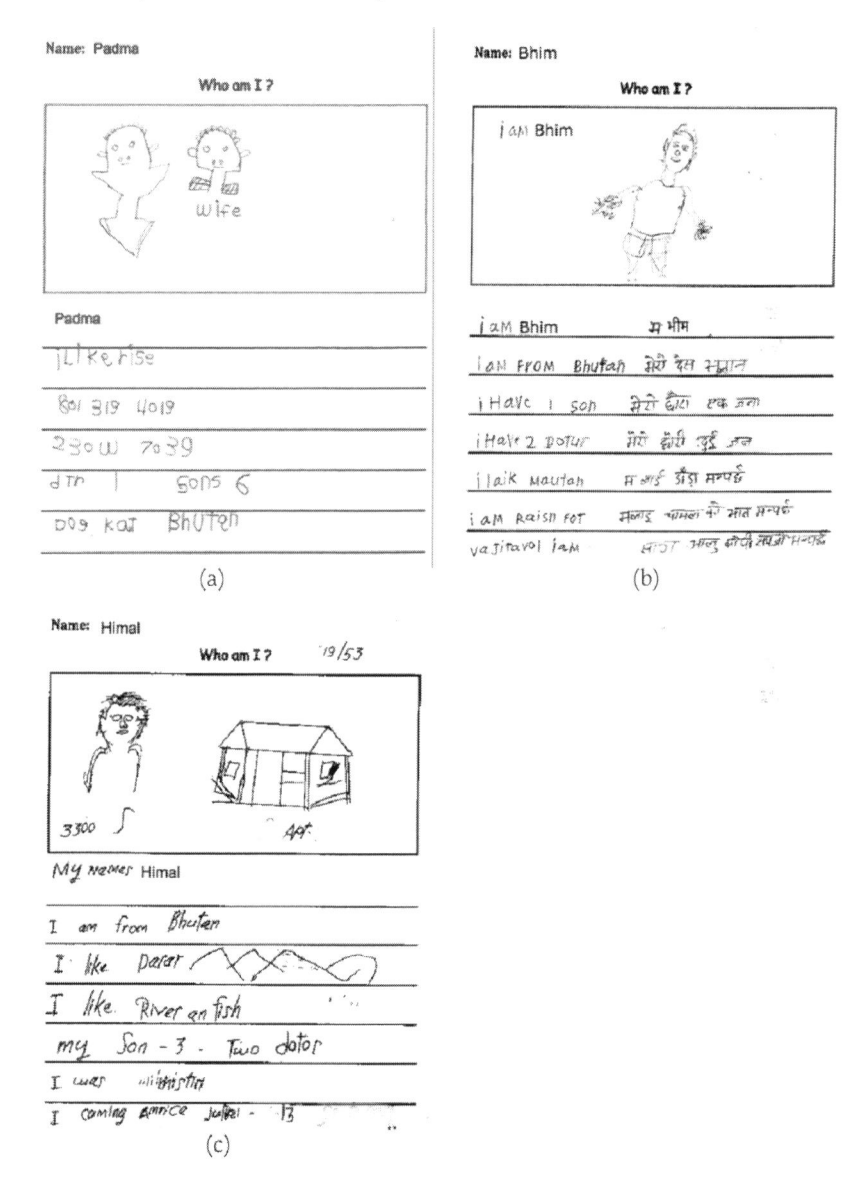

Figure 3.3 Students' writing illustrating their use of translanguaging

60 Part 1: Language and Literacy

speak simple phrases in English. He spoke Nepali at home, but did not know how to write it. Padma paid attention to linguistic details, building his metalinguistic awareness by often bringing questions to class about English signs and words he encountered outside of the classroom, wanting to figure out their pronunciation and meaning. As an example, during one class, he shared a note where he had written down the named logo of a local broadcasting channel 'UEN' that he saw on TV and asked the teacher what it was. The teacher then explained that it stood for 'Utah Education Network' (field note). This provided an opportunity for other students to learn not only the meaning of the logo, but also about acronyms by elaborating on other terms that were relevant to the students' surroundings and their lives (e.g. other TV channels, USA).

In the ESOL class, Padma preferred to work with numbers because he was more proficient with them. Thus, his writing incorporated a large amount of numbers more than other students. Since numeracy was part of his funds of knowledge and represented a form of literacy that he was comfortable with, he used numbers as important crosslinguistic codes to express who he was in English and to link to concepts introduced in the class writing activities. For example, to describe who he was in Figure 3.3a, Padma listed his cell phone number (Line 3), address (Line 4) and how many children he had (Line 5). His focus on numbers also showed up in his notebook, in which he listed his cell phone number on each page for several months and frequently wrote numbers from 1 to 100. He also drew on his knowledge of English kinship terms and his understanding of himself as a member of a family unit when he included a drawing of himself and his wife and listed the number of daughters and sons he had to express who he was. In Line 5, he illustrates his metalinguistic awareness by applying the English plural rule that he previously learned in class by adding the plural morpheme 's' to the word 'son' because he had six sons, whereas he treated the word 'dtr (daughter)' as a singular noun by not adding any suffix because he only has one daughter. Padma was the only student to apply this rule at the time despite its review in class. This example suggests Padma's attention to numeracy and linguistic detail sometimes helped him gain metalinguistic awareness faster than others in the class.

Extending English meaning using Nepali translations

Bhim was a 74-year-old male, which made him one of the oldest students in class; he also had the most advanced proficiency in English and in writing Nepali. Thus, he used translanguaging the most in class, particularly to help other students understand concepts. He also used his skills to fill in gaps that the teacher was not able to explain in Nepali. For instance, when the teacher used a facial expression to explain the word 'sad' during a lesson on feelings, some of the students asked if she meant the word 'cry' in Nepali. Bhim then intervened and explained the difference between the words to the students in Nepali. He indicated that *dukhi chu* means 'sad' while *rudai chu* means 'cry'. This helped other students learn the English words and the teacher learn new Nepali words.

In his writing (Figure 3.3b), Bhim wrote English sentences along with Nepali translations, highlighting his crosslinguistic knowledge. Bhim also used Nepali translation to expand on what he wanted to convey in sentences when he felt his English could not capture everything he wanted to say. For instance, in Line 7, he explained that he liked vegetables. In the English sentence, he wrote 'vajitavol i am', using invented spelling and unconventional syntax to convey that he liked vegetables. In Nepali, he wrote that he liked *saag* (spinach), *aloo* (potatoes), *gobi* (cauliflower) and *sabji* (vegetables). While Bhim exhibited translanguaging practices, he maintained a recognition of two separate languages as illustrated by the visual separation of the two languages in his writing. Instead of adding other linguistic or semiotic codes between English words, he provided a Nepali translation with extended information separate from the English sentences. For Bhim, Nepali translation of English words and sentences was a part of his translanguaging practice and an important tool for his English learning. These practices were also frequently found in his notebook, where he would write English words or sentences along with their Nepali equivalents. For example, he wrote 'I am happy' in his notebook along with the Nepali translation *ma* ('I') *chu* ('am') *khusi* ('happy'), with each Nepali word right above the English word. In fact, the right Nepali word order should be *ma khusi chu* (I happy am). This literal translation of each word signals his linguistic awareness of the difference in language structure between English and Nepali. This is another example of how translanguaging allowed him to use his crosslinguistic awareness to enhance his English learning.

Learning English phonetics and Roman script to write Nepali

Himal was a 63-year-old male and the second youngest student in class. In class, Himal would write Nepali words using Roman alphabet letters based on English phonetics as shown in Lines 3 (*darar*) and 6 (*mistiri*) of his writing (Figure 3.3c). He would then ask the teacher if he had correctly produced the words according to the English phonetic system. This is an illustration of his metalinguistic awareness, his ability to make letter–sound connections and his ability to do this using his impressive crosslinguistic knowledge of how sounds in Nepali correspond to the English letters of the alphabet. Himal's case illustrates how students' home languages can be employed to learn English phonetics and increase students' crosslinguistic and metalinguistic awareness. Using English phonetics to transcribe familiar vocabulary words in students' home language can keep them engaged in what is often a tedious linguistic exercise, helping them to make connections between oral and written language. Furthermore, Himal was not only learning English, but also developing his home language literacy through this translanguaging practice.

In Line 3 (Figure 3.3c), Himal did not know the word 'mountain/hill (specifically ones that are small without snow)' in English, so he wrote the Nepali word *darar* (*daada*) phonetically, along with a drawing of mountains. There are generally three words in Nepali that indicate mountains: *himal* (mountain covered with snow), *pahad* (mountain without snow) and *daada* (smaller mountain or hill without snow). Bhim wrote *daada* as a Nepali equivalent term for 'mountain' (Line 5 of Figure 3.3b) in his translation. Himal also knew the English word 'mountain'. However, Himal's choice to write the Nepali word *daada* instead of 'mountain' may indicate that he intended to find the equivalent term that better suits the condition of the mountain (*daada*) that he wanted to describe. This example shows his attempt to connect his metalinguistic awareness (differentiating the three Nepali terms) with crosslinguistic awareness (seeking their equivalent English terms). Similarly, to convey that he had previously been a house builder, he illustrated the use of his crosslinguistic awareness skills for meaning-making by drawing a picture of a house next to his portrait and writing the word *mistiri* (house builder in Nepali) in Line 6 of Figure 3.3c. Translanguaging allowed Himal to draw on his full linguistic repertoire to convey the complex aspects of his language knowledge and learning processes.

Conclusions and Implications

Older adults with refugee backgrounds, including those with interrupted or an absence of official schooling, have a great deal to contribute to their processes of English language learning. This research illustrates how the rich linguistic repertoires of older adults with refugee backgrounds can become evident as they engage with translanguaging practices to learn English and convey their understandings of themselves and their world. As this study illustrated, a teacher's strategically enacted translanguaging pedagogy can allow older adult students of refugee backgrounds to make meaning and increase their metalinguistic and crosslinguistic awareness as they are learning English. As educators, it is critical that we value and build upon our students' funds of knowledge and experience, including the funds of knowledge from which their linguistic repertoire is shaped. As the opening vignette reminds us, not doing so can stir up strong affective responses in students that can hinder their language learning. The strength of a translanguaging approach is that it offers a way for teachers to scaffold language learning and disrupts the deficit view of students' home languages and cultures, allowing them to be valued as assets.

In this study, it was the strategic creation of a translanguaging space for language learning by the teacher that allowed students to find ways to maintain and create new spaces for their learning. The classroom discussions and student writing that took place during the two classroom routines described here illustrate the ways that students used translanguaging, regardless of their age or level of English proficiency. The isolated examples offered in this chapter are not enough to showcase the comprehensiveness of this class's translanguaging curriculum. In addition, the absence of students' voices related to their experiences with a translanguaging pedagogy is another limitation of this study. However, we hope that this work contributes to an increase in awareness of language and literacy resources among older adults with refugee backgrounds.

In closing, it is worth noting that there is a widespread myth in the field of English language teaching that only native English speakers should be teaching English. This misconception was debunked by Phillipson (1992) who labeled it the *native speaker myth*. The marginality that Park experienced as a so-called non-native English-speaking teacher in the English teaching field inspired her to implement pedagogy that focused on their existing linguistic abilities and strengths. In other words, Park's marginalized position as a language minoritized individual helped her to empathize and understand the marginality of her students and seek ways to reverse that dynamic in her classroom. Recent studies show that translanguaging can also be practiced in a class of students from diverse language backgrounds and with a teacher who does not speak students' home languages (Ebe, 2016; Woodley, 2016). Underlying a translanguaging approach, whether the teacher shares students' home languages or not, is the willingness of a teacher to position herself as a language learner; to learn about students' linguistic codes, features and practices; and to use that knowledge in teaching English. By raising awareness of the linguistic resources, strategies and abilities that older adults from refugee backgrounds can draw on when learning English, we hope that this chapter inspires more educators to take up translanguaging in their classrooms.

References

Auerbach, E.R. (1993) Reexamining English only in the ESL classroom. *TESOL Quarterly* 27 (1), 9–32.

Capps, R., Newland, K., Fratzke, S., Groves, S., Auclair, G, Fix, M. and McHugh, M. (2015) *The Integration Outcomes of U.S. Refugees: Successes and Challenges*. Washington, DC: Migration Policy Center.

Collins, B.A. and Cioè-Peña, M. (2016) Declaring freedom: Translanguaging in the social studies classroom to understand complex texts. In O. García and T. Kleyn (eds) *Translanguaging with Multilingual Students: Learning from Classroom Moments* (pp. 118–139). New York: Routledge.

Denzin, N. and Lincoln, Y. (2011) *Handbook of Qualitative Research (4th edn)*. Thousand Oaks, CA: Sage.

Ebe, A.E. (2016) Student voices shining through: Exploring translanguaging as a literacy device. In O. García and T. Kleyn (eds) *Translanguaging with Multilingual Students: Learning from Classroom Moments* (pp. 57–82). New York: Routledge.

Evans, R. (2010) The perils of being a borderland people: On the Lhotshampas of Bhutan. *Contemporary South Asia* 18 (1), 25–42.

García, O. (2009) *Bilingual Education in the 21st Century: A Global Perspective*. Malden, MA: Wiley-Blackwell.

García, O. (2011) Theorizing translanguaging for educators. In C. Celic and K. Seltzer (eds) *Translanguaging: A CUNY-NYSIEB Guide for Educators* (pp. 1–6). New York: CUNY-NYSIEB. See http://www.nysieb.ws.gc.cuny.edu/files/2012/06/FINAL-Translanguaging-Guide-With-Cover-1.pdf (accessed 4 January 2018).

García, O. and Kano, N. (2014) Translanguaging as a process and a pedagogical tool for Japanese students in the US. In J. Conteh and G. Meier (eds) *The Multilingual Turn in Languages Education: Benefits for Individuals and Societies* (pp. 258–277). Bristol: Multilingual Matters.

García, O. and Wei, L. (2014) *Translanguaging: Language, Bilingualism and Education*. New York: Palgrave Macmillan.

García, O. and Wei, L. (2015) Translanguaging, bilingualism and bilingual education. In W.E. Wright, S. Boun and O. García (eds) *The Handbook of Bilingual and Multilingual Education* (pp. 223–240). Malden, MA: John Wiley & Sons.

García, O. and Kleyn, T. (2016) Translanguaging theory in education. In O. García and T. Kleyn (eds) *Translanguaging with Multilingual Students: Learning from Classroom Moments* (pp. 9–33). New York: Routledge.

García, O., Flóres, N. and Woodley, H. (2012) Transgressing monolingualism and bilingual dualities: Translanguaging pedagogies. In A. Yiakoumetti (ed.) *Harnessing Linguistic Variation to Improve Education* (pp. 45–75). Bern: Peter Lang.

García, O., Johnson, S.I. and Seltzer, K. (2016) *The Translanguaging Classroom: Leveraging Student Bilingualism for Learning*. Philadelphia, PA: Caslon.

González, N., Moll, L. and Amanti, C. (eds) (2005) *Funds of Knowledge: Theorizing Practices in Households, Communities and Classrooms*. Mahwah, NJ: Erlbaum.

Grognet, A.G. (1997) Elderly refugees and language learning. Center for Applied Linguistics, Washington, DC. See https://files.eric.ed.gov/fulltext/ED416721.pdf (accessed 4 January 2018).

Hirano, E. (2015) 'I read, I don't understand': Refugees coping with academic reading. *ELT Journal* 69 (2), 178–187.

Krashen, S.D. (1981) *Principles and Practice in Second Language Acquisition*. London: Prentice-Hall.

Miles, M.B., Huberman, A.M. and Saldaña, J. (2013) *Qualitative Data Analysis: A Methods Sourcebook*. Thousand Oaks, CA: Sage.

Moll, L., Amanti, C., Neff, D. and González, N. (1992) Funds of knowledge for teaching: Using a qualitative approach to connect homes and classrooms. *Theory Into Practice* 31 (2), 132–141.

Ortmeier-Hooper, C. (2013) 'She doesn't know who I am': The case of a refugee L2 writer in a high school English language arts classroom. In L.C. de-Oliveira and T. Silva (eds) *L2 Writing in Secondary Classrooms: Student Experiences, Academic Issues, and Teacher Education* (pp. 9–26). New York: Routledge.

Phillipson, R. (1992) *Linguistic Imperialism*. Oxford: Oxford University Press.

Prinsloo, M. and Street, B.V. (2014) Literacy, language and development: A social practices perspective. In H. McIlwraith (ed.) *Language Rich Africa: Policy Dialogue* (pp. 65–70). London: British Council.

Shrestha, M. (2008, March 25) First of 60,000 refugees from Bhutan arrive in US. *CNN.com*. See http://edition.cnn.com/2008/WORLD/asiapcf/03/25/bhutan.refugees/index.html (accessed 4 January 2018).

Swain, M. (2006) Languaging, agency and collaboration in advanced second language proficiency. In H. Byrnes (ed.) *Advanced Language Learning: The Contribution of Halliday and Vygotsky* (pp. 95–108). London: Continuum.

United Nations High Commissioner for Refugees (2015) *UNHCR's Statistical Yearbook 2014, 14th edition.* See http://www.unhcr.org/56655f4d8.html (accessed 4 January 2018).

Warriner, D.S. (2007a) 'It's just the nature of the beast': Re-imagining the literacies of schooling in adult ESL education. *Linguistics and Education* 18 (3–4), 305–324.

Warriner, D.S. (2007b) Language learning and the politics of belonging: Sudanese women refugees becoming and being 'American'. *Anthropology & Education Quarterly* 38 (4), 343–359.

Weinstein-Shr, G. (1993) *Growing Old in America: Learning English Literacy in Later Years.* Washington, DC: Center for Applied Linguistics. See http://www.cal.org/caela/esl_resources/digests/grow.html (accessed 4 January 2018).

Williams, C. (1996) Secondary education: Teaching in the bilingual situation. In C. Williams, G. Lewis and C. Baker (eds) *The Language Policy: Taking Stock* (pp. 39–78). Llangefni: CAI.

Woodley, H.H. (2016) Balancing windows and mirrors: Translanguaging in a linguistically diverse classroom. In O. García and T. Kleyn (eds) *Translanguaging with Multilingual Students: Learning from Classroom Moments* (pp. 83–99). New York: Routledge.

Wright, W.E. (2015) *Foundations for Teaching English Language Learners: Research, Theory, Policy, and Practice* (2nd edn). Philadelphia, PA: Caslon Publishing.

4 Girls with Refugee Backgrounds Creating Digital Landscapes of Knowing

Delila Omerbašić

This chapter presents findings from a qualitative study conducted in an urban community center in the western United States. It focuses on understanding how teenage girls who were resettled as refugees from Thailand engage in learning through multimodal literacy practices in digital spaces. The author draws on critical sociocultural theories of literacy and culturally sustaining pedagogy to consider how two girls in particular, Tait and Elizabeth, used digital tools in their out-of-school literacy practices to negotiate their knowledge, skills and resources. These participants created digital landscapes of knowing, crafted by designing, posting and interacting with digital texts that displayed a range of rich multilingual, translocal and technological knowledge typically marginalized in formal learning settings. This research contributes to emerging perspectives in education research that critique deficit-based representations of refugee-background students and offers implications for educators in formal and informal learning communities who work with this population of youth.

My language is Karen. And the second language I speak with my friend and my neighbor, is … Po, yea, the other, different Karen. And then my third language is Burmese and English. Next year I will learn Spanish. (Elizabeth, 13 years old)

Elizabeth (pseudonym) resettled to the United States with her family as a refugee from the Umpiem Camp in Thailand. Like many who resettle to the United States from various global locations, Elizabeth and her family were unable to return to their home in the Karen state in Burma (the country officially known as the Republic of the Union of Myanmar) because of fears of persecution and violence. While many refugee-background families find increased stability after resettlement, they may also continue to experience challenges across various social and economic contexts in their new homes, ranging from insufficient educational resources to racism and discrimination (Adams & Kirova, 2006; Roxas, 2011). This chapter highlights how girls with refugee backgrounds used out-of-school literacy practices to negotiate their complex experiences following resettlement to the United States.

Researchers have long recognized the importance of engaging with the home and community knowledge of immigrant communities (e.g. Moll *et al.*, 1992; Yosso, 2005), including young people's out-of-school literacy practices (e.g. Lam, 2009; Valdez & Omerbašić, 2015; Zentella, 2005). More recent studies have highlighted asset-based perspectives on the education of refugee-background youth (e.g. Roy & Roxas, 2011; Roxas, 2011; Shapiro, 2014), including their literacy practices that extend beyond formal learning settings (e.g. Gilhooly & Lee, 2014; Omerbašić, 2015). This chapter builds on this research by illustrating the skills and knowledge that refugee-background youth may develop and use in digital spaces through literacy practices. The findings come from a study that focused on refugee-background youth in a community afterschool program. This program was guided by highly structured learning activities that were aligned with the students' school curriculum. There were limited opportunities for the youth to contribute their out-of-school knowledge and expertise, as students were discouraged from using their home languages and digital learning resources such as smart phones and digital social networks. These restrictions reflected the center's ideologies that English and curriculum-based content were the key resources that students needed to acquire, while signifying that the students' home languages, practices and knowledge were not relevant for academic development. Consequently, the participants in this study considered learning to be solely linked to school activities, while they viewed their home and digital practices as forms of play. However, the findings reveal that the participants' out-of-school literacy practices were valuable resources with the potential to support academic learning and personal growth.

Focusing on the informal learning practices of two adolescent girls – Elizabeth and Tait (pseudonyms) – this chapter addresses the question: How do refugee-background students use digital tools in their out-of-school literacy practices to negotiate their cultural and linguistic knowledge, skills and resources? My analysis focuses on what I call *digital landscapes of knowing*, which were crafted as the two girls designed, posted and interacted with digital texts, displaying rich multilingual, translocal and technological knowledge typically marginalized in formal learning settings. Translocality in this study reflects participants' identification with multiple global locations based on real or imagined lived experiences in those spaces (Appadurai, 1996). These landscapes were digitally mediated in online spaces, co-constructed within peer networks and chronicled through snapshots over time. After presenting and discussing examples of these landscapes, I consider the implications for educators in formal and informal learning communities who work with youth with refugee backgrounds.

Conceptual Framing: Sociocultural Contexts of Literacy

This study uses the critical sociocultural theory of literacy (Lewis *et al.*, 2007) and the concept of culturally sustaining pedagogy (Paris, 2012) as frameworks for understanding learning across contexts. Critical sociocultural theory focuses on how power shapes the learning and literacy practices that are mediated by various factors, such as language, culture and technology (Lewis *et al.*, 2007). It considers literacy as a form of social practice that extends beyond reading and writing to focus on what young people do with literacy (Barton & Hamilton, 2000). As a social practice, literacy is thus ideological (Street, 1984) and reflects dialogic constructions of meaning through a variety of semiotic modes across learning spaces (Gee, 2012; Kress, 2003). In recent decades, these spaces have broadened to include digital settings, which support collaborative and socially distributed practices (Knobel & Lankshear, 2008). These settings allow young people to connect and engage with common interests and affinities (Gee, 2004), such as Korean dramas (Kim, 2016), family blogging (Lewis, 2014) and fan fiction narratives (Black, 2009). For immigrant communities, digital settings also provide important opportunities to make global connections through literacy practices that extend beyond national boundaries (Lam & Warriner, 2012). These settings provide critical affordances for (re)building cultural connections, language learning and maintenance and navigating post-resettlement contexts for people with refugee backgrounds (Gilhooly & Lee, 2014; Omerbašić, 2015; Siddiquee & Kagan, 2006). By providing opportunities for collaboration and community building, these digital settings carry the potential to serve as counterspaces where dominant narratives can be challenged or disrupted (Case & Hunter, 2012).

Culturally sustaining pedagogy offers opportunities to consider how literacy practices can be drawn upon as resources across learning spaces to accommodate the breadth of learners' knowledge landscapes. This approach to teaching and learning engages students' ways of knowing 'to perpetuate and foster – to sustain – linguistic, literate, and cultural pluralism as part of the democratic project of schooling' (Paris, 2012: 95). It builds on the wealth of asset-based literature that seeks to disrupt school-based inequities and deficit-oriented frameworks toward non-dominant youth in American classrooms. Examples of asset-oriented frameworks include resource-based pedagogies, such as funds of knowledge (Moll *et al.*, 1992), along with culturally relevant (Ladson-Billings, 1995) and culturally responsive (Gay, 2000) pedagogies. Paris (2012) builds on these approaches and argues for a culturally sustaining pedagogy that develops students' academic learning concurrently with cultural and linguistic ways of knowing in the classroom. Additionally, culturally sustaining pedagogy accounts for learning within dynamic local and global contexts (Paris & Alim, 2014). This perspective is especially important for youth with refugee backgrounds who often have translocal experiences across multiple lived and imagined global locations (Appadurai, 1996).

Methodology

The data for this eight-month qualitative study were gathered in a community center located in the Intermountain West. Situated in an urban housing complex, the community center's purpose was to meet the needs of the families who were resettled as refugees from East Asia, Africa and the Middle East. The center was run by the local government and guided by a group of diverse staff members and volunteers, including several with immigrant and refugee experiences. In addition to gathering data for this project, I was engaged with this community center for nearly six years, primarily as a volunteer working in the afterschool program for secondary school students, which included supporting students with their homework assignments and through one-on-one mentoring.

My interest in working with students with refugee backgrounds is rooted in my own experience with war, displacement and resettlement. I was born and raised in Sarajevo, Bosnia and Herzegovina, where I lived under a violent siege for nearly two years before being evacuated on a convoy for women and children in the mid-1990s. After resettling to the United States, I quickly became aware of the ways in which dominant discourses diminish the strength, resilience and heterogeneity of people with refugee experiences. As these dominant discourses, which Tuck (2009) refers to as narratives centered on 'damage', are reflected in much of the education research with immigrant and refugee-background students (Ngo *et al.*, 2014), my research goals include disrupting these deficit perspectives and working with youth to highlight the skills, resources and knowledge they share in their daily lives.

Study participants included nine 13- to 17-year-old girls who self-identified as Karen, Burmese Muslim and Po Karen. At the time of the study, they had been in the United States between two and six years. Participants were selected from a group of youth who regularly attended the afterschool program at this community center, based on their (1) engagement with digital technology, (2) identification as female and (3) basic communication skills in English. This chapter highlights the literacy practices of two participants, Elizabeth and Tait, who were selected to illustrate trends evident within the larger community. Both Elizabeth and Tait have roots in Burma (now Myanmar) and were members of persecuted groups: Elizabeth identified as Karen, while Tait identified as Muslim. At the beginning of the study, Elizabeth was 13 years old and had been living in the United States for two years, while Tait was 17 and had been in the United States for five years.

Data were gathered using an ethnographic approach, focusing on youth's literacy practices (Barton & Hamilton, 2000). Data collection included participant observation, semi-structured, in-depth interviews and screenshots of the girls' literacy activities. Data gathering also included multimodal interviews, which I defined as 'interviews that purposefully use multiple modalities, such as aural and visual, and resources, such as digital media, to communicate meaning in a qualitative research process' (Omerbašić, 2015: 475). The multimodal interviews included simultaneous audio and screen recordings of the girls' literacy engagement in digital settings. Field notes, interview transcripts and documents were analyzed through theme analysis (Saldaña, 2009) and multimodal analysis (Jewitt, 2009). Data were initially coded to identify similarities and differences, followed by developing categories and themes, such as 'literacy as schoolwork' and 'literacy as play'. Examining the students' multimodal texts in relation to their interview narratives revealed important contextual cues that were necessary for better understanding their literacy practices. Participants were encouraged to provide feedback on the research process and analysis through informal conversations and member-check interviews. The following section presents findings that emerged from the data analysis.

Findings: Digital Landscapes of Knowing

> Being different is what it makes me special between these two very different world. Even if I miss my old world, I know that my new world is safer for my life. However, these two world are my world and I loved it. So many things have change to me. My education, language, cultural, and my life. I am happy that I have my both world besides me. (Tait, 17)

The following two examples reveal how Tait and Elizabeth created digital landscapes of knowing that reflected translocal knowledge and skills developed across global contexts, or what Tait referred to as 'different worlds'. The examples begin with sociocultural framings, before recounting the stories that each girl told about herself through snapshots over the course of the study. These snapshots were shared in digital spaces, particularly on Facebook. In these digital landscapes, the two girls asserted themselves as multilingual and translocal knowledge holders.

Elizabeth: 'I have a smart brain.'

Elizabeth was one of the youngest participants in the study, as well as one of the most recent arrivals at the time. She turned 14 during the study and was excited to know her 'real' birthday, which was three months earlier than what was listed on her official documents. During two interviews, she talked about learning about her real birthday by finding paperwork in her mother's documents. While many families with refugee backgrounds are assigned estimated birth dates after resettling to the United States, Elizabeth reclaimed her actual birthday by drawing on her multilingualism and literacy and by researching her personal history. Reclaiming her birthday was not only an important symbol of her connectedness to her culture and family, but also a form of resistance to an identification that was imposed on her upon arrival to the United States.

Elizabeth was born to Christian Karen parents in a Thai refugee camp. She was a top student there, attending a Karen school through the US equivalent of fifth grade. She resettled to the United States in 2011 and enrolled in sixth grade. The next summer, she moved with her parents and three siblings, while a brother and a sister remained in a neighboring state. Her extended family lived in yet another state, while some relatives remained in camps at the Thailand/Burma border. Her parents had not received formal schooling and were not able to read or write. She noted about her mother: 'When she was young, younger than me, she always had to work'. Although her parents were employed after resettlement, they struggled financially, so Elizabeth's older brother provided financial support.

These moves, as well as family separation, were difficult for Elizabeth and she missed her older siblings and friends. During informal conversations, she noted that although she cried a lot privately, people around her were unaware of her sadness, as she smiled a lot in public. Her nickname was 'Smiley Elizabeth', but she was also known as 'Peace Elizabeth', because of her ability to resolve conflicts among friends. In fact, Elizabeth was heavily involved in volunteering at the community center and her school. In her volunteer work, she moved easily across multiple languages: 'I go to school, sometimes when people need translate, they call me'. She spoke Karen, along with 'Po, the other, different Karen', as well as Burmese and English. Multilingualism was an important resource for Elizabeth in rebuilding and maintaining connections that were lost or interrupted through displacement, thereby supporting her adjustment to her new life in the United States. Toward the end of the study, she was feeling more comfortable in her new community, as she developed new friendships and maintained old ones in physical and digital settings through translocal language and literacy practices. For example, she used Facebook to connect with peers from her school and neighborhood, along with her Karen church community, siblings and mentors who resided in a different state.

Digital settings offered opportunities to enact Elizabeth's translocal ways of knowing through literacy practices, while negotiating personal interests with family expectations. Elizabeth's family discouraged her from using social media, including Facebook and YouTube, because they were concerned that she would engage in romantic relationships that could potentially interfere with her achievement in school. Consequently, Elizabeth was not allowed to interact with boys or listen to love songs until she had completed formal schooling, including college. Elizabeth's older brother was responsible for monitoring her digital literacies and had access to all of her social media accounts. She explained that although her brother did not allow her to download the Facebook app on her iPod, she was able to access her account through an internet browser.

> Elizabeth: My brother don't let me download Facebook.
> Delila: No?
> Elizabeth: But I have a smart brain. I go to Safari, here, and then I go to Facebook.
> Delila: Oh, hehe. So you have ways around it.
> Elizabeth: But my brother still know that I use Facebook, and then he know my Facebook password. He don't let me change it.

By noting that she had 'a smart brain', Elizabeth indicated that she saw negotiating the limitations imposed by her family in digital settings as a reflection of herself as a knowledge holder. Her multimodal literacy practices in digital spaces mediated the enactment of a 'smart' identity, which is especially important in a post-resettlement context in which youth with refugee backgrounds are often positioned as lacking skills and knowledge (Adams & Kirova, 2006; Roxas, 2011).

As a consequence of her brother's monitoring, Elizabeth's social media participation generally included making postings of which her family would approve. Her digital literacy practices frequently included shared images with religious messages or excerpts from religious scriptures in Karen or English. While these images demonstrated her Christian beliefs, they also highlighted her multilingualism. Elizabeth was one of the few participants who was able to read and write Karen fluently, using Karen orthography. However, like other participants, Elizabeth also used Romanized representation of Karen in her digital literacy practices. This practice was learned through collaboration among the resettled youth in digital spaces, as there is no formalized representation of Karen or Burmese languages in the Latin alphabet. Elizabeth noted that she learned how to read and write using Romanized Karen by interacting with her peers and watching YouTube videos of Karen songs with Romanized captioning. An example is evident in Figure 4.1 – a multimodal image that she composed for her friend. She described this figure in our multimodal interview:

Figure 4.1 Elizabeth's use of Romanized Karen in a multimodal composition

E: See this one, like, I write in my language.
D: Aha, what does it say?
E: *Ya eh na lar tha tha boe*, it mean 'I love you my dear, like my dear', something like that. I just wrote it for fun, I didn't even do anything with it.
D: How did you make that?
E: Uh, I go to edit picture, and I just do like that, just color. It's take a long time.

This example shows how Elizabeth combined multilingualism with multimodal composition skills. On her iPod, she had several apps that she used to edit photographs, including DecoAlbum, SmilePhoto, MoreBeaute2 and DecoBlend.

Although her family and the afterschool program discouraged Elizabeth from using social networks and smart phones, these digital tools fostered multimodal literacy practices that supported a wealth of learning opportunities. For Elizabeth, engaging in multimodal composition with photo-editing apps supported the development of the 21st-century skills that have become essential for learning in our globalized society (Black, 2009).

Elizabeth's engagement in digital spaces illustrates the social and ideological nature of literacy practices (Gee, 2012). Situated in social and historical contexts, Elizabeth's digital literacy practices reflected a tension between her interests and her family's expectations. While negotiating these tensions, Elizabeth constructed a digital landscape of knowing in which she demonstrated her multilingualism and technological savvy. In this landscape, she engaged in multilingual multimodal composing, interaction with various apps and digital content, and communication with peers and family. These literacy practices were representative of collaborative meaning-making (Knobel & Lankshear, 2008), such as learning how to communicate in Romanized Karen. These instances of collaborative learning with people who shared her cultural and linguistic background supported Elizabeth's maintenance and (re)building of connections that were disrupted during displacement and resettlement, such as relationships with friends and siblings in other states. Fostering these connections served an important role in supporting Elizabeth's emotional well-being post-resettlement. Moreover, in this dialogically constructed landscape, Elizabeth positioned herself as a knowledge holder, demonstrating a variety of 21st-century skills that can support learning beyond informal digital settings (Black, 2009). Thus, this landscape served as a counterspace (Case & Hunter, 2012) in which deficit-oriented discourses surrounding young people with refugee backgrounds could be disrupted. The following section reveals how another participant, Tait, crafted a digital landscape of knowing by engaging with a range of cultural and linguistic skills and resources.

Tait: 'I'm like a mirror.'

Tait was born and raised in the Mae La refugee camp at the Thailand/Burma border. She spent 12 years there, before resettling to the United States with her mother, stepfather and three siblings, while her two oldest siblings remained in Thailand. She identified ethnically as Muslim, a highly persecuted group of people in Burma. Her mother and stepfather had two more children following resettlement, thus Tait was one of eight children. Her mother was one of the few parents in the community who was able to read and write in her home language, Burmese.

Tait was one of the oldest girls in the study and one of the most outgoing. She had many friends in the community, school and online and prided herself on having friends from different cultures. At the community center, she enjoyed volunteering and helping younger students, but over time she became less engaged. She rarely attended the afterschool activities, which she attributed to changes in the environment, such as schedules and rules for attendance. For example, the schedule changed at the beginning of 2013 in order to provide focused attention to two different adolescent age groups. However, the implementation of this new schedule was ineffective, as the time for attendance was not consistent across days for each age group. As a result, many of the teens would arrive during a time when they were not scheduled to attend and they would be sent home. Tait did not like this, as she explained:

Tait: [whispers] I don't like Jasmine [pseudonym for a staff member].
Delila: [whispers] Why?
Tait: [whispers] She is mean. And she says 'Tait, go home, go home' and 'why don't you come here anymore?' And I don't come, because I don't want it. And 'you better come'. When I come, I bring all my homework, and she says 'you see, I told you, you should come more, because now you have a lot of work and we don't have much time'. I just hate it.

Tait did not like the highly structured environment that was created in the community center, particularly how this structure was enforced by some staff members. She hoped to be able to get help when she needed it and not be turned away or chastized for accumulating too much homework. Thus, she made the choice to withdraw from participating in the afterschool program. Although this decision diminished support for her academic learning, her choice exemplified an assertion of power by refusing participation in a space where she did not feel welcome.

In online spaces, Tait interacted regularly with other youth through her iPod, visiting Facebook, ooVoo (a video chatting application) and GChat (Google Chat) on a daily basis. Although she did not have internet access at home, she logged on to her friends' or neighbors' wireless networks.

Delila: So your iPod, it has internet on it, right?
Tait: Not really. I steal people's internet.
Delila: Okay
Tait: [laughing] But I have to stay outside.
Delila: Ohh
Tait: Inside, it don't work so much. It's so slow.
Delila: But if you open the window?
Tait: No. I open the door, and I sit on the... [steps]
Delila: That's cool.
Tait: If I don't, one day, if I can't sleep, [laughing]. I'm like, into it.
Delila: That's why you do it outside?
Tait: All the time. My mom say, 'Tait come inside!' 'Wait a minute!' [laughing] I'm still like, 'Let me download something' and I'm chatting people... [laughing].

In these digital spaces, Tait was able to broaden her network of friends to include those in local communities as well as many others who lived in states across the United States, including Oregon, Texas and Colorado. As most of her online friends were also Burmese Muslim, she communicated with them using Burmese, English and a Romanized version of Burmese, which she called Burglish: 'It's like Burmese sound, and the... English word. We use alphabet, we use our Burmese language sounds, so we just combine it'. Without internet access at home, she drew on her skills and technical knowledge to navigate this limitation to maintain and build relationships in digital settings.

Tait identified as someone who always tells the truth, which was reflected in the way that she openly participated in social media spaces. On Facebook, she shared thoughts, opinions, photos of her drawings and photographs of self and others. Her postings frequently reflected her current experiences or challenges; for example, she openly shared struggles that she was having with her boyfriend, challenges at home and joyful moments with her friends. She also expected others to share their honest opinions. For example, the images she shared were frequently modified with text, or represented as collages, and followed with an invitation for feedback. Figure 4.2 is a drawing she shared on Facebook in which she tagged 69 friends, asking for feedback.

In this example, Tait positioned herself in her digital landscape of knowing as not only someone who is very social and open to feedback, but also an artist. Forty-two of her friends 'liked' her drawing; some also commented that her drawing was 'nice'. In this case, her friends' feedback affirmed her artistic knowledge and expertise, which she acknowledged by thanking them for their friendship and respect.

Figure 4.2 Tait's request for feedback on her drawing

While identifying as someone who always tells the truth, Tait also identified as a 'mirror' in every interview: 'I'm like a mirror, you know. If I meet like really funny one, I'd be fun... You know, just be the way of the other'. She demonstrated what this looked like in her literacy practices in digital spaces. When her friends joked with her, she would joke back. When they wrote in English, she would write back in English. If they used 'Burglish', she would respond accordingly. Thus, Tait purposefully modified the way in which she communicated through literacy to align with the communication and writing style of the other person. The 'mirror' is a powerful metaphor alluding to the concept of literacy as a social practice (Gee, 2012) that is mediated by dialogic relationships with people and resources, such as language and technology (Bakhtin, 1981; Lewis *et al.*, 2007). As such, the metaphor also reflected Tait's recognition of ideologies within literacy and other social practices (Janks, 2010; Street, 1984). She was proud of her ability to interact with many different people in this way, and this awareness shaped her digital landscape of knowing as multilingual, highly interactive and dialogic.

Sustaining Multilingual and Multiliterate Knowledge

As these examples illustrate, the participants' literacy practices in digital spaces were situated in sociocultural contexts that included the girls' experiences with displacement and resettlement, their multiple identity enactments in digital settings and their family, school and community networks. These situated practices were important to the girls' development and maintenance of multilingualism, translocal relationships and technical expertise, enabling them to construct digital landscapes of knowing. However, these landscapes of knowing were not acknowledged, developed or encouraged in formal learning settings like school and the afterschool program. As a result, the girls' languages and cultures were marginalized within formal learning settings in which a prescribed curriculum and the English language were dominant and the girls perceived their skills in digital settings as something they did solely for fun and not as part of learning.

Applying a culturally sustaining pedagogical (Paris, 2012; Paris & Alim, 2014) approach in formal learning can serve to bridge formal and informal learning spaces. This approach builds on the heterogeneity of students' knowledge and identities (Paris, 2012). For example, while the girls in this study recognized the situatedness of their experiences in the broader context of displacement, these were not the sole experiences that defined their everyday practices. Instead, the girls drew on their experiences before and after resettlement, or what Tait referred to as her 'two different worlds', to make meaning in daily lives. Engaging with students' cultural and linguistic practices and lived experiences could allow educators to resist discourses that typically homogenize youth with refugee backgrounds. For example, although Elizabeth and Tait had roots in the same geographic region, with similar experiences of displacement and resettlement, their cultural and linguistic identities, religious affiliations and learning resources differed. These differences were enacted through their multimodal literacy practices in digital settings. For example, by creating and sharing multimodal images using both the traditional and Romanized Karen orthography, Elizabeth asserted her knowledge of multiple forms of written Karen. On the other hand, while Tait was very comfortable with 'Burglish', she was not as familiar with traditional written Burmese, but was able to practice it in her interactions with peers. Thus, academic activities that rely on students' home languages need to take into account the multiple dimensions of students' multilingual literacies, while providing opportunities to develop those literacies through collaboration.

Digital spaces in this study offered students important affordances to engage with and develop the breadth of their skills and knowledge through meaning production in their digital landscapes of knowing. Engaging with this knowledge in formal learning spaces would provide opportunities for students to take positions as knowledge holders and producers (Pandya & Ávila, 2014). This engagement would reflect the students' participation in digital spaces in which knowledge is distributed (Knobel & Lankshear, 2008). However, in efforts to support students' formal learning experiences with out-of-school, interest-driven literacy practices, it is important to resist co-opting these literacies in instruction (Gustavson, 2007). Doing so may reduce the students' motivation and engagement with such literacies. Instead, educators can encourage students to draw on their interests and skills developed out of school, without specifying which topics or resources the students must use (Moje et al., 2008; Skerrett & Bomer, 2011). For example, students can choose to use preferred multimodal composing apps, incorporate artistic drawings or engage with popular culture content that they find meaningful in order to enhance academic projects or support the development of content-area comprehension.

Engaging with students' out-of-school interests requires broadening of the definitions of what constitutes knowledge and literacy. In contrast to dominant damage-centered discourses (Tuck, 2009) of refugee-background students, it is important to recognize that students have a range of access to technology that can include opportunities to practice 21st-century skills such as collaboration and multimodal composing. In addition to recognizing the wealth of knowledge that students practice in their lives out of school, it is also important to provide opportunities for students to learn how these skills can be used in formal learning spaces. For example, most of the participants were able to quickly navigate apps, modify and produce multimodal texts and share content with each other using their mobile devices. These same skills can be applied to creating multimodal presentations for coursework or to preparing study guides that can be co-constructed and shared among students. However, explicit instruction that links the students' digital practices between formal and informal learning settings would be important. Linking these two settings would allow both students and educators to acknowledge the types of learning across spaces as equally meaningful.

Conclusion

This study considered how two girls who resettled as refugees used multimodal literacy practices in digital spaces to create landscapes of knowing that engaged with a range of cultural and linguistic skills and resources. These digital settings provided opportunities to sustain cultural and linguistic ways of knowing that were not available to the participants in formal learning settings. Students with refugee backgrounds would benefit from opportunities to bridge out-of-school literacies and formal learning settings. To promote learning opportunities that sustain knowledge from students' everyday lives, it is important that educators working with refugee-background youth learn from their students about meaningful practices that can be used to support academic learning in formal educational settings. Future research might address the following questions: (1) What are the affordances of the out-of-school linguistic and literacy practices of youth with refugee backgrounds for supporting academic learning? (2) What is the transformative potential of new media for academic learning within the context of students' translocal identities and experiences? and (3) How can educators integrate students' digital landscapes of knowing in formal learning settings without appropriating students' varied knowledge and expertise? Addressing these questions in greater depth could contribute to disrupting deficit-based perspectives of youth, and particularly girls, with refugee backgrounds.

References

Adams, L.D. and Kirova, A. (2006) Introduction: Global migration and the education of children. In L.D. Adams and A. Kirova (eds) *Global Migration and Education: School, Children, and Families* (pp. 1–10). Mahwah, NJ: Lawrence Erlbaum.

Appadurai, A. (1996) *Modernity at Large: Cultural Dimensions of Globalization.* Minneapolis, MN: University of Minnesota Press.

Bakhtin, M.M. (1981) *The Dialogic Imagination: Four Essays.* M. Holquist (ed.) (C. Emerson and M. Holquist, trans.). Austin, TX: University of Texas Press.

Barton, D. and Hamilton, M. (2000) Literacy practices. In D. Barton, M. Hamilton and R. Ivanič (eds) *Situated Literacies: Reading and Writing in Context* (pp. 7–14). London: Routlege.

Black, R. (2009) English-language learners, fan communities, and 21st century skills. *Journal of Adolescent and Adult Literacy* 52 (8), 688–697.

Case, A.D. and Hunter, C.D. (2012) Counterspaces: A unit of analysis for understanding the role of settings in marginalized individuals' adaptive responses to oppression. *American Journal of Community Psychology* 50 (1–2), 257–270.

Gay, G. (2000) *Culturally Responsive Teaching: Theory, Practice and Research*. New York: Teachers College Press.

Gee, J.P. (2004) *Situated Language and Learning: A Critique of Traditional Schooling*. New York: Psychology Press.

Gee, J.P. (2012) *Social Linguistics and Literacies* (4th edn). London: Routledge.

Gilhooly, D. and Lee, E. (2014) The role of digital literacy practices on refugee resettlement. *Journal of Adolescent & Adult Literacy* 57 (5), 387–396.

Gustavson, L. (2007) *Youth Learning on Their Own Terms: Creative Practices and Classroom Teaching*. New York: Routledge.

Janks, H. (2010) *Literacy and Power*. New York: Routledge.

Jewitt, C. (2009) *Handbook of Multimodal Analysis*. London: Routledge.

Kim, G.M. (2016) Transcultural digital literacies: Cross-border connections and self-representations in an online forum. *Reading Research Quarterly* 51 (2), 199–219.

Knobel, M. and Lankshear, C. (2008) Digital literacy and participation in online social networking spaces. In C. Lankshear and M. Knobel (eds) *Digital Literacies: Concepts, Policies, and Practices* (pp. 249–278). New York: Peter Lang.

Kress, G. (2003) *Literacy in the New Media Age*. London: Routledge.

Ladson-Billings, G. (1995) Toward a theory of culturally relevant pedagogy. *American Educational Research Journal* 32 (3), 465–491.

Lam, W.S.E. (2009) Multiliteracies on instant messaging in negotiating local, translocal, and transnational affiliations: A case of an adolescent immigrant. *Reading Research Quarterly* 44 (4), 377–397.

Lam, W.S.E. and Warriner, D.S. (2012) Transnationalism and literacy: Investigating the mobility of people, languages, texts, and practices in contexts of migration. *Reading Research Quarterly* 47 (2), 191–215.

Lewis, C., Enciso, P. and Moje, E.B. (2007) Introduction: Reframing sociocultural research on literacy. In C.J. Lewis, P. Enciso and E.B. Moje (eds) *Reframing Sociocultural Research on Literacy: Identity, Agency, and Power* (pp. 1–14). Mahwah, NJ: Lawrence Erlbaum Associates.

Lewis, T.Y. (2014) Apprenticeships, affinity spaces, and agency: Exploring blogging engagements in family spaces. *Journal of Adolescent and Adult Literacy* 58 (1), 71–81.

Moje, E., Overby, M., Tysvaer, N. and Morris, K. (2008) The complex world of adolescent literacy: Myths, motivations, and mysteries. *Harvard Educational Review* 78 (1), 107–154.

Moll, L.C., Amanti, C., Neff, D. and Gonzalez, N. (1992) Funds of knowledge for teaching: Using a qualitative approach to connect homes and classrooms. *Theory Into Practice* 31 (2), 132–141.

Ngo, B., Bigelow, M. and Lee, S.J. (2014) Introduction to the special issue: What does it mean to do ethical and engaged research with immigrant communities? *Diaspora, Indigenous, and Minority Education* 8 (1), 1–6.

Omerbašić, D. (2015) Literacy as a translocal practice: Digital multimodal literacy practices among girls resettled as refugees. *Journal of Adolescent & Adult Literacy* 58 (6), 472–481.

Pandya, J. and Ávila, J. (2014) Introduction. In J. Pandya and J. Ávila (eds) *Moving Critical Literacies Forward: A New Look at Praxis Across Contexts* (pp. 1–16). New York: Routledge.

Paris, D. (2012) Culturally sustaining pedagogy a needed change in stance, terminology, and practice. *Educational Researcher* 41 (3), 93–97.

Paris, D. and Alim, H.S. (2014) What are we seeking to sustain through culturally sustaining pedagogy? A loving critique forward. *Harvard Educational Review* 84 (1), 85–100.

Roxas, K. (2011) Tales from the front line: Teachers' responses to Somali Bantu refugee students. *Urban Education* 46 (3), 513–548.

Roy, L.A. and Roxas, K.C. (2011) Whose deficit is this anyhow? Exploring counter-stories of Somali Bantu refugees' experiences in 'doing school'. *Harvard Educational Review* 81 (3), 521–541.

Saldaña, J. (2009) *The Coding Manual for Qualitative Researchers*. Los Angeles, CA: Sage.

Shapiro, S. (2014) 'Words that you said got bigger': English language learners' lived experiences of deficit discourse. *Research in the Teaching of English* 48 (4), 386–406.

Siddiquee, A. and Kagan, C. (2006) The internet, empowerment, and identity: An exploration of participation by refugee women in a community internet project (CIP) in the United Kingdom (UK). *Journal of Community & Applied Social Psychology* 16 (3), 189–206.

Skerrett, A. and Bomer, R. (2011) Borderzones in adolescents' literacy practices connecting out-of-school literacies to the reading curriculum. *Urban Education* 46 (6), 1256–1279.

Street, B.V. (1984) *Literacy in Theory and Practice*. Cambridge: Cambridge University Press.

Tuck, E. (2009) Suspending damage: A letter to communities. *Harvard Educational Review* 79 (3), 409–428.

Valdez, V.E. and Omerbašić, D. (2015) Multimodal self-authoring across bi/multilingual educator and student learning spaces. *Bilingual Research Journal* 38 (2), 228–247.

Yosso, T.J. (2005) Whose culture has capital? A critical race theory discussion of community cultural wealth. *Race, Ethnicity and Education* 8 (1), 69–91.

Zentella, A.C. (2005) Perspectives on language and literacy in Latino families and communities. In A.C. Zentella (ed.) *Building on Strength: Language and Literacy in Latino Families and Communities* (pp. 1–12). New York: Teachers College Press.

5 Sociocultural Literacy Practices of a Sudanese Mother and Son in Canada

Katerina Nakutnyy and Andrea Sterzuk

This chapter examines the literacy practices of Sahal and Aheu, a refugee-background son and mother living in Canada, originally from what is now the Republic of South Sudan. By studying their evolving literacy practices, we learn how schools might better align in-school learning with the existing literacy practices of refugee-background students. Our findings confirm that significant changes in participants' lives during and since migration have affected their access to previous literacy practices, and that literacy mediation or brokering often takes place through community networks. These findings add to the conversation on refugee resettlement, educational integration and culturally relevant pedagogy.

'This my Arabic name', Sahal said to his fellow classmates, holding a paper filled with wavy lines. He wanted his classmates to believe that he could write his name in Arabic, his first language. Unfortunately, he had never had an opportunity to fully develop print literacy in Arabic so he could only approximate the look of this script. Although he had arrived in Canada as a Sudanese refugee only a few months earlier, the importance placed on print literacy in this classroom was already apparent to Sahal. Indeed, an individual's ability to communicate with others through the medium of written language is a valued practice in Canadian classrooms, as it is in many places around the world. In this chapter, we draw on a theoretical perspective that sees literacy as more than just reading and writing and includes an understanding of literacy as a sociocultural practice, an interactive activity between people (Barton & Hamilton, 1998). Referred to as New Literacy Studies, this paradigm for theory and research (e.g. Barton & Hamilton, 2000; Luke, 2003; Purcell-Gates, 2007) posits that 'literacy is what people do with reading, writing, and texts in real world contexts and why they do it' (Perry, 2012: 54). This view of literacy guides our focus on the meaning-making practices of Sahal and Aheu, his mother, both before migration and after resettlement. By studying Sahal and Aheu's evolving literacy practices, we can better understand how schools might better align in-school learning with the existing literacy practices of refugee-background students.

Our study adapts a research design used in the Cultural Practices of Literacy Study (CPLS). Created by Victoria Purcell-Gates and now under the direction of Kristen Perry, CPLS is a large ethnographic project consisting of a collection of case studies which primarily examine literacy in communities that have been historically marginalized.[1] One of the key conclusions of the CPLS project (Purcell-Gates, 2007) and of other educational research (e.g. González *et al.*, 2005) is that students from marginalized communities are more likely to learn when their curriculum is related to their out-of-school lives. But what if their out-of-school lives include tremendous upheaval because of resettlement? If, as Blommaert (2007) suggests, literacy texts, events and practices are tied to the local, it is important to consider what happens when local literacy practices are disrupted through migration. Exploring Sahal and Aheu's literacy practices through the tradition of CPLS and extending this focus to include consideration of their previous and present locations helps us to understand how forced migration affected their access to meaning-making.

Literature Review

Literacy practices develop through culture and lived experiences, and these practices change over an individual's lifetime. Moreover, the emergence of new literacy forms can alter the life of the individual. Barton and Hamilton (1998: 12) describe this relationship, explaining that 'people use literacy to make changes in their lives; literacy changes people and people find themselves in the contemporary world of changing literacy practices'. As Prinsloo (2013: 1) points out, there is 'remarkable diversity in the ways that people read and write for the performance of widely varying personal, social, and economic functions'. However, upon arrival in new countries, many refugee-background students encounter formal educational systems which devalue their knowledge (Li, 2008; Omerbašić, 2015; Roxas, 2011; Schroeter & James, 2014). Recent research has raised concerns about the prevalent deficit orientation that positions refugee-background youth in ways that do not recognize or develop their pre-existing academic skills (Emert, 2013; Shakya *et al.*, 2010). Some of these specific types of often-devalued knowledge include: (1) the languages and writing systems they already know; (2) their previous life experiences, including informal and formal learning experiences; (3) their resilience; (4) the ability to co-construct knowledge in groups; and (5) memory and oracy practices. As educational researchers, we share an interest in complicating the notion of literacy that positions learners like Sahal and Aheu in deficit ways (Menken, 2013; Roy & Roxas, 2011; Shapiro, 2014).

An early but key study that complicates understandings of literacy and illustrates the range of out-of-school literacy practices available to individuals and community is Street's (1984) ethnographic work in an Iranian village. This research determined that while outside agencies such as state education and national literacy campaigns discounted the literacy practices of this community, positioning the villagers as illiterate, a closer look revealed a variety of literacy practices, including record-keeping, public communication and engagement with religious texts. Similarly, Cruickshank (2006) conducted an ethnographic study of the home and school literacy practices of Arab teenagers in Australia, whose parents hired Qur'anic literacy tutors and arranged stays in their home countries in order to improve fluency in Arabic literacies. Teachers considered a lack of English reading material at home as a sign of parental disregard for education, whereas parents saw the development of culturally meaningful relationships as a key responsibility. Cruickshank's study highlights the potential discontinuities between home and school literacy practices of newcomer students.

Research has also shown that literacy has oral and multimodal components. In many communities, meaning-making includes print literacy as well as drawings and pictures, gestures and music (Blommaert, 2007; Kress, 2010). A noteworthy example is Lorenzatti's (2013) case study of the literacy practices of a Bolivian woman named Marta Graciela living in Argentina. Dominant representations might have characterized Marta Graciela as illiterate, but a closer look revealed a variety of meaning-making activities in her daily life, including using drawings and photographs to help her sell cosmetics.

New Literacy Studies also conceptualizes the bond between written and oral language as flexible (Lorenzatti, 2013). Within orality-based social networks, some individuals may act as literacy mediators for others. Literacy mediation, also known as literacy brokering, can be understood as 'the act of seeking out help in understanding texts and their purposes and uses in the real world' (Perry, 2007: 4). Research into literacy mediation, according to Papen (2012: 114) 'confirms the importance of the learners' social context and the collaborative nature of informal learning'. Recognition of these processes is an important way to resist deficit narratives about individuals who have not had access to formal schooling: While it is often assumed that 'adults without schooling are a homogeneous mass of socially disabled people' (Prinsloo & Breier, 1996: 11), research on literacy mediation highlights the agentive actions taken by such individuals in pursuing resources and relationships that contribute to literacy.

Methodology

This qualitative study investigates two research questions: (1) In what ways do Sahal and Aheu draw on literacy mediation in meaning-making? and (2) In what ways do changing contextual factors both impede and support Sahal and Aheu's access to meaning-making and social networks? In 2008, Aheu, a single mother in her mid-forties, came to Canada from a refugee camp in Egypt with five children and her mother. Previously, the family lived in an area of sub-Saharan Africa which is now the Republic of South Sudan. Prior to the family's arrival in Canada, Aheu's children, including Sahal, had some schooling in the Egyptian refugee camp, but no formal education in their home region or using the variety of Arabic spoken in the family. The Canadian city in which Sahal and Aheu have settled has a population of approximately 200,000 people. Katerina (first author) met Sahal in 2008 as his teacher in his first Canadian school. Andrea (second author) is a professor of language and literacies education at a university in the same Canadian province as the school.

Data collection included conducting interviews, gathering literacy artifacts (samples of print literacy used by participants in their daily lives) and keeping a researcher's journal over the three months during which the interviews were completed. Three semi-structured interviews were conducted – one with Sahal, one with Aheu and one with both participants. At the time of the interviews, Sahal was in Grade 9. Because Sahal frequently answers for his mother, the first two interviews were conducted separately, in order to ensure sufficient interview data from both participants. All interviews were completed in English; attempts were made to involve an Arabic-English translator in the interview process, but these arrangements fell through, due to winter storms and scheduling conflicts. The interview questions were designed by drawing on Perry's (2007) study of Sudanese refugee-background students in the United States. Following this model, the interview questions were organized to elicit data about background/demographic information, life histories, culture, literacy practices, types of text used and encountered, literacy brokering and feelings about learning English.

The goal of artifact collection was to collect evidence of print literacy engaged in by the participants. For a number of reasons, including the limited availability of the participants to meet and their difficulty with locating examples, only one text was shared during the interviews – a form from Sahal's school. However, Sahal and Aheu were able to discuss other artifacts from memory. Finally, Katerina's researcher's journal includes additional details and personal reflections, to contextualize the findings.

Interviews were transcribed and coded according to the seven categories in the interview protocol, with some overlap. After initial coding of interview data, each category was reviewed to determine subcategories and commonalities. As writing began, the categories changed; themes began to emerge, and additional reading of the data led to new ideas. In the following section, we discuss two themes: (1) the changing social networks of information-sharing and (2) the alignment of home and school literacy practices.

86 Part 1: Language and Literacy

Findings and Discussion

It is important to understand Sahal and Aheu's history in order to appreciate the degree of change in their living conditions and the significance of this change for our argument about literacy and the loss of social networks. Because our analysis considers how forced migration has changed Sahal and Aheu's access to meaning-making, we begin with a macro-level overview of contextual factors, including the history and political climate of their home country (Sudan) and the participants' life histories and linguistic repertoires. After this overview, we discuss their literacy practices and implications of the findings for formal education.

Beginning in 1955, with the development of a southern Sudanese independence movement, Sudan has undergone many years of conflict (Collins, 2008). The first Sudanese civil war lasted until 1972. A period of peace ensued until the discovery of large oil fields in southern Sudan. Disputes over control of the oil fields contributed to a second civil war, which began in 1983 and lasted for over 20 years. At the same time, Sudanese President Gaafar Nimeiry instituted an Islamicization campaign, designed to transform Sudan into a Muslim state. This campaign led to mutinies, and rebel forces increased in the South. Simultaneously, the Sudanese People's Liberation Army (SPLA) formed in Ethiopia and the civil war continued with the SPLA attempting to gain control. Throughout southern Sudan, villages were obliterated, slavery became common and famine occurred in some parts. Eventually, many southern Sudanese began to flee and take refuge in Egypt, Kenya and Ethiopia before ultimately resettling in Canada, the United States, Australia and Great Britain. The second civil war ended in 2005 and in 2011, southern Sudan formed an independent nation, known as the Republic of South Sudan, but only after approximately two million Sudanese people had died and four million had been displaced (Morrison & de Wael, 2005). This exodus included Aheu and Sahal, who first fled to Egypt and then to Canada. This series of events and the mass scale of displacement that resulted are important for this study to highlight the degree of change that Sahal and Aheu experienced. Their former communities no longer exist and, as the following data excerpts show, their former approaches to meaning-making have been disrupted.

Changing social networks of information-sharing

The following three data excerpts highlight some ways in which Aheu and Sahal are impacted by changes to their social networks. The common thread in this section is their use of orality and community networks as part of literacy and information-sharing. The most striking finding about Aheu and Sahal's literacy practices is perhaps the interruption to community channels of information-sharing. Aheu, Sahal and their family fled from the second Sudanese civil war to a refugee camp in Egypt. Before this displacement, Aheu stayed home and took care of her family, while her brother made money for the family. Aheu describes daily life in South Sudan as including a lot of daily visitors, which allowed for the exchange of oral information. 'In Africa', she reported, 'people coming more ... You come, your house busy'. Even in their refugee camp in Egypt, Sahal and Aheu explained that people would often congregate outside to sit and talk much more than people do in their new environment in Canada. Hence, robust social networks were an integral part of information-sharing in Sahal and Aheu's lives.

When Sahal and Aheu moved to Canada and began living within a new and different culture, their daily life practices – including literacy practices – changed from a community-mediated approach that relied heavily on oral communication, to a more individualistic and writing-based social reality. Although Aheu still lives near many Sudanese immigrants in Canada, her practice of receiving daily visitors and her access to exchanging information through oral interaction have been altered. Asked whether people in the family or community helped out with English, Aheu responded:

> No, cause the people is busy ... Some people working two job, three job. No time, in Africa the community help you because you working one job. You go in the morning seven o'clock, two o'clock at home, maybe three... not time, running, running, all the time busy.

This strategy of accessing knowledge through community is no longer accessible to Aheu. She must find new ways to make meaning within a new environment, illustrating again how changes in the participants' lives affect their literacy practices.

Since literacy is closely tied to oracy in these participants' lives, personal relationships take on an important function in literacy mediation. In order to gain agency and make meaning in a new context, Aheu relies on family and friends to understand texts and their purposes. While at their refugee camp in Egypt, Aheu's children were given some Arabic-medium education. While Sahal claims that he is no longer able to read in Arabic, his older sister, described by her mother as more studious, has retained this ability; the sister therefore helps her mother a great deal with communicative tasks, such as filling out forms and making phone calls. As Aheu explains, 'Yeah, sometime, I want to call at home, make the appointment, my daughter to helping me'. Elsewhere in the interview, she mentions another brother who also mediates, translates and scribes in English. 'Sometime I can't understand good', she says. 'I take my son because now it is difficult for me'. A significant aspect of literacy mediation worth noting here is its 'close relation to power distribution' (Thériault, 2016: 163). This is particularly true when considering traditional family relationships: In one sense, Aheu's distribution of literacy to include her children as brokers can be seen as empowering, as children become a valuable literacy resource. In another sense, however, this sort of familial dynamic can be disempowering, as it reverses the age hierarchy, causing parents to depend on their children (Dorner *et al.*, 2008; Perry, 2014).

Aheu's literacy network and literacy mediators also extend beyond family; an older Sudanese man from the community, who reads and writes Arabic, assists her at times. Moreover, when she first arrived in Canada, she had the support of a social worker to help with new tasks, such as banking, healthcare appointments and phone calls to social service programs. Hence, this social worker became a cultural, linguistic and literacy broker for Aheu. In this way, Aheu navigated unfamiliar structures and entered into new spheres of social and economic activity. Her use of literacy brokering is more than a 'stop-gap' approach to meaning-making; it provides access to social structures that would be inaccessible otherwise (Prinsloo & Breier, 1996).

Alignment of home and school literacy practices

Since arriving in Canada, Sahal has been a student in primary and secondary schools and Aheu has accessed adult English classes through a local newcomer center. In discussions with Aheu and Sahal about their experiences of school in Canada, we noted the importance of classroom community for Sahal, just as community, as discussed earlier, is an important part of information-sharing within Sudanese culture. Sahal reports feeling competent in activities that focus on team work and group strengths. He praises two teachers who frequently employ group work, and he points to his enjoyment when he is permitted to interact with his classmates, saying, 'Yeah, she lets us do things. She lets us talk and all that stuff. It makes it funner'.

Sahal's description of this type of classroom interaction as 'funner' suggests that he is contrasting this type of educational experience with others in which it is not permitted to speak or interact with peers. The pleasure he takes from interacting with others and learning through community could be understood as the result of a pedagogy that more closely aligns with the socially mediated literacy practices present in Sahal's background than other lessons he encounters at school. If, from a sociocultural view, 'literacy is what people do with reading, writing, and texts in real world contexts and why they do it', then collective activities which allow for group interaction seem to be better aligned with Sahal's real world experiences (Perry, 2012: 54).

Like her son, Aheu also discusses learning moments that she finds valuable. Asked about what activities from her adult English language classes were most helpful, Aheu referenced a class field trip to the grocery store. This answer serves as an important reminder that students may be more likely to perceive the value in an activity when tasks are seen as having worth in their daily lives. This activity may have included literacy events that look similar to those of the school, such as writing on pieces of paper or reading information from a sign. Yet, literacy is not just about the act itself; it is the context of the act that gives meaning to its practitioner. Hence, performing these acts within the context of an actual grocery store likely made the learning more meaningful. Moreover, visiting the store with the group, rather than going alone, allowed Aheu to draw on the social network of support from her English instructor and classmates. The social aspect of this activity likely positioned Aheu more effectively for successful meaning-making outside of class.

Conclusion

This chapter has examined the literacy practices of Sahal and Aheu, a refugee-background son and mother. We find that for Sahal and Aheu, community and literacy are interconnected, and changes in their lives during and since migration have affected their literacy practices. Before coming to Canada, both participants relied on a community network to share knowledge through spoken language. When they became disconnected from these networks, therefore, their previous strategies for information-sharing were no longer viable. However, they began to forge new networks, in addition to relying on familial relationships, to mediate literacy in the new context. Both participants appreciated opportunities to forge and utilize new social networks in the classroom as well.

Our findings echo results from other studies of refugee resettlement which find that refugee-background students benefit from community-based programs that allow them to make use of their existing literacy practices, while simultaneously adding new meaning-making resources (Duran, 2016; Singh *et al.*, 2015; Thériault, 2016). This line of inquiry suggests that schools and teachers must learn about 'existing knowledges, beliefs and practices of those we aim to teach in order to create a relevant curriculum and pedagogy for the development of their literacy' (Street, 2012: 223). The findings from this study therefore add to the ongoing conversation on refugee resettlement, educational integration and culturally relevant pedagogy.

This study has several limitations. First, this is a case study of a son and a mother from one area of the world. The experiences of Sahal and Aheu are not the experiences of every refugee-background person and, as such, generalizations from these findings are not possible. Another limitation of this study is our inability to speak Arabic. In the case of Aheu, in particular, not conducting the interviews in Arabic or even with the assistance of an English-Arabic translator limited the depth of the conversation. While Katerina developed a good relationship with Sahal and Aheu, the study could have been strengthened if participants had been given the choice of conducting the interviews in English or Arabic.

More studies that expand our understanding of what counts as literacy are necessary, as are studies that delve further into how refugee-background students respond to strengths-based, culturally relevant literacy pedagogy (e.g. González et al., 2005). This sort of pedagogy begins with understanding their life histories, literacy practices and strategies for meaning-making, including literacy mediation and oral language. Our study highlights the importance of teacher awareness of students' prior literacy practices and use of literacy activities that align with the meaning-making experiences that students bring with them.

Note

(1) For more information, see http://sites.education.uky.edu/cpls/.

References

Barton, D. and Hamilton, M. (1998) *Local Literacies: Reading and Writing in One Community*. New York: Routledge.
Barton, D. and Hamilton, M. (2000) Literacy practices. In D. Barton, M. Hamilton and R. Ivanič (eds) *Situated Literacies: Reading and Writing in Context* (pp. 7–15). New York: Routledge.
Blommaert, J. (2007) Grassroots literacy: Writing, identity and voice in central Africa (Paper 2). Working Papers in Language Diversity, University of Jyväskylä.
Collins, R.O. (2008) *A History of Modern Sudan*. New York: Cambridge University Press.
Cruickshank, K. (2006) *Teenagers, Literacy and School: Researching in Multilingual Contexts*. New York: Routledge.
Dorner, L., Orellana, M. and Jiménez, R. (2008) 'It is one of those things that you do to help the family': Language brokering and the development of immigrant adolescents. *Journal of Adolescent Research* 23 (5), 515–543.
Duran, C.S. (2016) 'I want to do things with languages': A male Karenni refugee's reconstructing multilingual capital. *Journal of Language, Identity & Education* 15 (4), 216–229.
Emert, T. (2013) 'The Transpoemations Project': Digital storytelling, contemporary poetry, and refugee boys. *Intercultural Education* 24 (3), 355–365.
González, N., Moll, L.C. and Amanti, C. (eds) (2005) *Funds of Knowledge: Theorizing Practices in Households, Communities, and Classrooms*. New York: Routledge.
Kress, G. (2010) *Multimodality: A Social Semiotic Approach to Contemporary Communication*. New York: Routledge.
Li, G. (2008) *Culturally Contested Literacies: America's 'Rainbow Underclass' and Urban Schools*. New York: Routledge.
Lorenzatti, M. (2013) When illiterate isn't illiterate: Reading reality in a multimodal way. In J. Kalman and B. Street (eds) *Literacy and Numeracy in Latin America: Local Perspectives and Beyond* (pp. 81–94). New York: Routledge.
Luke, A. (2003) Literacy and the other: A sociological approach to literacy research and policy in multilingual societies. *Reading Research Quarterly* 38 (1), 132–141.
Menken, K. (2013) Emergent bilingual students in secondary school: Along the academic language and literacy continuum. *Language Teaching* 46 (4), 438–476.
Morrison, J.S. and de Waal, A. (2005) Can Sudan escape its intractibility? In C.A. Crocker, F.O. Hampson and P. Aall (eds) *Grasping the Nettle: Analyzing Cases of*

Intractable Conflict (pp. 161–182). Washington, DC: United States Institute of Peace Press.

Omerbašić, D. (2015) Literacy as translocal practice: Digital multimodal literacy practices among girls resettled as refugees. *Journal of Adolescent & Adult Literacy* 58 (6), 472–481.

Papen, U. (2012) Informal, incidental and ad hoc: The information-seeking and learning strategies of health care patients. *Language and Education* 26 (2), 105–119.

Perry, K. (2007) Sharing stories, linking lives: Literacy practices among Sudanese refugees. In V. Purcell-Gates (ed.) *Cultural Practices of Literacy: Case Studies of Language, Literacy, Social Practice, and Power* (pp. 57–84). Mahwah, NJ: Lawrence Erlbaum.

Perry, K.H. (2012) What is literacy?: A critical overview of sociocultural perspectives. *Journal of Language and Literacy Education* 8 (1), 50–71.

Perry, K. (2014) 'Mama, sign this note': Young refugee children's brokering of literacy practices. *Language Arts* 91 (5), 313–325.

Prinsloo, M. (2013) Literacy in community settings. In C. Chapelle (ed.) *The Encyclopedia of Applied Linguistics* (pp. 1–7). Oxford: Blackwell.

Prinsloo, M. and Breier, M. (eds) (1996) *The Social Uses of Literacy: Theory and Practice in Contemporary South Africa*. Amsterdam: John Benjamins.

Purcell-Gates, V. (2007) *Cultural Practices of Literacy: Case Studies of Language, Literacy, Social Practice, and Power*. Mahwah, NJ: Lawrence Erlbaum Associates.

Roxas, K. (2011) Tales from the front line: Teachers' responses to Somali Bantu refugee students. *Urban Education* 46 (3), 513–548.

Roy, L.A. and Roxas, K.C. (2011) Whose deficit is this anyhow? Exploring counter-stories of Somali Bantu refugees' experiences in doing school. *Harvard Educational Review* 81 (3), 521–542.

Schroeter, S. and James, C.E. (2014) 'We're here because we're Black': The schooling experiences of French-speaking African-Canadian students with refugee backgrounds. *Race Ethnicity and Education* 18 (1), 20–39.

Shakya, Y.B., Guruge, S., Hynie, M., Akbari, A., Malik, M., Htoo, S., Khogali, A., Abiyo Mona, S., Murtaza, R. and Alley, S. (2010) Aspirations for higher education among newcomer refugee youth in Toronto: Expectations, challenges, and strategies. *Refuge* 27 (2), 65–78.

Shapiro, S. (2014) 'Words that you said got bigger': English language learners' lived experiences of deficit discourse. *Research in the Teaching of English* 48 (4), 386–406.

Singh, S., Sylvia, M.R. and Ridzi, F. (2015) Exploring the literacy practices of refugee families enrolled in a book distribution program and an intergenerational family literacy program. *Early Childhood Education* 43 (1), 37–45.

Street, B.V. (1984) *Literacy in Theory and Practice*. Cambridge: Cambridge University Press.

Street, B.V. (2012) Society reschooling. *Reading Research Quarterly* 47 (2), 216–227.

Thériault, V. (2016) Literacy mediation as a form of powerful literacies in community-based organisations working with young people in a situation of precarity. *Ethnography and Education* 11 (2), 158–173.

6 Narratives of Trauma and Self-healing Processes in a Literacy Program for Adolescent Refugee Newcomers

M. Kristiina Montero

Positive school experiences are critical to the successful resettlement of students with refugee backgrounds, yet the locus of responsibility for responding to these students' mental health and well-being seems to remain largely outside the school and classroom. Despite many studies highlighting the increased risk for mental health concerns among children and youth with refugee backgrounds during permanent resettlement, little research considers their specific needs in educational contexts. For this study, the trauma narratives of five Rohingya youth, aged 18–20, from Burma (Myanmar) were collected and analyzed using methods of structural narrative analysis to understand the meanings the youth ascribed to their experiences. The findings highlight how the youth exhibited prosocial behaviors – the observable elements of self-healing from trauma – when talking about their traumatic life events. These behaviors include engagement with school and/or work, altruism and social activism, and spirituality. The findings presented in this chapter suggest that trauma stories, when appropriately received within the context of classroom instruction, could help all educators, but specifically those who support children and youth from refugee backgrounds, to better understand the process of recovery from trauma.

In recent years, child and youth mental health and well-being have become a major focus in educational research, in general, and more specifically in research related to the schooling of students with refugee backgrounds in resettlement countries. However, despite many studies highlighting the increased risk for mental health concerns (e.g. depression, anxiety, post-traumatic stress disorder) among child and youth refugee newcomers during permanent resettlement (e.g. Bronstein & Montgomery, 2011; Fazel *et al.*, 2014; Kia-Keating & Ellis, 2007), few studies have considered their specific needs in educational contexts. For example, the Ontario Ministry of Education's (2013) mental health implementation strategy for K-12 schools, *Supporting Minds*, calls for school-based personnel to develop their 'cultural competence' and to recognize that ethnicity and culture can significantly impact mental health-seeking behavior by newcomers and impede their uptake of community mental health services. While cultural competence is critical when working with non-dominant culture populations, that alone may not be sufficient for fostering positive mental health and well-being for refugee newcomers.

The underlying assumption in the *Supporting Minds* document, as in many similar documents put forth about support for refugee-background students, is that educators need to be more attuned to refugee newcomers' signs of adjustment difficulties[1] and/or psychological distress in the classroom. Yet, the locus of responsibility for responding to such difficulties seems to remain largely outside the school and classroom. While the existing literature demonstrates that it is essential that those working with refugee newcomers consider the impact of trauma on learning, behavior and relationships in school (Cole *et al.*, 2013), most school districts offer few if any comprehensive professional development opportunities to better support refugee newcomers' mental health in the classroom (MacNevin, 2012; Miller *et al.*, 2005; Woods, 2009).

Viewing educational practice through a trauma-informed lens (Cole *et al.*, 2013; Phifer & Hull, 2016; Substance Abuse and Mental Health Services Administration [SAMHSA], 2014) may help educators understand their role in supporting refugee newcomers' recovery from trauma within their academic mission. A trauma-informed approach requires all members of the school (e.g. teachers, administrators, educational assistants, support staff, settlement workers) to understand the impact of trauma, recognize the signs of trauma, respond in ways that help resolve trauma-related issues and avoid dehumanizing practices that might result in the re-traumatization of students (SAMHSA, 2014). To take a trauma-informed approach in the classroom, an educator does not need to be a trained therapist (Bath, 2008), but simply needs the ability (and desire) to respond to another human being who is suffering and to offer support in a humane manner (World Health Organization, 2011).

The study presented in this chapter examines how, by welcoming students' trauma stories into the curriculum, educators might re-envision their academically oriented classrooms as spaces that support refugees' self-healing processes and therefore contribute to their positive mental health. Self-healing has both psychological and social dimensions that help a person recover from traumatic life events and construct new meaning out of violence (Mollica, 2014). Recovery from trauma has been shown to be positively associated with engaging in prosocial behaviors such as volunteering, work/school, advocacy, charitable work, other-oriented empathy (altruism), spirituality and humor (Frazier *et al.*, 2013; Mollica, 2006; Mollica *et al.*, 2015). These prosocial behaviors are the more observable elements of self-healing; the trauma story, therefore, can be an entry point in this healing process (Mollica, 2006).

This study is grounded in an understanding of the importance of trauma stories, the distressing and painful narratives about personal and/or social events whose function is 'not only to heal the survivor, but also to teach and guide the listener – and, by extension, society – in healing and survival' (Mollica, 2006: 37). In particular kinds of relationships, such as between teacher and student, the listener learns about the trauma survivor's life events and forms of resilience in response to these events; the storyteller, in turn, becomes more comfortable with the storytelling process when his or her story is told to an empathic listener (Mollica, 2006, 2014).

In this chapter, I address the following research question: What role can trauma stories that are voluntarily told in the non-therapeutic context of the classroom have in supporting refugee newcomers' mental health and well-being? To this end, I describe an early reading program designed for low literacy adolescent refugee newcomers, in which trauma stories were collected and documented from five Rohingya[2] youth from Burma/Myanmar[3] using the principles of digital language experience approach (D-LEA) (Labbo *et al.*, 2002). I then establish how the trauma stories served as a window for educators to witness students' self-healing processes. I conclude the chapter with a discussion about how trauma-informed stances might help educators re-envision their classrooms as healing environments that support the mental health and well-being of refugee newcomers who have experienced traumatic life events.

Research Context

The research took place in an English literacy development (ELD) program at a secondary school in Ontario, Canada. ELD programs, generally speaking, combine language learning with literacy and numeracy development and aim to support students' transition to mainstream high school programs and see them through to graduation. The program is offered across five developmental levels, A through E, with entry into the program dependent on students' dominant language print literacy and previous formal schooling experiences. Students in ELD Level A, for example, have normally had significant interruptions to their formal schooling experiences (six years or more), as well as limited dominant language print literacy and low English proficiency. Each Ontario school board is responsible for interpreting the ELD policy and designing programming to suit students' needs, teachers' pedagogical expertise and school budgets. The ELD programming at the research site focused on early reading instructional methods (e.g. guided reading, running records, literature circles, listening centers) to advance the English language and print literacy development of low literacy adolescent refugee newcomers whose formal education was limited or significantly interrupted. (See Montero *et al.*, [2014] for more information about the reading program and impact on students' reading development.)

Educators in the early reading ELD program enhance reading instruction by creating age-appropriate, culturally sustaining and developmentally appropriate reading materials using the D-LEA texts[4] (Labbo *et al.*, 2002). Supported by mentor texts and writing/speaking scaffolds, students were prompted to recount narratives of important events in their lives. Some students told narratives about part-time jobs, what made them happy and free-time activities such as playing soccer or using social media. Others recounted narratives about their lives in their country of origin, fleeing war and/or resettling in Canada. Where students did not have sufficient print literacy skills to write the stories themselves, teachers or other assistants scribed their stories. To create texts for the purposes of print literacy instruction, these narratives were transliterated using Standard English writing conventions. The intention was not to colonize students' oral stories, but rather to restructure them according to a narrative structure valued in school, which helped storytellers (and readers) learn the linguistic conventions necessary to experience success in what Delpit (1988: 283) calls the 'culture of power' – the ways of talking, writing, dressing and interacting used by middle- and upper-class segments of society.

Using PowerPoint, the written stories were then typeset, illustrated with digital photos and printed as books.[5] The student-created texts then served as reading and instructional materials in the early reading ELD program. These texts supplemented the collection of high interest, age-appropriate, culturally sustaining and developmentally appropriate books in the program's collection. Gathering students' narratives opened up opportunities for students to share their trauma stories, as was the case with the Rohingya youth who participated in this research. These narratives also provided insight into the refugee newcomers' self-healing processes.

Research Methodology

I used an instrumental case study design – a method which seeks to provide insight into a particular issue or phenomenon (Stake, 2005) – for this inquiry into narrative. This design allowed me to closely examine the youths' trauma stories and to consider how they might help guide teachers' roles in students' recovery from trauma. This study's research methodology is also informed by action research, where 'social inquiry aims to generate knowledge and action in support of liberating social change' (Greenwood & Levin, 2000: 94) and classroom action research, where inquiry is used (often with the help of academics) by teachers to make data-informed decisions on ways to improve their own pedagogical practices (Kemmis & McTaggart, 2005).

Furthermore, this instrumental case study is informed through narrative methods of inquiry, which seek to understand experience as lived and told through stories (Clandinin & Connelly, 2000). Narratives are co-constructed texts between researcher and participant (Riessman, 2008) and as such, can draw on a social constructivist (Vygotsky, 1978) theoretical frame that values the role of social actors – in this case the Rohingya youth and the university-based researcher-teacher – in the co-creation of knowledge. This work explores the narratives of lived experiences, represents the data as stories and interprets them through the lens of trauma-informed practices.

Participants

I met the five Rohingya men (aged 18–20) who participated in this study in January 2015. They were students in the ELD program (Level A) at a secondary school in Ontario, Canada, and were recruited to be part of the larger print literacy study described earlier. These young men resettled to Ontario from Burma as government-assisted refugees. They fled Burma on overcrowded, non-seaworthy fishing boats, because of deep religious and ethnic persecution and lack of freedom in their country. They preferred to risk dying at sea rather than to live under an oppressive regime in which the Rohingya people experienced physical violence and segregation, rampant hate speech, denial of citizenship, arbitrary violence, arrest, detention and other egregious human rights violations (United States Holocaust Memorial Museum, n.d.).

Data collection

I did not initially set out to document refugees' trauma stories; they naturally emerged in the context of the storyteller–listener relationship that had been established during the larger print literacy research program. Set within this context, I began to document the Rohingya youth's life stories upon their request and to help classroom teachers create instructional materials for the early reading program. Through interviews and language experience approach methods, I co-constructed the students' life narratives with them. In this sense, I became a researcher-teacher, although my official role in the classroom was that of researcher. (Research ethics approval was obtained for this study and permission was obtained by each of the participants.)

As I got to know the young men and earned their trust, they began disclosing details about their lives in Burma and their journey to Canada. One of the young men, Nagu (pseudonym), wanted to document his story after he saw that other students in the program had published D-LEA books, which were being used in the reading program. Nagu wanted to document his journey to Canada and be able to share his story of survival through this book. While I was working with Nagu, the other Rohingya students expressed an interest in sharing their stories with a broader audience, including teachers, peers and the public. To this end, I interviewed each Rohingya youth at least two times using an open-ended interview format, from January to August 2015. The interviews were audio-recorded and transcribed to facilitate the creation of the D-LEA texts. I began each interview asking: What would you like to tell me about your life and journey to Canada? The young men generally began by summarizing the difficult lives they had left behind in Burma. For example, Mozu (pseudonym) said:

> My story is sad and happy at the same time. I want to start my story with Burma. What I did in Burma, why I left Burma, what happened there, how long I stayed at sea, and how I came to Canada. I don't have many happy memories from Burma because it was too dangerous.

I aimed to conduct the interviews in a way that would offer a 'brave space' (Arao & Clemens, 2013) for stories to evolve organically. I probed for clarification when necessary, but did not interfere in general with how the stories unfolded. I was not concerned with the historical accuracy of the stories; rather, I was interested in the meaning the young men were making of their narrated lives. I was mindful not to solicit trauma stories directly, but listened to them empathically when they arose.

At times, I helped students find appropriate words and/or images to tell their stories. For example, in his first interview, Mozu found it difficult to describe the conditions of the Burmese jails and showed me a picture of a jail online that represented the abhorrent conditions he had experienced. Another example where online images were used to help the young men tell their stories was when Nagu told about being rescued by the Sri Lankan Navy from the drifting fishing boat he was on in the Bay of Bengal. He found a Reuters image published in *Time* (Rauhala, 2013) to show how frail and ill the passengers were when rescued. These examples highlight how the narratives were co-constructed between the researcher and participant.

Data analysis

I used structural narrative analysis (Labov & Waletzky, 1997/1967; Riessman, 2008) for two purposes: (1) to craft participants' orally related narratives into written texts and (2) to understand the functions of students' oral narratives. Structural narrative analysis helped me understand what the young men were trying to articulate, and it provided structure to the stories that were often told in fractured or disjointed ways. Labov and Waletzky (1997/1967) note that people engage in storytelling for two reasons: (1) to give a straightforward report of the events as they occurred (referential narrative) or (2) to communicate the meaning of the narrative by connecting it to a level of personal perspective and meaning (evaluative narrative). I restructured each of the narratives according to Labov and Waletzky's six-part structure: abstract, orientation, complicating action, resolution, evaluation and coda. Doing so organized the participants' stories in a way supported by dominant-culture school literacies, as explained earlier. Furthermore, the restructured narratives allowed me to highlight the evaluation or the 'so what' statements, which, according to Labov and Waletzky, emphasizes the reason for which the story was told. (See the Appendix for an example.) These evaluative statements provided insights related to how the Rohingya youth made sense of their lived experiences through a socially constructed understanding of life experiences; when viewed through a trauma-informed lens, these statements could be interpreted as an expression of social healing via prosocial behaviors.

Findings

As I analyzed the stories told by the youth using Labov and Waletzky's (1997/1967) structural narrative analysis methods, viewing the evaluation elements through a trauma-informed lens of healing and recovery, the narratives revealed how the young men ascribed meaning to their experiences. Their stories highlighted prosocial behaviors related to the themes of school/work, altruism and spirituality, thereby signaling their self-healing pathway from trauma. I discuss these themes in turn.

School/work

Children and youth can find purpose in meaningful schooling experiences. Education contributes to human flourishing and well-being through the ability to contribute to civic, political and community life. Schools can play an important role in promoting students' successful adaptation and recovery from trauma (Fazel *et al.*, 2009, 2016). These understandings of the value of education emerged in the participants' narratives.

The Rohingya youth individually and collectively expressed regret that they had been prohibited from getting a formal education in Burma. They would often begin interview/work sessions by attributing their low literacy and limited schooling experiences to the oppression of the Rohingya, explaining that they were only taught to write their names in Burmese, and did not have print literacy or basic freedoms. As Mozu explained, 'Rohingya, they don't [have] power because the government [is] all Burmese people, no Rohingya... Rohingyas are not allowed to go to school. We are not allowed to have children. We have to pay money for every child that is born'.

In each narrative, the young men discussed the importance of school in their lives. They saw attending school as a way to get a good job, contribute to the financial stability of family members they left behind and pursue social and economic mobility and freedom. Nagu, for example, expressed pride in being able to attend school in Canada and learn literacy. He noted,

> The teachers [in Canada] are helping us learn to read and write in English and teaching many important things. When I was in Burma, I didn't know how to write my story because I was not allowed to go to school to learn to write. The government doesn't allow the Rohingya people to go to school. In Canada, I can go to school and learn to read and write.

Similarly, Mozu noted,

> I hope to finish high school and get a good job to support my family in Burma. I don't have any idea what kind of job I would like. Maybe I would like to work with car parts, or at a bank. I want to make a good salary so that I can send money home to my family.

The opportunity for formal education was critical to the self-healing processes for these young men. Schooling has the potential to provide refugee newcomers with the hope of upward mobility in their resettlement country, as well as to provide financial assistance to their families. These benefits echo the research about the important role that schools play in resettlement: Successful school experiences help refugee youth develop a positive sense of school belonging, which helps with their psychosocial adjustment in resettlement (Kia-Keating & Ellis, 2007) and helps to create a stable social milieu that contributes to the quality of daily life (Fazel *et al.*, 2014).

Altruism

Altruism, defined as the 'motivation to engage in prosocial behavior such as helping, sharing, and cooperating that increases others' welfare' (Puvimanasinghe *et al.*, 2014: 314), can be fostered through exposure to caring and supportive relationships that serve as role models. Altruism and other prosocial behaviors are associated with resilience, post-traumatic growth and recovery from traumatic experiences (Agaibi & Wilson, 2005; Mollica *et al.*, 2015; Puvimanasinghe *et al.*, 2014). Because trauma disrupts the ordinary and destroys the social systems of care that support mental health and well-being (Herman, 1992), altruism can help return a sense of power and control to survivors, allowing them to build supporting relationships and to create a foundation on which to build a new life (Mollica, 2006).

In each narrative, the Rohingya youth insisted that because they had survived mass violence and now had the opportunity to make a good life, they wanted to give back to their communities by offering financial support, sponsoring family members' resettlement to Canada and engaging in social activism. Each young man talked about the need to raise awareness about the plight of the Rohingya people. Mozu noted, 'It is important for me to tell my story because some Canadian people don't know about the Rohingya situation. If they know our story, maybe Canadians can help the Rohingya people'.

To help the young men tell their stories and engage in acts of altruism and social activism, I taught them 'discourse of power' (Delpit, 1988) words such as 'discrimination', 'survivor', 'violence', 'extermination' and 'hunger strike'. They learned these words during the co-writing sessions where they would describe a thought or feeling and I taught them a power word, which they would study and learn to use in the context of retelling their stories. For example, Nagu talked about going on a hunger strike when he was jailed in Sri Lanka:

Nagu: And then we can eat, we can walk, and put in jail [laughter] because we don't have passport, we don't have visa, that's why... that jail had five people in one room, that jail not good. You know mosquito bites, so difficult to live there, after one year is finished, we are stop the food, no eating, they told us 'Why did you stop the food'. This problem to here. How can we live with that? We escape the country. Same life in Sri Lanka, so no need for my life.
Kristiina: So you went on a hunger strike.
Nagu: So we are hungry, we stop eating. We told them that [we] need UNHCR, then they provide UNHCR.

As Nagu shared his story about going on a hunger strike, we also researched and talked about other political figures like Gandhi, whose hunger strikes were a form of non-violent resistance and political pressure. These stories of trauma, recovery and resilience therefore became the students' *testimonial narrative* (Beverly, 2008: 547) – 'a novel or novella-length narrative, produced in the form of a printed text, told in the first person by a narrator who is also the real protagonist or witness of the events she or he recounts'. By telling teachers and classmates about their testimonial narratives, the young men spread awareness about the human rights violations occurring against the Rohingya and collectively pleaded with Canadian and international communities to help the Rohingya. In essence, the classroom provided a brave space, in which students could make others aware about the injustices occurring in their homeland.

Spirituality

Survivors of trauma often instinctively turn to their self-healing capabilities, which may include calling upon divine authorities. Spiritual practices such as prayer and meditation provide positive physical and psychological benefits (Mollica, 2006). The importance of spirituality to the Rohingya youth was evidenced in their trauma narratives. For example, Mozu and I co-constructed a narrative about the business he ran in Burma. He explained that his mother had given Mozu and his brother money to start a store; they had built shelves to house the produce and general merchandise, and reported that 'everyone loved our store!'. He ended his story this way:

> Then one day I had to sell my store because it was too dangerous. The police were arresting and putting young Rohingya men in jail. I had to leave my store, my family, and my country. Insha'Allah [If God wills it so], one day I will be with my family again.

In this excerpt, Mozu gives the listener a point of entry to his trauma story and expresses hope that he will be reunited with his family someday. As the young men talked about their harrowing journeys and new lives in Canada, they made a point to thank Allah for the blessings bestowed upon them. They often linked this gratitude to their appreciation of the Canadian people for welcoming them to the community and to their altruistic intentions. For example, Nagu noted, 'I want to thank the Canadian government for helping me. Thank you Allah and God for helping us'.

Discussion

When educators create school and classroom environments that are safe, 'brave' and welcoming, refugee-background newcomers may be likely to reveal their trauma stories, whether in small chunks or all at once, within the context of classroom instruction or private conversation, as the Rohingya youth in this chapter did. The narratives may be able to provide insight into their prosocial behaviors that signal self-healing. The findings presented herewith suggest that educators working directly and indirectly with refugee youth have the potential to contribute to the self-healing processes of youth who voluntarily share their trauma stories in school spaces. Trauma stories can therefore have a space in formal learning environments.

I am not suggesting, however, that educators should systematically collect and analyze the sorts of trauma stories presented in this chapter. In fact, it is imperative that educators do not go 'fishing' for trauma stories and that they understand the boundaries and limits of their professional practice. On the other hand, when students volunteer such stories, educators might be reluctant to acknowledge the trauma for fear of retraumatizing the teller or hearing the traumatic details of another person's life.[6] This study suggests that making space for the telling of these stories in the classroom can be part of students' processes of self-healing. If educators can learn to recognize expressions of prosocial behaviors in students' trauma stories, as evidenced in this study, then perhaps they can support these behaviors within the context of the school and classroom. Of course, educators should also learn to recognize signs of psychological distress that are severe, prolonged and/or interfering with students' day-to-day functioning that require professional mental health assistance, so they can help students access care.

Clearly, teachers should not be solely responsible for students' mental well-being. Self-healing from trauma must be socially supported and therefore a holistic, community effort. Provincial policies that support the academic, socioemotional and psychosocial needs of refugee newcomers, such as the *Supporting Minds* and ELD policies referenced earlier, are useful starting points to becoming able to service these children and youth in the school and classroom. However, teachers also need the professional space to learn about and develop programs and curricula to address refugee newcomers' needs.

Through the D-LEA activities described in this chapter, the Rohingya youth were not only able to improve their proficiency in English and literacy, but were also given the linguistic and cultural tools to tell, retell and share their stories of resistance and resilience that may contribute to self-healing from trauma. More research is required to understand how teachers can engage in trauma-informed pedagogies to support the self-healing processes of trauma survivors.

Notes

(1) For signs of adjustment difficulties among refugee newcomer children and youth, consult the 'Welcoming Syrian Newcomer Students & Families to School' info-brief (School Mental Health Assist, 2016).
(2) The Rohingya are a Muslim minority ethnic group living in the northern coastal region of Burma. The United Nations has acknowledged that the Rohingya are one of the most persecuted people in the world. They became stateless with the passing of the 1982 citizenship law that requires minority groups to prove ancestry to pre-1823 Burma.
(3) With the military takeover of government in 1989, Burma's name was changed to Myanmar to reject Burma's colonial history. Because the name was changed undemocratically, many nation states refuse to recognize Myanmar as the country's official name. In this chapter, I refer to the country as Burma, because participants did so.
(4) The D-LEA books can be turned into digital stories by adapting the content to personal multimedia presentations with voice, image, video and sound. See Yoon (2013), Miller and Kim (2015) and Angay-Crowder *et al.* (2013) for examples used with English language learners.

(5) See Newmaster *et al.* (2014) for sample student-generated or student-inspired LEA books used in the program.
(6) Listening to students' trauma stories and/or witnessing signs of psychological distress can be emotionally hard. It is therefore critical that educators acknowledge their mental health needs and engage in self-care to reduce vulnerability to compassion fatigue or vicarious trauma and bolster one's energy and strength.

References

Agaibi, C.E. and Wilson, J.P. (2005) Trauma, PTSD, and resilience. *Trauma, Violence, and Abuse* 6 (3), 195–216.
Angay-Crowder, T., Choi, J. and Yi, Y. (2013) Putting multiliteracies into practice: Digital storytelling for multilingual adolescents in a summer program. *TESL Canada Journal* 30 (2), 36–45.
Arao, B. and Clemens, K. (2013) From safe spaces to brave spaces: A new way to frame dialogue around diversity and social justice. In L.M. Landeman (ed.) *The Art of Effective Facilitation: Reflections from Social Justice Educators* (pp. 135–150). Sterling, VA: Sylus Publishing.
Bath, H. (2008) The three pillars of trauma-informed care. *Reclaiming Children and Youth* 17 (3), 17–21.
Beverly, J. (2008) Testimonio, subalternity, and narrative authority. In N.K. Denzin and Y.S. Lincoln (eds) *The Sage Handbook of Qualitative Research* (3rd edn; pp. 547–557). Thousand Oaks, CA: Sage.
Bronstein, I. and Montgomery, P. (2011) Psychological distress in refugee children: A systematic review. *Clinical Child and Family Psychology Review* 14 (1), 44–56.
Clandinin, D.J. and Connelly, F.M. (2000) *Narrative Inquiry: Experience and Story in Qualitative Research*. San Francisco, CA: Jossey-Bass.
Cole, S.F., Eisner, A., Gregory, M. and Ristuccia, J. (2013) *Helping Traumatized Children Learn: Creating and Advocating for Trauma-Sensitive Schools*. See http://traumasensitiveschools.org/tlpi-publications/ (accessed 6 January 2018).
Delpit, L.D. (1988) The silenced dialogue: Power and pedagogy in educating other people's children. *Harvard Educational Review* 58 (3), 280–299.
Downey, L. (2007) Calmer classrooms: A guide to working with traumatised children. See https://www.communities.qld.gov.au/resources/childsafety/foster-care/calmer-classrooms.pdf (accessed 6 January 2018).
Fazel, M., Doll, H. and Stein, A. (2009) A school-based mental health intervention for refugee children: An exploratory study. *Clinical Child Psychology and Psychiatry* 14 (2), 297–309.
Fazel, M., Garcia, J. and Stein, A. (2016) The right location? Experiences of refugee adolescents seen by school-based mental health services. *Clinical Child and Psychology and Psychiatry* 21 (3), 368–380.
Fazel, M., Reed, R.V., Panter-Brick, C. and Stein, A. (2014) Mental health of displaced and refugee children resettled in high-income countries: Risk and protective factors. *The Lancet* 379 (9812), 266–282.
Frazier, P., Greer, C. and Gabrielsen, S. (2013) The relation between trauma exposure and prosocial behaviour. *Psychological Trauma: Theory, Research, Practice, and Policy* 5 (3), 286–294.
Greenwood, D.J. and Levin, M. (2000) Reconstructing the relationships between universities and society through action research. In N.K. Denzin and Y.S. Lincoln (eds) *The Sage Handbook of Qualitative Research* (3rd edn; pp. 85–106). Thousand Oaks, CA: Sage.
Herman, J. (1992) *Trauma and Recovery: The Aftermath of Violence – from Domestic Abuse to Political Terror*. New York: Basic Books.

Kemmis, S. and McTaggart, R. (2005) Participatory action research: Communicative action and the public sphere. In N.K. Denzin and Y.S. Lincoln (eds) *The Sage Handbook of Qualitative Research* (3rd edn; pp. 559–603). Thousand Oaks, CA: Sage.

Kia-Keating, M. and Ellis, B.H. (2007) Belonging and connection to school in resettlement: Young refugees, school belonging, and psychosocial adjustment. *Clinical Child Psychology and Psychiatry* 12 (1), 29–43.

Labbo, L.D., Eakle, A.J. and Montero, M.K. (2002) Digital language experience approach: Using digital photographs and software as a language experience approach innovation. *Reading Online* 5 (8). Abbreviated version available at https://laulima.hawaii.edu/access/content/user/kavitar/Articles/Readings/DigitalLEAArticleShortVersion.pdf (accessed 19 January 2018).

Labov, W. and Waletzky, J. (1997/1967) Narrative analysis: Oral versions of personal experience. *Journal of Narrative and Life History* 7, 3–38. (Reprinted from *Essays on the Verbal and Visual Arts: Proceedings of the 1966 Annual Spring Meeting of the American Ethnological Society*, J. Helm (ed.), 1967, pp. 1912–1944. Seattle, WA: University of Washington Press.)

MacNevin, J. (2012) Learning the way: Teaching and learning with and for youth from refugee backgrounds on Prince Edward Island. *Canadian Journal of Education* 35 (3), 48–63.

Miller, J. and Kim, S. (2015) Digital storytelling as an integrated approach to second language learning and teaching. *Language and Communication Quarterly* 4 (3–4), 41–55.

Miller, J., Mitchell, J. and Brown, J. (2005) African refugees with interrupted schooling in the high school mainstream: Dilemmas for teachers. *Prospect: The Australian Journal of TESOL* 20 (2), 19–33.

Mollica, R.F. (2006) *Healing Invisible Wounds: Paths to Hope and Recovery in a Violent World*. Vanderbilt, TN: Vanderbilt University Press.

Mollica, R.F. (2014) The new H5 model trauma and recovery: A summary. See http://hprt-cambridge.org/wp-content/uploads/2015/09/THE-NEW-H5-MODEL-TRAUMA-AND-RECOVERY-09.22.14.pdf (accessed 6 January 2018).

Mollica, R.F., Brooks, R., Ekblad, S. and McDonald, L. (2015) The new H5 model of refugee trauma and recovery. In J. Lindert and I. Levav (eds) *Violence and Mental Health* (pp. 341–378). New York: Springer.

Montero, M.K., Newmaster, S. and Ledger, S. (2014) Exploring early reading instructional strategies to advance the print literacy development of adolescent SLIFE. *Journal of Adolescent and Adult Literacy* 58 (1), 59–69.

Newmaster, S., Robinson, J., Bartlett, M., Hambleton, J., Dunham, P., Gerland, M., Petrus, M., Savelli, J., Wattie, B. and Woomert, A. (2014) Making good choices: Financial literacy series. See http://www.ergo-on.ca/ - !making-good-choices/c1ynv (accessed 6 January 2018).

Ontario Ministry of Education (2013) *Supporting Minds: An Educator's Guide to Promoting Students' Mental Health and Well-Being* (draft 2013). Ontario: Ministry of Education. See http://www.edu.gov.on.ca/eng/document/reports/SupportingMinds.pdf (accessed 6 January 2018).

Phifer, L.W. and Hull, R. (2016) Helping students heal: Observations of trauma-informed practices in the schools. *School Mental Health* 8 (1), 201–205.

Puvimanasinghe, T., Denson, L.A., Augoustinos, M. and Somasundaram, D. (2014) 'Giving back to society what society gave us': Altruism, coping, and meaning making by two refugee communities in South Australia. *Australian Psychologist* 49 (5), 313–321.

Rauhala, E. (2013) Horror at sea: Adrift for months, starving asylum seekers threw 98 bodies overboard. *Time*. See http://world.time.com/2013/02/19/horror-at-sea-adrift-for-months-starving-asylum-seekers-threw-98-bodies-overboard/ (accessed 6 January 2018).

Riessman, C.K. (2008) *Narrative Methods for the Human Sciences*. Thousand Oaks, CA: Sage.

School Mental Health Assist (2016) Welcoming Syrian newcomer students and families to school, info sheet. See http://www.edugains.ca/resourcesMH/ClassroomEducator/AdditionalResources/InfoSheet_Newcomers.pdf (accessed 6 January 2018).

Stake, R.E. (2005) Qualitative case studies. In N.K. Denzin and Y.S. Lincoln (eds) *The Sage Handbook of Qualitative Research* (3rd edn; pp. 443–466). Thousand Oaks, CA: Sage.

Substance Abuse and Mental Health Services Administration (2014) *SAMHSA'S Concept of Trauma and Guidance for a Trauma-Informed Approach*. HHS publication No. (SMA) 14-4884. Rockville, MD: Substance Abuse and Mental Health Services Administration.

United States Holocaust Memorial Museum (n.d.) 'They want us all to go away': Early warning signs of genocide in Burma. See http://www.ushmm.org/m/pdfs/20150505-Burma-Report.pdf (accessed 6 January 2018).

Vygotsky, L. (1978) *Mind in Society: The Development of Higher Psychological Processes*. Cambridge, MA: Harvard University Press.

Woods, A. (2009) Learning to be literate: Issues of pedagogy for recently arrived refugee youth in Australia. *Critical Inquiry in Language Studies* 6 (1–2), 81–101.

World Health Organization (2011) *Psychological First Aid: Guide for Field Workers*. See http://apps.who.int/iris/bitstream/10665/44615/1/9789241548205_eng.pdf (accessed 6 January 2018).

Yoon, T. (2013) Are you digitized? Ways to provide motivation for ELLs using digital storytelling. *International Journal of Research Studies in Educational Technology* 2 (1), 25–34.

Appendix: Structural Narrative Analysis of Nagu's Trauma Story

Abstract (summary of the substance of the narrative): We tried to escape from Burma to Malaysia because we didn't have any freedom in our country. We could not travel, go to school, vote or get married. If we wanted to get married, we had to pay a lot of money. If somebody died we had to pay a lot of money. If a child was born, we had to pay a lot of money. It was not fair.

Orientation (time, place, situation, participants): When we left Myanmar, there were 138 people crammed in a very small fishing boat. There were too many people to fit comfortably in the boat. We could only sit in the boat. We could not lie down to sleep.

Complicating action (sequence of events): On our way to Malaysia, the Thai Navy caught us and pushed us back to the sea. We did not have any food or water for about thirty days. Ninety-eight people died on our journey. The Sri Lankan Navy rescued me, and the other 31 survivors. They took us to Colombo. The Sri Lankan Navy helped us a lot and we are grateful to them. When we arrived in Sri Lanka we were very sick. The Sri Lankan doctors gave us saline fluids and helped us recover so that we could walk and eat again. Once our health recovered, the Sri Lankan government put us in jail for nine months. Then we decided to go on a hunger strike to force the government to contact UNHCR. The United Nations took us out of jail and they provided everything for us – food, clothing, housing, teachers. Muslim Aid also helped us. We stayed in Sri Lanka for almost two years.

Resolution (what finally happened): Then, the UNHCR resettled me and my five friends from the fishing boat to Canada.

Evaluation (significance and meaning of the action, attitude of the narrator): Canadian people have also helped us a lot. I want to thank the Canadian government for helping me. I am very happy to be in Canada. Thank you Allah/God for helping us. I will never forget to help others.

Coda (returns the perspective to the present): We only get money from the government for one year, then we have to find jobs to support ourselves. I made a lot of friends from Burma and from Canada.

7 The Role of English as a Foreign Language in Educating Refugees in Norway

Anne Dahl, Anna Krulatz and Eivind Nessa Torgersen

Like other Western European countries, Norway has seen a steady influx of refugees in the last two decades. As elsewhere in Europe, dominant ideologies of language and language learning affect refugees in complicated ways. Government regulations state that refugees in Norway are expected to develop proficiency in Norwegian and obtain jobs in the community of settlement. However, despite English being Norway's most important foreign language – one which is often required for higher education and employment – the role of English is downplayed in refugee education programs. Seeking to explore refugee-background students' voices and to empower them to shape their futures in Norway, we examine how refugees and their teachers in schools in the two small communities of Storbu and Laksvær perceive the role of English in their educational and employment opportunities. Using semi-structured, face-to-face interviews with teachers and refugee education coordinators, as well as a short survey administered to selected adult refugees in the two communities, we compare how these groups envision refugees' educational and professional success and the role of English education and proficiency in that success. The findings suggest a hidden curriculum, with discrepancies between educational and career goals set by the refugee-background students and those of the Norwegian authorities, teachers and administrators.

In the last two decades, the number of new refugees to Norway, as with other Western European countries, has been rising steadily (Statistics Norway, 2015). Refugees constitute 3.6% of the total population of Norway and 28% of all immigrants to Norway (Statistics Norway, 2015). As of January 1, 2015, 188,100 persons with refugee status were living in Norway, with citizens from Somalia, Eritrea, Syria and Iraq constituting the largest groups (Statistics Norway, 2015). Many of the recent refugees are culturally and ethnically dissimilar from the majority of the Norwegian population. They tend to come from war-affected countries and may have disrupted schooling backgrounds. Few have the advanced academic degrees and professional skills that are recognized as economically valuable in the West (Kanu, 2008). Occupational and economic adjustment has therefore been deemed one of the most important aspects of acculturation for adult refugees (Stein, 1979): it constitutes a key to financial independence, has a positive impact on self-esteem and offers opportunities for language development and social contact in the country of settlement.

In an attempt to increase adult refugees' employability and financial independence, the Norwegian government grants them both the right and the obligation to attend a two-year introduction program that covers the Norwegian language and civics. The program aims to 'provide basic Norwegian language skills, provide basic insight into Norwegian social conditions, [and] prepare for participation in working life' (Lovdata, 2015 [translation by Ministry of Foreign Affairs, 2006: 3]). To achieve this, the program must at least include 'Norwegian language training, social studies, [and] measures that prepare the participant for further education or access to working life' (Lovdata, 2015). Refugee-background individuals are expected to develop the necessary language skills to 'obtain employment and [...] provide for themselves' and to fully 'participate in community life' (Samfunnskunnskap, 2015: para. 1). The program may offer a number of additional components, including classes toward an exit diploma from the obligatory school system,[1] based on each participant's needs, and the exact contents of the program are agreed upon by the program coordinator and the participants (Directorate of Integration and Diversity, n.d.). Nevertheless, instruction in English is only included in the program insofar as it is an obligatory subject toward this diploma (Norwegian Directorate for Education and Training, 2013).

The lack of instruction in English in the program is noteworthy, given the important role of English in Norway. This role is underscored by the national curriculum for lower-secondary schools, which states that 'to succeed in a world where English is used for international communication, it is necessary to be able to use the English language and to have knowledge of how it is used in different contexts' (Norwegian Directorate for Education and Training, 2013, n.p.). The ability to use English is a requirement, in fact, for many jobs in Norway. In addition, English proficiency enables broader access to tertiary education, as textbooks written in English are often used at Norwegian universities, and students are often expected to write master's theses and doctoral dissertations in this language (e.g. Ljosland, 2007). Thus, refugees who have only received instruction in Norwegian may be at a disadvantage when competing for jobs with applicants who have both Norwegian and English proficiency.

In the present study, we compare the perspectives of refugee-background students to those of teachers and administrators, regarding the perceived importance of the two languages.

Language Learning as Part of Refugees' Integration in Society

The degree to which refugees have access to educational, economic and social opportunities is affected by social, political and historical factors in the country of settlement; national ideologies that shape access to language education can either enable belonging or perpetuate exclusion of refugee groups (Warriner, 2007). Proficiency in the dominant language of the country of resettlement and basic knowledge of that nation's history, institutions and culture are often assumed to be sufficient to create a sense of belonging, membership and empowerment (Cooke, 2009; Warriner, 2007). Little support is given, for example, to the maintenance of languages spoken by minorities, including immigrants and refugees (May, 2001).

Although language and citizenship courses are offered to refugees in an increasing number of Western countries, exclusion and marginalization continue to dominate refugees' experiences, which may be due in part to limited access to educational options. Homogeneity, the model of society which perceives differences as undesirable and threatening and views a monolingual, monoethnic, monoreligious and mono-ideological society as ideal (Blommaert & Verschueren, 1998), is an additional obstacle faced by many refugees in contexts across Europe. Refugees are typically expected to acquire the majority language and adapt to the social norms of the country of resettlement, and cultural integration is seen as an important objective to be promoted through proficiency in the national language (Stevenson, 2006). In a country such as Norway, the focus on learning the national language may thus have consequences not just for minority language maintenance, but also for whether learning English is seen as necessary or even desirable. This perspective in turn may effectively exclude refugees from many areas of society, by limiting access to employment and higher education, for example.

These dominant ideologies of language and language learning affect refugees in complicated ways. Previous research suggests that adult refugees may feel disadvantaged compared to native-born citizens and other immigrants in the educational domain, because of inadequate or absent support systems and programs (Earnest *et al.*, 2010). In the United Kingdom, research has found that English language and citizenship programs are often perceived as a barrier rather than a support in the process of becoming a citizen, because such programs are not easily accessible and are subject to time limitations within which the programs have to be completed (Cooke, 2009; Kaiwan, 2008; see also Khan, this volume). Studies involving refugees in the United States suggest that proficiency in the country's dominant language, English, 'does not necessarily confer the social, cultural, economic or political capital' needed to fully participate in various aspects of social life (Warriner, 2007: 355).

Although, arguably, knowledge of a national language is a useful first step toward accessing social, cultural, economic and political resources (McBrien, 2005), understandings about what is essential for the successful acculturation of refugees vary among government officials, researchers and the public. In Norway, the consensus appears to be that knowledge of Norwegian social norms and proficiency in the Norwegian language are two key factors in integration (Hayfron, 2001; Krulatz & Torgersen, 2016). Nevertheless, research suggests that proficiency in the dominant language does not always guarantee economic self-sufficiency (Blommaert, 2006; Warriner, 2007), and that other factors need to be taken into consideration.

In Norway, one such factor may be proficiency in English, which plays an important role in many areas of society. In contrast to languages spoken by non-EU migrants, English as a global language enjoys high status (Stevenson, 2006) and has been recognized as an important medium of communication in the Nordic countries (Brock-Utne, 2001; Hayfron, 2001). However, as far as we know, no official documents in non-English-dominant countries in Europe specifically recognize the importance of providing English instruction to refugee-background students who do not already speak the language, and no research has examined the perceived usefulness of English proficiency from the refugee perspective in these countries. If proficiency in English is an important commodity enabling better access to tertiary education and jobs, refugee-background students without English proficiency would appear to be linguistically and economically disadvantaged. Our study therefore compares how refugee-background students and their teachers and administrators in two small communities in mid-Norway perceive the role of English versus Norwegian in their educational and employment opportunities. We used semi-structured, face-to-face interviews with teachers and refugee program coordinators, as well as a short survey (see Appendix) administered to selected adult refugee-background students, to understand these perceptions.

Research Questions and Methodology

This study is part of a larger project that examines the available and preferred educational and career paths for refugees in two communities of resettlement in Norway. In this chapter, we focus on three research questions:

(1) What are the main institutional learning goals for adult refugee-background students in Norway?

(2) To what extent do these goals overlap with those that the students set for themselves?
(3) What is the perceived importance of developing Norwegian and English proficiency by adult refugee-background students in Norway in achieving the above goals?

Data collection took place in two rural communities, Laksvær and Storbu.[2] These locations were chosen because of the authors' links to and engagement with the local schools. Both communities are municipalities in mid-Norway with populations of between 4500 and 7500, with former refugees comprising between 3% and 4.5% of the population (Statistics Norway, 2015). The majority of refugee-background residents come from Eritrea, Iraq, Sudan, Bosnia and Herzegovina, Morocco, Congo, Myanmar, Afghanistan, Somalia, Sri Lanka and Ethiopia. Storbu's main industries, and thus employers include agriculture, tourism and light manufacturing. Laksvær is a coastal community where the main industries are fish farming, deer hunting and tourism.

Semi-structured interviews with seven teachers and two program administrators were used to gain insight into perspectives on educational and professional goals for adult refugee-background students. The interviews were conducted in Norwegian and focused on policies, educational programs, professional career choices and perceptions of the importance of Norwegian and English. Each interview lasted about 40 minutes and was audio-recorded and transcribed using the ELAN[3] or Praat programs.[4]

In addition, a short two-part survey was used to obtain information from 40 adult refugee-background students, 18 females and 22 males. The first section focused on the participants' demographic information, and the second on their views on educational and professional needs and goals, and the perceived role of proficiency in Norwegian and English in achieving those goals (see Appendix). Respondents came from Afghanistan, Eritrea, Ethiopia, Somalia and Sudan. They were between 19 and 45 years old and had been residing in Norway between nine days and three years. The following native languages were listed: Amharic, Arabic, Belin, Dari, Fur, Oromo, Saho, Somali, Tigre and Tigrinya. Because of the high number of languages spoken by the refugee-background students and limited access to translators and research resources, the surveys were administered in Norwegian. Teachers of Norwegian as a second language assisted in the process and explained any unknown words and phrases. The students were not interviewed because of their limited language proficiency.

To draw findings from the dominant themes in the data, an inductive approach to data analysis was implemented (Mackey & Gass, 2016). We coded the interview transcripts using the following key words, drawn from the research questions: 'introductory program', 'Norwegian', 'proficiency in Norwegian', 'obligation', 'career goals', 'educational goals', 'English', 'proficiency in English'. The thematic analysis of the interview materials produced additional subcategories for the theme 'English': 'instrumental use of English', 'English as a school subject', 'English as a possible hurdle' and 'English as a communicative tool'. Next, we identified patterns by which to group key words into themes. Finally, we created a matrix of the central themes that emerged. The findings suggest that while both structural and individual factors affect educational and career paths available to adult refugees in Norway, discrepancies exist in perceptions of the role of English proficiency among refugee-background adults, compared with their teachers and program administrators. A detailed report follows, including quotes and vignettes from the data, which we translated into English.

Researcher positionality

It is important to acknowledge that as researchers in this study, we were not just neutral observers, but human agents who can effect change on the population we investigated, a phenomenon referred to as the 'observer's paradox' in sociolinguistic research (Labov, 1972). Although we attempted to remain neutral and objective during the interviews, and we were not physically present while the students filled out the survey, we may have prompted teachers and administrators to increase their conscious reflection on issues pertaining to refugee education and the amount of control they exert on the programs and the students during and following the study. Similarly, by asking the students to answer questions about the role of Norwegian and English in their career options, we may have increased their level of reflection on their educational and career activities. Our professional experience as applied and educational linguists who work in English teacher education programs also affected our interpretation of the findings. Our biases and assumptions led us to focus on particular aspects of adult refugee-background student education, namely the roles of English and Norwegian.

Findings

Restricted institutional goals

As stated above, participation in the introduction program is mandatory for refugees to Norway. Although the program consists of stable key components, teachers and administrators have freedom to differentiate based on student needs. However, our findings suggest that the refugee-background adults in Laksvær and Storbu have little choice in the educational and occupational paths available to them. To quote one of the respondents, Monica: 'It is limited what you can do here. ... So to take the subjects they want in high school, [students] move. Here [you get to choose] general studies, and health studies, and construction studies… It is [a bit limited]'.

Because of the small size of both communities, with limited access to university and college education, which is only available through long-distance learning, educational opportunities are restricted to those offered through adult education programs. Similarly, because there are few local industries, employment options are scarce. According to the interviewees, these factors tend to affect the degree to which students can act upon their agency and achieve their educational and professional dreams and goals. One goal of the program is to prepare students for upper-secondary school; thus, obtaining a lower-secondary exit diploma in order to enter upper-secondary school and enter professional life was a common goal agreed on between the coordinators and teachers. In the words of Ida, a teacher, '[they] should make it through high school, and [they] should get a vocational certificate'. The teachers and the administrators seemed to assume uniformly that the students should aim to obtain jobs that are available in the local communities, such as in the fish industry, in stores, in healthcare and at local businesses. For instance, Marthe, a teacher, mentioned transport, cleaning and restaurants, as well as the possibility of becoming a native language teacher. She added, however, that for that last career choice '[students'] Norwegian must be very good and they need additional training', which implies that she does not see employment in a profession requiring a college degree as a likely option for these students.

School authorities do attempt to meet the individual needs of the students, however, and there is evidence in the interviews that individual plans are made through dialogue between coordinators and students, as mandated by the program guidelines. For instance, Tonje, an administrator, stated that 'both the content and the length of the program can be individualized; it's actually quite flexible'. Furthermore, Kari, another program administrator, commented: '[they receive instruction] depending on their needs, whether it's work experience at a company, language experience at a work place, or whether it's other measures that have to do with children and family life'. Kari also explained that refugee-background adults at her school have varied educational backgrounds, with some lacking primary school education, whereas others hold university degrees. The educational levels of the students before arrival in Norway ranged from no former schooling to graduate education. More than 50% of the students reported completing varying degrees of elementary education, between three and eight years, and about 25% stated that they had high school education. The remaining participants reported vocational education, a college degree, a graduate degree or no former schooling (one each).

The teachers reported that students had large variation in their literacy skills, from absent and emerging native language literacy to university-level literacy, as well as variation in their level of proficiency in Norwegian. Marthe stated that often instruction has to address basic skills: 'teach the alphabet is what we often do, and we have a literacy support group for those who have learned the basics but are not functional readers'. Nevertheless, all participants receive instruction in Norwegian and civics in the introductory program, as well as in other content areas such as mathematics and social studies, if they take lower-secondary education as part of the program. This is because, as one teacher pointed out, the students will not be able to enroll in upper-secondary education if they do not develop an adequate knowledge of academic concepts. While these comments suggest a certain degree of course adaptability to individual student needs, regardless of previous educational background, obtaining a lower-secondary diploma is perceived as necessary in order to secure future employment, education and training. Students already holding a university degree are expected to focus on developing the proficiency in Norwegian that would allow them to obtain employment.

The teachers and administrators noted that at least some students are highly aware of the importance of education as a means of improving their employment opportunities. To quote Silje, a teacher, 'Some want to continue their education, they have clear goals, are driven by internal motivation'. Additionally, according to the interviewees, competition with work immigrants from Eastern Europe, who possess desirable professional skills, is an additional obstacle for refugee-background adults. The responses of four of the participants suggest a general perception of economic immigrants as hard-working and possessing 'the strengths needed in the Norwegian society', which makes them more competitive on the job market than refugees. For instance, one administrator stated that 'Poles are sought after due to their good work ethic' and one of the teachers commented that Poles and Lithuanians manage to obtain jobs even if they do not speak a word of Norwegian, as long as they have the necessary professional qualifications. This positive stereotype of Eastern European workers is contrasted with a negative stereotype of refugee-background job seekers for whom 'to get up at six am, well, is a bit outrageous', as one teacher put it. While not all teachers and administrators made such comments, this bias suggests some discrimination and negative stereotyping. A spread of similar views in the local community may have serious implications for the employability of the refugees.

Varied student goals

In contrast to the teachers and the administrators, who seem to assume that most refugees will seek jobs related to the fishing industry and healthcare, the student survey respondents indicated a variety of educational and professional goals, ranging from finishing primary education (11 participants) and high school (8 participants), to obtaining graduate degrees (2 participants), with Master of Arts (MA) and PhD each mentioned once. Seventeen students stated that they wanted to obtain a vocational or professional education. The professions mentioned in the survey responses included unskilled jobs that do not require formal qualifications, such as custodian and elderly or child caretaker; manual labor jobs such as electrician, painter, plumber, carpenter, car mechanic, cook, hairdresser and bus driver; and professional positions such as teacher, teacher's assistant, interpreter, nurse and physician. Thus, we observe a mismatch between societal and individual goals with respect to education and career, as students reported higher occupational aspirations than those assumed by institutional representatives.

The perceived role of proficiency in Norwegian and English

The perceived importance of learning Norwegian for refugee-background adults in Norway was clearly reflected in our data. All of the students agreed that gaining proficiency in Norwegian is very important, and 90% agreed that it would help them obtain work. All teachers and administrators agreed that learning Norwegian is the most important educational goal for the refugee-background students and likely the most important factor in obtaining employment and integration into Norwegian society. This perspective is illustrated in the following comment by Marthe: 'Overall to manage in the Norwegian society it is Norwegian, it is Norwegian, and it is Norwegian [...] We talk among ourselves here and we are so uniform on that they must know Norwegian'.

The teachers and administrators consciously articulated the reason for prioritizing Norwegian – that is, its importance for employment and integration. In the interview data, a number of participants provided accounts of how they focus on Norwegian language development in their classes, including their reasons for doing so. For instance, Hanne stressed that it is 'my goal that they will learn Norwegian', and Ingvild commented that 'it is Norwegian that they require [to obtain work] in the stores'. Again, these comments reflect on the skills that will help the refugees obtain jobs in the local community – jobs requiring relatively little education – rather than on what is needed to pursue students' long-term educational goals.

Most of the student survey respondents (90%) agreed that learning Norwegian is a very important goal and that they believe it will help them obtain employment. There is also indirect evidence in the interview data that the students see Norwegian as important for gaining economic independence. For instance, Ingvild, a teacher, noted, 'It seems that they understand how important it is to learn Norwegian'. Tonje, an administrator, commented, 'They clearly want to learn sufficient Norwegian to be able to practice their profession'. Thus, there appears to be consensus among policymakers, teachers, program administrators and refugee-background students themselves that it is important to learn Norwegian.

Focus on competence in English, in contrast, was virtually non-existent among the teachers and administrators. Although English was mentioned by many as one of the subjects necessary to pass lower-secondary education, the focus seemed to be mainly on achieving a passing grade, not on developing communicative competence. Our data confirm that the role of developing English proficiency is marginalized within the programs in the two communities studied. Indeed, English is not a component of the introduction program. It is a required subject for those continuing with the lower-secondary and upper-secondary program, but beyond secondary school requirements, Norwegian is the only language seen as important by the program teachers and administrators. As Ingvild commented: 'We did not focus on English as a language to be learned at all [in the Introductory Program]. It is only at the primary/lower-secondary education level that we do'. For students who have no previous English learning experience, English is perceived, in another teacher's words, as 'yet another language to be learned' and thus a potential challenge. Ingvild raised this issue of English constituting a hindrance in the process of acquiring Norwegian: 'Some of them have huge problems learning Norwegian. And then they are poor in English, and so if we were to introduce the sound system of English, well, I don't think that would be good'.

However, when prompted, some of the teachers admitted that instrumental knowledge of English could be beneficial in certain jobs related to tourism – for example, as a cashier at a supermarket or in construction, where many workers from Eastern Europe are employed, and thus the common language is often English. Nevertheless, lack of proficiency in English is not perceived as a disadvantage, as evidenced in the following comment by Ingvild: 'But I have never ever heard from the manager at Rema [a local store] that we should have taught them more English. It is Norwegian. We have heard that'. As another teacher commented, knowledge of English is considered advantageous mostly because it implies familiarity with the Latin alphabet, which is seen as beneficial in the process of learning to read and write in Norwegian. Several other interviewees mentioned that individual factors, for example ambition and motivation, may contribute to professional success more significantly than knowledge of English.

However, nearly all of the student survey participants (97.5%) stated that it is important to learn English; 37.5% of students indicated that they believe knowledge of English would certainly help them obtain a better job in Norway, with an additional 57.5% stating that English might be helpful. The participants were not asked to compare the importance of Norwegian and English, yet they rate the importance of English and Norwegian as similar, in contrast to teachers and administrators, who foreground the importance of Norwegian.

Agentive behaviors for achieving goals

Despite high educational and professional aspirations on the part of students, the teachers and administrators we interviewed perceived students' involvement and motivation as lacking. While the Norwegian government and the schools set goals for the refugee-background students, they also expect that these adults should manifest some independence in advancing these goals. The teachers noted differences in the level of independence that students display. For instance, Ingvild commented that 'it is the personality, and there are big differences, we have some in the introduction program who already sit and write their own job applications'. However, according to the teachers, some students appeared unmotivated and unable to set goals for themselves. 'I have to motivate [the students] to not think negatively if [employers] do not contact them, they have to be a little proactive, not be afraid to speak with mistakes', said Marthe, as she commented on the challenges that refugees face when looking for a practicum or permanent employment. Similarly, Tonje, an administrator, mentioned a lack of initiative on the part of the students as a concern: 'Some of them show insufficient motivation and effort to learn the language'. These observations may signal student resistance to learning Norwegian, however, rather than lack of ambition – a possibility worthy of further research.

Conclusion

This research has explored perspectives on educational and career opportunities for refugee-background adults in Norway, with a focus on English proficiency. Our analysis reveals discrepancies between the ways in which refugee-background students and their teachers and program administrators interpret their roles and goals. Similar to Warriner (2007: 354), we conclude that the adult refugees in the two communities we studied 'are positioned by the program as well as the influence of the dominant ideologies of language and language learning'.

The most important findings of our research can be summarized as follows: Norwegian law and the content of the introductory program sanction the key importance of developing advanced proficiency in Norwegian. The monolingual majority language ideology is perpetuated through the actions and attitudes of the program administrators and teachers, as well as the refugee-background students themselves. Secondly, there is a discrepancy in terms of the types of employment that the communities envision for refugee-background adults, compared with the professional goals these adults set for themselves. Moreover, despite its important role in Norway, English is marginalized in educational programs for adult refugees, because the sole focus is on learning Norwegian, and proficiency in English is not seen as an important goal for this group.

As a result, refugees may face challenges as far as English proficiency is concerned, and may therefore have a lower chance of succeeding within certain sectors of the Norwegian job market.

A lack of support in developing English proficiency could perhaps be perceived as reinforcing educational inequality. Similar to previous research, which has concluded that educational programs serving refugee and immigrant populations often assume low-level employment goals for students (e.g. Curry, 2001), the findings of the present study suggest that there is a 'hidden curriculum' – i.e. a set of implicit social, cultural and academic messages transmitted to students – embedded in the introductory program for refugees in the two communities where the data were collected. Judging from the formal setup of the introduction program, it is likely that the situation is similar in other communities in Norway.

This study has some limitations, which can be taken as a point of departure in future research. Most important, while focusing on teacher and administrator perspectives sheds important light on the issues in question, more in-depth data from the students themselves would enable a better understanding of the refugees' views. Additionally, this project was conducted in two rural communities with particular local economies and employment options, which beyond a doubt influence the available adult education paths. Adult refugees in urban areas of Norway likely face different realities. Future research should therefore examine refugees' education paths in larger, urban communities with more diverse employment opportunities.

Nonetheless, we feel that this research constitutes an important contribution in the Scandinavian context, as it supplies information about the potential mismatches in conceptions of the role of different languages in professional and educational success, and it should enable government agencies and schools to better respond to the needs of refugee populations. The Norwegian authorities should make sure that when the contents of the introduction program are determined, the goals of such programs are made clear to refugee students, and student perspectives on what should be included in the curricula are considered. Thus, the possibility of adding English instruction to the program should be a point of discussion in these two communities.

Warriner (2007: 356) argues that changes are needed in 'teaching and learning practices that facilitate the transformations required for genuine educational access and inclusion, long-term economic self-sufficiency and stability, and social mobility for [...] recently arrived refugees'. Our findings indicate a similar need for educational changes in our context. If the introduction program for refugees is aimed at preparing them for further education and access to working life in Norway, its curriculum should arguably include instruction toward English proficiency. While proficiency in the language of the host community is indisputably a key factor in integration, focusing on its importance can overshadow the complexity of the social, psychological, cultural and educational factors that affect the integration of refugee-background students in their country of resettlement.

Notes

(1) The lower-secondary education in Norway comprises Grades 8–10. Education through tenth grade is mandatory. Upper-secondary education (Grades 11–13) is optional.
(2) To protect the privacy of participants, participant names and place names are pseudonyms.
(3) https://tla.mpi.nl/tools/tla-tools/elan/.
(4) http://www.fon.hum.uva.nl/praat/.

References

Blommaert, J. (2006) Language policy and national identity. In T. Ricento (ed.) *An Introduction to Language Policy: Theory and Method* (pp. 238–254). Malden, MA: Blackwell Publishing.
Blommaert, J. and Verschueren, J. (1998) The role of language in European nationalist ideologies. In B.B. Schieffelin, K.A. Woolard and P.V. Kroskrity (eds) *Language Ideologies: Practice and Theory* (pp. 189–210). Oxford: Oxford University Press.
Brock-Utne, B. (2001) The growth of English for academic communication in the Nordic countries. *International Review of Education* 47 (3), 221–233.
Cooke, M. (2009) Barrier or entitlement? The language and citizenship agenda in the United Kingdom. *Language Assessment Quarterly* 6 (1), 71–77.
Curry, M.J. (2001) Preparing to be privatized: The hidden curriculum of community college ESL writing classes. In E. Margolis (ed.) *The Hidden Curriculum in Higher Education* (pp. 175–192). New York: Routledge.
Directorate of Integration and Diversity (n.d.) Introduksjonsprogram. [Introduction Program] See http://www.imdi.no/opplaring-og-utdanning/introduksjonsprogram (accessed 23 January 2017).
Earnest, J., Joyce, A., de Mori, G. and Silvagni, G. (2010) Are universities responding to the needs of students from refugee backgrounds? *Australian Journal of Education* 54 (2), 155–174.
Hayfron, J.E. (2001) Language training, language proficiency and earnings of immigrants in Norway. *Applied Economics* 33 (15), 1971–1979.
Kaiwan, D. (2008) A journey to citizenship in the United Kingdom. *International Journal on Multicultural Societies* 10 (1), 60–75.
Kanu, Y. (2008) Educational needs and barriers for African refugee students in Manitoba. *Canadian Journal of Education* 31 (4), 915–940.
Krulatz, A. and Torgersen, E. (2016) The role of the EFL classroom in maintaining multilingual identities: Issues and considerations in Sør-Trøndelag public schools. In K. Amanti, J. Álvarez Valencia, S. Keyl and E. Mackinney (eds) *Critical Views on Teaching and Learning English Around the Globe* (pp. 53–68). Charlotte, NC: Information Age Publishing.
Labov, W. (1972) *Sociolinguistic Patterns*. Oxford: Blackwell.
Ljosland, R. (2007) English in Norwegian academia: A step towards diglossia? *World Englishes* 26 (4), 395–410.
Lovdata (2015) *Lov om introduksjonsordning og norskopplæring for nyankomne innvandrere (introduksjonsloven)* [Act on an introductory program and Norwegian language instruction for newly arrived immigrants (Introduction Act)]. See

https://lovdata.no/dokument/NL/lov/2003-07-04-80#KAPITTEL_1 (accessed 5 January 2018).

Mackey, A. and Gass, S.M. (2016) *Second Language Research: Methodology and Design* (2nd edn). New York: Routledge.

May, S. (2001) *Language and Minority Rights: Ethnicity, Nationalism and the Politics of Language.* New York: Longman.

McBrien, L.J. (2005) Educational needs and barriers for refugee students in the United States: A review of the literature. *Review of Educational Research* 75 (3), 329–364.

Ministry of Foreign Affairs (2006) Act on an introductory programme and Norwegian language instruction for newly arrived immigrants [Introduction Act]. Translation. See http://app.uio.no/ub/ujur/oversatte-lover/data/lov-20030704-080-eng.pdf (accessed 5 January 2018).

Norwegian Directorate for Education and Training (2013) English subject curriculum. See https://www.udir.no/kl06/ENG1-03?lplang=http://data.udir.no/kl06/eng (accessed 5 January 2018).

Samfunnskunnskap [Civics] (2015) New immigrant in Norway. See http://www.samfunnskunnskap.no/?page_id=245&lang=en (accessed 5 January 2018).

Statistics Norway (2015) Immigrants by reason for immigration. See https://www.ssb.no/en/befolkning/statistikker/innvgrunn/aar/2015-06-18 (accessed 5 January 2018).

Stein, B.N. (1979) Occupational adjustment of refugees: The Vietnamese in the United States. *International Migration Review* 13 (1), 25–45.

Stevenson, P. (2006) 'National' languages in transnational contexts: Language, migration, and citizenship in Europe. In C. Mar-Molinero and P. Stevenson (eds) *Language Ideologies, Policies and Practices* (pp. 147–161). New York: Palgrave Macmillan.

Warriner, D.S. (2007) Language learning and the politics of belonging: Sudanese women refugees *becoming* and *being* 'American'. *Anthropology and Education Quarterly* 38 (4), 343–359.

Appendix: Survey Administered to Refugees (English Translation)

(1) What is your gender? Please circle.   M   F
(2) What is your age?
(3) What is your home country?
(4) What languages do you speak? For each language, please specify the level (native tongue, native-like, advanced, intermediate, beginner).
(5) How long have you lived in Norway?
(6) What is your level of education from your home country?
   (a) Elementary education
   (b) High school education
   (c) Vocational education
   (d) Associate's degree
   (e) Bachelor's degree
   (f) Master's degree
   (g) PhD
   (h) Other. Please state.

(7) What language(s) were used for instruction during your former education in your home country? Please specify what languages were used for each level of education:
   (a) Primary:
   (b) High school:
   (c) Beyond high school:
(8) How long did you study English in your home country?
(9) What program of study are you currently attending in Norway?
(10) What are your current educational goals?
(11) What are your current professional goals?
(12) What knowledge and skills do you think you need to obtain a job in Norway?
(13) How important is it for you to become proficient in Norwegian?
   (a) Very important
   (b) Somewhat important
   (c) Not important
(14) Do you think proficiency in Norwegian would help you obtain a better job in Norway?
   (a) Yes
   (b) Maybe
   (c) No
(15) How important is it for you to learn English?
   (a) Very important
   (b) Somewhat important
   (c) Not important
(16) Do you think that knowledge of English would help you obtain a better job in Norway?
   (a) Yes
   (b) Maybe
   (c) No

Part 2
Access and Equity

8 Bridges and Barriers: Karen Refugee-background Students' Transition to High School in Australia

Amanda Hiorth and Paul Molyneux

This chapter reports on research into the experiences of six Karen refugee-background adolescents as they made the social, academic and institutional transition from a supported, short-term English as an additional language (EAL) school to mainstream high school in Melbourne, Australia. A longitudinal ethnographic case study design enabled the collection of rich, cross-cultural and multivoiced data, allowing a deep and trusting relationship between researcher and students to evolve. A core data source was the collection of eight themed pictures hand-drawn by each of the students at critical times of their transition. The drawings depict student perspectives on different elements of transition, enabling participants to voice their hopes, concerns, frustrations, confusions and successes in a non-threatening and creative manner. The study reveals that the students' transition to mainstream schooling was very complex, individual, long-term and non-linear. The student artwork and accompanying testimonies, along with observed school and classroom practices, reveal the inadequacy of many well-intentioned transition programs. An urgent need emerges for schools and teachers to better understand the immense social, academic and institutional adjustments that refugee-background adolescents are expected to make, as well as the enormous reserves of strength, determination and resourcefulness they possess.

In the ranking of countries accepting refugees for permanent resettlement, Australia is third (United Nations Refugee Agency, 2016). In Australia, around 14,000 refugee-background applicants are accepted for permanent protection and residency each year through the Refugee and Humanitarian Program. In 2014–2015, the highest number of refugee visas was granted to applicants born in Iraq, Syria, Burma (Myanmar) and

Afghanistan. Many among these newcomers are children and adolescents encountering the English language and a formal school system for the first time.

While programs designed to support EAL learners differ from state to state in Australia, there is often some educational support in the form of English language schools (ELS) that accommodate newcomers for 6–12 months before they enroll in mainstream schools. There is a paucity of research internationally investigating the transition experiences of these students (particularly adolescents) as they move from sheltered, intensive language-support settings to mainstream schools. Investigations of refugee-background students' transitions are needed to identify the social, academic and institutional challenges they face, and the supports that are most helpful.

This chapter reports on a qualitative study of six refugee-background students from the Karen ethnic group whose families relocated to Melbourne, Australia. These students had all experienced warfare and persecution in their homelands on the Thai/Burmese border. Amanda, the key researcher in this study, closely followed the six students as they made the transition from an ELS to mainstream high school. Our research questions were:

- What are the social, academic and institutional experiences of Karen EAL learners as they transition from ELS to mainstream schooling?
- What factors facilitate or inhibit their transition?

After a review of the academic literature related to refugee-background adolescents and their schooling, this chapter discusses symbolic capital (Bourdieu, 1986) and funds of knowledge (González et al., 2005), theories that frame this research. After that, we discuss the research design, the participants, and the data collection devices for this study – in particular, an innovative visual data collection tool. This leads into reporting and discussing our findings around the social, institutional and academic transitions of the six students. We conclude with a focus on the lessons learned and ways to move forward.

Literature Review

Transition for EAL students entering mainstream education can be a time of mixed emotions and multiple challenges, particularly so for students with refugee backgrounds (Gifford et al., 2009). It typically involves 'leaving one location, settling into another, leaving old friends, making new friends, and continuing learning and development' (Catholic Education Office, 2010: 1). The transitional challenges faced by refugee-background students extend beyond academic and linguistic issues to include social and institutional aspects (Gifford *et al.*, 2009; Hos, 2012). Other research has provided valuable insights into broader issues that refugees face, such as acculturation and adaptation, in their new countries of resettlement (Ager & Strang, 2008; Ghaffar-Kucher, 2006). Research in the Australian context, however, has tended to focus on academic challenges, overlooking social and institutional factors (Miller & Windle, 2010; Taylor, 2008; Weekes *et al.*, 2011).

Students with interrupted schooling and low literacy in particular have been the focus of a growing body of international research (Brown *et al.*, 2006; DeCapua & Marshall, 2011). Brown *et al.*'s (2006) research involving Sudanese students new to Australia highlighted the potential connections that could be made between students' existing cultural and social practices and their literacy learning. Karen refugee-background students and their families have often experienced similar levels of interrupted schooling and, in some cases, arrive with limited first language literacy, though there has been little research into their specific needs.

At the time of this study in 2013, there were approximately 1500 ethnic Karen people living in Melbourne's Western Metropolitan Region, the largest Karen community in Australia and the location of this research. In fact, more than half of all Karen students in the state of Victoria were enrolled in schools in the region of this study (Department of Education and Early Childhood Development, 2011). Karen learners have been portrayed as compliant, passive and less orally engaged in classroom learning than other groups of learners (Barron *et al.*, 2007; Bodde, 2011). In the socially dynamic Australian classroom, Karen students might therefore easily be overlooked. Our study extends this research, foregrounding the voices of Karen-background students and providing insights into their lived experiences of transition from ELS to mainstream secondary schooling.

Theoretical Framework

This research uses a theoretical framework drawing on notions of linguistic, cultural and symbolic capital (Bourdieu, 1991). Symbolic capital, in Bourdieu's (1986) terms, refers to the actual or potential resources an individual possesses and the degree to which these are perceived and recognized as legitimate. Bourdieu (1991) argued that possession of certain forms of linguistic and cultural capital or knowledge can be highly advantageous in negotiating schools and institutional learning. He asserted that school systems, like wider society, accord high status to the cultural knowledge and linguistic competencies that reflect the dominant culture, and typically overlook or deride minority languages and non-dominant forms of cultural expression. These ideas have been influential in educational research on the experiences of immigrant, refugee or low socioeconomic status children and their families. This line of research has also led to the understanding of *funds of knowledge* (González et al., 2005; Moll et al., 1992) as the resources and practices of students' home communities and consideration of how these resources can be drawn on in the classroom. The goal of viewing diverse forms of linguistic and cultural knowledge as an asset, rather than a deficit, informed the design of this study.

Research Design

We employed a qualitative case study methodology. A group of six Karen-background adolescents made up the case. We investigated their experiences of transition from one ELS to three mainstream high schools in a suburban area of metropolitan Melbourne. All schools were co-educational and catered to Grades 7 through 12 in relatively low socioeconomic communities. All schools and participants in the study have been ascribed pseudonyms. The ELS was purposively selected, being located in a region with the largest Karen community in Australia, with close to 25% of the total student cohort being of Karen ethnicity. The three destination high schools in this study (Wills Secondary College, Howard Secondary College and Goodwin High) ranged in size with student populations of 764 (Wills), 1321 (Howard) and 1777 (Goodwin). Approximately one-third of students at each school were from language backgrounds other than English, with an average of 15% from Karen backgrounds.

After receiving human research ethics clearance from our university, we collected data over the course of one school year. The primary researcher maintained extensive field notes; undertook regular classroom observations; conducted student, parent and staff interviews; and gathered artifacts such as student work and school documents. We drew on these multiple data sources to develop an understanding of the process of transition and to make audible the voices of those who are often marginalized and silenced in educational research (Fine & Weis, 2003; Liamputtong, 2007). In addition, we asked student participants to produce eight drawings at different periods of their transition. In line with the study's theoretical framework around funds of knowledge, we saw this interest in drawing as an asset they brought to the research. Visual devices have been shown to be a powerful means of expression, particularly for culturally diverse and/or marginalized people (Alerby, 2003; Einarsdottir, 2007; Liamputtong, 2007). Visuals provide an alternative mode of communication to the linguistic mode, reducing pressure and offering an innovative means to capture participant stories (Darbyshire et al., 2005; Yates, 2010). Scholars note that children's drawings 'are not just illustrations of a verbal text, not just "creative embellishment"; they are part of a "multimodally" conceived text' (Kress & Van Leeuwen, 2006: 113), where the visual and the verbal play different and defined roles.

The six students had three to four weeks to complete the drawings, which we then used as part of two individual interviews to stimulate communication and enable deep reflection on transition. In essence, students interpreted and analyzed their own artwork during the interviews. The first four pictures were drawn by the students at the end of their time at the ELS. They brought the pictures to an individual interview session on their final day at the ELS. The prompt given for drawing each picture was as follows:

Picture 1:   My first day at the ELS.
Picture 2:   My last day at the ELS.
Picture 3:   How I imagine my first day at my new school.
Picture 4:   How I imagine me in the future.

The other four pictures were drawn by students six months after they transferred to the mainstream high school. They brought the pictures to an individual interview on the final day of the school year. The prompt for drawing each picture in this second set was as follows:

Picture 5:   Me in my first week at school/Me at school now.
Picture 6:   A place I like at school/A place I don't like at school.
Picture 7:   Something to help a student from the ELS coming to my school.
Picture 8:   My weekends.

Our analysis of students' pictures was guided by Callow's (2013) frameworks for interpreting visual texts, allowing us to explore aspects such as isolation and connection, as represented by features of placement, distance and proximity between figures.

The participants

Four female students and two male students participated in this study, ranging from 12 to 15 years of age, corresponding to Years (or Grades) 7–9 in the Victorian secondary schooling system. All students were of Karen ethnicity, born in refugee camps along the Thai/Burmese border and experienced interruptions in prior camp schooling.

Our research drew on other data sources including formal interviews with other significant people involved in the students' transition, such as family members, school staff and community leaders. These interviews assisted in providing multiple voices and also helped us piece together an understanding of the bigger picture (Janesick, 2000) of transition. This form of triangulation (Stake, 2000; Yin, 2009) added reliability and rigor to this study.

Findings

We have used the social, institutional and academic domains of transition as a framework for analysis and reporting. We define the social domain as the personal interactions and connections the students made among themselves and with other members of the school community, and the level of comfort and security they felt in the new setting. The institutional domain relates to the students' engagement with the school as an institution: how they understood its formal and informal structures and its policies and patterns of practice. The academic domain encompasses the students' learning across the curriculum, particularly the language and literacy demands of their schooling.

The social domain of transition

Little attention to social interaction (such as strategies for entering conversations, conducting personal introductions, etc.) was evident in the curriculum at the ELS. Similarly, this area of transition was essentially ignored at each of the high schools. Nonetheless, all students in this study, on leaving the ELS, expressed hope and optimism that a larger school environment would enhance their social contact with many more adolescents their age and result in a more heterogeneous friend group. Participants' pictures drawn before leaving the ELS imagined themselves in the new school environment.

Figure 8.1, for example, shows Lili being hopeful for social connections. Lili depicts herself (on the left) smiling and happily gazing at the viewer; her use of color in the original drawing adds to the optimism of the image. In her discussion of this illustration, she imagined the other student coming up to her with the positive greeting that appears in the speech bubble, complete with emoticons. In an interview before transition, she reported that although she had 'butterflies in [her] stomach', she felt 'very happy to have new friends and new teachers'. Lili's optimism and nervousness mirrored that of other students, who commented that they were nervous but excited for the new opportunities high school would provide, particularly for friendship.

The reality was a lot more complicated, as the students' social transition was not well supported by the mainstream schools. Although Howard Secondary College had an informal 'buddy system' set up on Orientation Day, this approach was not pursued further, nor did any of the schools designate staff members as contacts for students or organize whole-school welcome activities which might have facilitated a sense of belonging and decreased anxiety levels. All students reported feeling immediate pressure

Figure 8.1 Lili imagines her social transition to high school

to establish friendships with peers as a symbol of having transitioned successfully into the new school. However, they instead experienced isolation and loneliness, as depicted in Figures 8.2 and 8.3.

Both Hsar Hsar and Law Lu Eh's pictures employ similar visual conventions to depict circumstances of isolation, distance and powerlessness during the transition. In their drawings, they are dwarfed by large objects placed to their left (an elaborate tree with branches, fruits and birds, in Hsar Hsar's case, and the edge of the school building, in Law Lu Eh's). The decision by both boys to draw themselves and the other students without visual markers of expression or individuality may be artistic convenience, but equally conveys feelings of depersonalization. The isolated individual contrasts with the tightly bunched groups of friends in both pictures. Law Lu Eh's comments about his first day reinforce the sense of isolation:

132   Part 2: Access and Equity

Figure 8.2 Hsar Hsar recalls his first day at his new school and his sadness at not having any friends.

> I come to the high school … and I have no friend. I look the people play … but I'm not play [with] them – just looking. I don't know them and like, I little bit scared. I have to do myself. I have to try really hard, you know. (Interview)

The two Year 9 students (Hsar Hsar and Gay Paw) established new but superficial friendships. Students talked of these friendships as convenient for lunchtime company, but stated that they were often not pursued or deepened out of school. Although these friendships were tentative, having a peer group to spend break time with and an appropriate place for building social connections in the school aided in their transition journeys. While Hsar Hsar at times boasted of his popularity, he more often commented on the difficulties of making and sustaining friendships. He expressed confusion that friendships outside the Karen-speaking student group were difficult to establish and, for him as well as for Gay Paw, this was a source of frustration, since friendships with Australian-born, English-speaking students were seen as a marker of acceptance within the Australian school system. More pragmatically, he was disappointed that the failure to establish these friendships reduced the social opportunities he needed to improve his English.

Like the other four students, Mi Mi Moe and Moo Dar Eh found the social transition to Howard Secondary College a challenge. They displayed high levels of anxiety, affecting all aspects of their transition. Both

Figure 8.3 Law Lu Eh depicts his unhappiness at not having friends on his first day at his new school.

reported feeling scared to speak to new people, and therefore gravitated to girls from Karen-speaking backgrounds, but found this situation limiting. Mi Mi Moe quickly established herself as the leader of the Karen-background girls in Year 8 and exerted a somewhat controlling influence over these girls. In this way, Mi Mi Moe found status among other Karen students, yet still felt excluded among the larger population of students at the school. Law Lu Eh, however, was entirely satisfied with his new group of Karen-background friends, with sports during break times being an effective means of establishing and maintaining social connections. Sport was also a vehicle for bonding with teachers, as observed by his physical education teacher, who recognized and encouraged Law Lu Eh's physical skills and strengths. Hence, although students reported overall feelings of isolation, positive social connections with Karen peers and some teachers provided a much-needed bridge in the transition journey.

Although Lili was just as shy as her transitioning peers, she was the only Karen student at Goodwin High. With no same-language peers, she was forced to establish relationships with a diverse range of other students. While Lili expressed a perhaps unrealistic expectation of making instant friendships, she was nonetheless successful over time in forging positive relationships with other students, using her knowledge of four languages and her intercultural communication skills. By the end of her first term, she had formed a solid and heterogeneous friendship group who would meet in the library to socialize during break times. Here again, a designated place for social interaction facilitated the development of important social connections. It was these friendships that became a strong bridge in Lili's transition and enabled her to develop a sense of belonging and well-being. Lili deemed her social transition a great success, as defined by her playful and busy lunchtimes and the large number of classmates who arrived at a weekend birthday party and a Halloween party she held.

The institutional domain of transition

When these students transitioned into mainstream high school, they were required to make sense of how school itself functioned, without explicit explanation or ongoing guidance. Two of the three schools offered the students a single Orientation Day prior to starting the school term, which involved a school tour, an information packet (in English, containing complex information about school rules, procedures and timetables) and some visits to the classes they would soon attend. However, this was insufficient to orient students to the culture and processes of their new schools. The students' limited understandings of how their new schools operated as institutions proved to be a barrier in their transition, as has been found in other research (Hos & Curry, 2013). While the schools were attentive to some aspects of the institutional transition, they did not have a broad enough understanding of the length and complexity of the transition and adjustment process.

Moo Dar Eh, in a drawing completed two terms after her arrival at Wills Secondary College, reflected on her first day at the new school (Figure 8.4). She draws the school as imposing and official, herself glumly standing in front, revealing her unhappiness. The viewer's eye is drawn to both her in the foreground and the school in the background. The level of detail in the depiction of the school (including its commanding portals and elaborate architecture) creates a sense of institutional power and authority. Moo Dar Eh, by contrast, appears daunted and overwhelmed and – literally – without a pathway by which to enter. This illustration is more than symbolic: her first day was spent wandering around the exterior of the school grounds in an attempt to find the entry gate.

In Moo Dar Eh's picture, there is also a sense that without human support, the task of transitioning and integrating herself into the school community had become wholly her responsibility. There is little sense of welcome, nor any expectation that the school might attempt to integrate Moo Dar Eh's culture and traditions, something reflected in the experiences

Figure 8.4 Moo Dar Eh at her new high school, without a known path to enter the building

of the other five students. When discussing this image later in the year, Moo Dar Eh reflected:

136 Part 2: Access and Equity

I got lost. When I come to this school I be like (widens her eyes and moves her head around quickly). I don't know how to come in school ... walk around, and I don't know how to go out. I lost. (Interview)

While Moo Dar Eh's experience – and her stark illustrative representation of it – was more extreme than the other students, they all experienced considerable difficulty in the first few weeks locating classrooms, arriving on time, wearing the correct uniform or bringing the necessary textbooks and equipment. Law Lu Eh, for example, was admonished for wearing the wrong clothing to physical education and received a reprimand for being late to another class (when locating the room was the cause of his tardiness). Institutional unfamiliarity, in this case, resulted in an unfair and insensitive reprimand.

The academic domain of transition

All six students were both excited and apprehensive about beginning their academic studies at a mainstream high school. Like the participants in Harklau's (2000) study, the Karen students imagined themselves as 'the good student': one who is motivated, attentive and involved in class. Harklau's focus was specifically on participants' in-class learning and understandings of their teachers' expectations across the curriculum. Our study took a

Figure 8.5 Hsar Hsar imagines his first day of high school.

similar focus with our understanding of the students' academic transition drawing on both in-class and out-of-class sources.

Hsar Hsar's picture (Figure 8.5) depicts an optimistic orientation toward learning – a perspective shared by other participants. In placing his own image in a central position, Hsar Hsar uses layout conventions to draw attention to himself as 'the good student' in his imagined new classroom. Even though facial features are obscured, he has attracted the gaze of the classroom teacher and their proximity suggests engagement and mutual respect. The other students are barely in the frame – it is all about the teacher, Hsar Hsar and his learning. The classroom is depicted as a place of warmth and belonging, symbolized by the wall pictures of flowers and sunlit landscapes that create a feeling of optimism. When discussing this image, Hsar Hsar commented, 'I learn [so] much the English. The teacher teach me something I don't understand. I listen and thinking how to write, how to know, yeah. I think it's not too much hard' (Interview).

In reality, the students' experiences were somewhat different from Hsar Hsar's idealistic image. Their experiences of classroom learning, the curriculum demands and low levels of teacher empathy and support proved to be barriers – rather than bridges – to a smooth academic transition. In terms of cultural expectations, all students had imagined a more traditional and didactic form of instruction similar to that depicted in Hsar Hsar's drawing. As found in other studies (Arkoudis & Love, 2004; Lee, 2005), students imagined learning as structured around copying notes from the board, filling in workbooks and memorizing lists for tests, something linked not to their learning at the ELS, but to their previous schooling in refugee camps. While a lot of teacher instructional talk was observed in the high school classrooms, many of the students' assumptions were inaccurate. There was an element of critical thinking and reflection required that the students did not anticipate and were quite unprepared for, given that the ELS focused more on the basics of English communication and understanding. In addition, their assumptions of what it meant to be a 'good student' were incorrect, as teachers expected more active engagement in classroom dialogue.

Students also had unmet expectations about their classmates. To their surprise and distress, other students' behavior was often disruptive, disrespectful of the teachers and the subject content, and not conducive to learning. Reflecting on what disappointed her about the transition, Mi Mi Moe drew a picture of her reaction to student misbehavior in class (Figure 8.6).

Mi Mi Moe employs a bird's-eye perspective to her picture of the classroom, which removes her emotionally from the image (it is unclear which student is in fact Mi Mi Moe). As her written comment makes

Figure 8.6 Mi Mi Moe depicts common happenings inside the classroom.

clear, Mi Mi Moe found conflict in the classroom disturbing. A bookcase appears on one side of the illustration, symbolizing learning and knowledge, and the more compliant students sit in front, facing the two students involved in a physical altercation. The teacher appears distant and powerless. When discussing this picture, Mi Mi Moe stated that the fighting she had witnessed had left her feeling scared for her safety and unable to concentrate.

The academic expectations of their schools also proved challenging for students. All participants reported difficulties with language, literacy and content in different schools and subject classrooms. Based on both classroom observations and interviews, many teachers were ill-equipped to cater to these newcomer EAL learners and had received little or no professional development in supporting these students. Additionally, these learners' quietness and compliance in the classroom meant that their needs were often overlooked. Hence, there was a significant mismatch between teachers and students in terms of cultural expectations about learning. Law Lu Eh commented some months after arriving:

> I wanna go back to the language school, you know. You know why? Because the language school is not hard for me [and] I got a lot of friends in there. [The work here is] so hard, you know. I got [my results] so little. (Interview)

These feelings of frustration characterized many of the students' experiences. A number of participants commented that extended time at the ELS would have enabled a smoother academic transition. Even subjects in which the students had previously been successful posed significant challenges, as evident in Moo Dar Eh's comment: 'I love Math, but I always fail Math. I don't know [why] – because I not study or something? I study, but when I do the test I will fail'. This suggests that Moo Dar Eh was not receiving the instructional support necessary for her to succeed academically.

Not all aspects of the students' academic transition caused such frustration, however. Subjects that do not typically present the same academic demands and allow for greater student-centered instruction proved to be a relief for many of the students. In physical education, for example, Law Lu Eh's adeptness and agility enabled him to quickly master new skills that resulted in success in that subject, and improved his social connections. Gay Paw's creativity and dexterity allowed her to quickly learn new skills in woodworking and textiles, which endowed her with symbolic capital in that learning space. All the students attended art classes at their mainstream high schools, and they valued this opportunity to advance their artistic skills.

Discussion: The Complex Nature of Transition

Analysis of the participating students' artwork and accompanying testimonies provides insights into the complexities of transition. Our findings add to the research showing that transition brings a multitude of challenges for adjustment. Although undoubtedly true for all students (native English speakers and EAL learners), for these refugee-background adolescents, transition was found to be a particularly complex, multifaceted, long-term and non-linear process. It is a process which is perhaps more appropriately pluralized as *transitions*. Students were found to face multiple challenges across all stages of the social, institutional and academic domains of transition. While discussing the domains of transition highlights the myriad demands that the students face, we must emphasize that these domains are closely interrelated: The degree of success that students achieved in their social transition to high school was deeply influenced by (and had an impact on) their academic transition. So too, their understanding of how schools work as institutions (such as their awareness of typical modes of classroom interaction) was implicated in their social and academic transitions.

The students' expectations of a smooth transition to a high school where they would expand their friendship group, successfully master English and achieve academic success and a positive institutional affiliation were not fulfilled to the degree they had expected. Students' early excitement and enthusiasm often turned to disappointment well into the period in which they had imagined being at ease in their new environment. The early transition challenges – finding classrooms, reading timetables and accessing school facilities – were typically overcome speedily. Indeed, schools seemed more successful in recognizing and addressing these early challenges. In contrast, the more protracted and somewhat hidden challenges related to socialization and student behavior were largely overlooked. These findings suggest that schools need to engage more actively with the long-term, complex group and individual needs of refugee-background adolescents as they make transitions into and through high school. We recommend that schools recognize the social, academic and institutional domains of transition, and review their policies and practices to better accommodate refugee-background students.

This study also demonstrates that the schools overlooked various resources, talents and skills that the students brought to their learning. Ultimately, the schools – strapped for resources as they were – needed to better understand the refugee-background students that they enrolled, and to use the students' existing funds of knowledge, such as Law Lu Eh's adeptness at sports or Gay Paw's dexterity in sewing and woodwork, as a way to recognize and build symbolic capital. The value of visual arts programs to the identity development of EAL learners has been documented in other studies (Wielgosz & Molyneux, 2015) and this investigation reaffirms these connections. Student artwork as a source of data in this study provided a non-linguistic method for students to reflect on their lives and learning, and to share their hopes and frustrations. Schools may wish to consider the use of visual modalities to open up dialogue with their newcomer, refugee-background learners.

The study also reveals the importance of places (libraries, gymnasiums, sheltered seating areas, music rooms, etc.) conducive to the development of social connections, academic and non-academic skills and institutional bonds and affiliations. In such spaces, students' often under-recognized funds of knowledge can be affirmed, shared and extended.

Conclusion

This study revealed various factors that could help schools to better bridge students' transition. First and foremost, the students themselves brought a positive, aspirational orientation to school and to life. Properly harnessed, this could serve as an effective vehicle for successful social, academic and institutional transition. In addition to affirming the students' existing knowledge and orientation to learning, schools and teachers need to acknowledge and explicitly teach the cultural knowledge necessary to traverse Australian schooling, thereby allowing students such as those in this study who are often not in the know, to become players in the game (Curry, 2007). Professional development is needed to help school staff:

- recognize and affirm the hopes and goals of refugee-background learners;
- identify the linguistic and cultural resources these students already possess and build on these in classroom planning;
- teach refugee-background students the necessary cultural knowledge to successfully negotiate mainstream schooling.

This study also points to the need for longitudinal research. For example, researchers could track refugee-background students from their entry into mainstream schooling through to their subsequent educational or vocational pathways. This would allow us to understand the long-term impact of transition initiatives implemented in schools. In addition, case studies of high-quality transition programs that take heed of student and family resources would be highly valuable contributions to knowledge in this field, and could aid schools to develop more clearly articulated transition policies and practices. The six students discussed here displayed enormous generosity in being involved in this research over a long period. Working with them has highlighted for us the complexities of the transition process, and the need for a student-centered conception of transition, one which meaningfully and respectfully foregrounds their experiences, needs and assets.

References

Ager, A. and Strang, A. (2008) Understanding integration: A conceptual framework. *Journal of Refugee Studies* 21 (2), 1–26.

Alerby, E. (2003) 'During the break we have fun': A study concerning pupils' experience of school. *Educational Research* 45 (1), 17–28.

Arkoudis, S. and Love, K. (2004) They're all over the shop: Chinese international students in the VCE. *TESOL in Context* 14 (1), 10–14.

Barron, S., Okell, J., Yin, S.M., VanBik, K., Swain, A., Larkin, E., Allott, A.J. and Ewers, K. (2007) Refugees from Burma: Their backgrounds and refugee experience. Center for Applied Linguistics. See http://www.culturalorientation.net/content/download/1338/7825/version/2/file/refugeesfromburma.pdf (accessed 7 January 2018).

Bodde, R. (2011) *Karen Refugee Ministries: Needs and Priorities Study*. Melbourne: Anglican Diocese of Melbourne.

Bourdieu, P. (1986) The forms of capital. In J.G. Richardson (ed.) *Handbook of Theory and Research for the Sociology of Education* (pp. 241–258). New York: Greenwood Press.

Bourdieu, P. (1991) *Language and Symbolic Power*. Cambridge: Polity Press.

Brown, J., Miller, J. and Mitchell, J. (2006) Interrupted schooling and the acquisition of literacy: Experiences of Sudanese refugees in Victorian secondary schools. *Australian Journal of Language and Literacy* 29 (2), 150–162.

Callow, J. (2013) *The Shape of Text to Come: How Image and Text Work*. Newtown, NSW: Primary English Teaching Association of Australia.

Catholic Education Office (2010) *Transition and Engagement*. Melbourne: Author.

Curry, M.J. (2007) A 'head start and a credit': Analyzing cultural capital in the basic writing/ESOL classroom. In J.A.A. Luke (ed.) *Pierre Bourdieu and Literacy Education* (pp. 279–298). New York: Routledge.

Darbyshire, P., MacDougall, C. and Schiller, W. (2005) Multiple methods in qualitative research with children: More insight or just more? *Qualitative Research* 5 (4), 417–436.

DeCapua, A. and Marshall, H. (2011) *Breaking New Ground: Teaching Students with Limited or Interrupted Formal Education in U.S. Secondary Schools*. Ann Arbor, MI: University of Michigan Press.

Department of Education and Early Childhood Development (2011) *English as a Second Language in Victorian Government Schools 2010*. Melbourne: DEECD.

Einarsdottir, J. (2007) Research with children: Methodological and ethical challenges. *European Early Childhood Education Research Journal* 15 (2), 197–211.

Fine, M. and Weis, L. (2003) Introduction: Silenced voices and extraordinary conversations. In M. Fine and L. Weis (eds) *Silenced Voices and Extraordinary Conversations: Re-Imagining Schools* (pp. 1–8). New York: Teachers College Press.

Ghaffar-Kucher, A. (2006) Assimilation, integration or isolation? (Re)Framing the education of immigrants. *Current Issues in Comparative Education* 9 (1), 3–7.

Gifford, S., Correa-Velez, I. and Sampson, R. (2009) *Good Starts for Recently Arrived Youth with Refugee Backgrounds*. Melbourne: La Trobe Refugee Research Centre.

González, N., Moll, L.C. and Amanti, C. (eds) (2005) *Funds of Knowledge: Theorizing Practice in Households, Communities, and Classrooms*. Mahwah, NJ: Lawrence Erlbaum Associates.

Harklau, L. (2000) From the 'good kids' to the 'worst': Representations of English language learners across educational settings. *TESOL Quarterly* 34 (1), 35–67.

Hos, R. (2012) The experiences of refugee students with interrupted formal education in an urban secondary school newcomer program. Unpublished doctoral dissertation, University of Rochester, New York.

Hos, R. and Curry, M.J. (2013) 'Transitions': Collaboratively developing a curriculum on future educational choices for English learners. In J.F. Nagle (ed.) *English Learner Instruction through Collaboration and Inquiry in Teacher Education* (pp. 101–115). Charlotte, NC: Information Age Publishing.

Janesick, V. (2000) The choreography of qualitative research design. In N. Denzin and Y. Lincoln (eds) *Handbook of Qualitative Research* (2nd edn; pp. 379–399). Thousand Oaks, CA: Sage.

Kress, G.R. and Van Leeuwen, T. (2006) *Reading Images: The Grammar of Visual Design*. London: Routledge.

Lee, S. (2005) Learning about race, learning about 'America': Hmong American high school students. In L. Weis and M. Fine (eds) *Beyond Silenced Voices: Class, Race and Gender in United States Schools* (pp. 133–145). Albany, NY: SUNY Press.

Liamputtong, P. (2007) *Researching the Vulnerable*. London: Sage.

Miller, J. and Windle, J. (2010) Second language literacy: Putting high needs ESL learners in the frame. *English in Australia* 45 (3), 31–40.

Moll, L.C., Amanti, C., Neff, D. and González, N. (1992) Funds of knowledge for teaching: Using a qualitative approach to connect homes and classrooms. *Theory into Practice* XXXI (2), 132–141.

Stake, R. (2000) Case studies. In N. Denzin and Y. Lincoln (eds) *Handbook of Qualitative Research* (2nd edn; pp. 435–454). Thousand Oaks, CA: Sage.

Taylor, S. (2008) Schooling and the settlement of refugee young people in Queensland: '...the challenges are massive'. *Social Alternatives* 27 (3), 58–65.

United Nations Refugee Agency [formerly United Nations High Commissioner for Refugees] (2016) *Global Trends: Forced Displacement in 2015*. Geneva: UNHCR. See http://www.unhcr.org/576408cd7 (accessed 7 January 2018).

Weekes, T., Phelan, L., Macfarlane, S., Pinson, J. and Francis, V. (2011) Supporting successful learning for refugee students: The Classroom Connect project. *Issues in Educational Research* 21 (3), 310–329.

Wielgosz, M. and Molyneux, P. (2015) 'You get to be yourself': Visual arts programs, identity construction and learners of English as an additional language. *Journal of Language, Identity & Education* 14 (4), 275–289.

Yates, L. (2010) The story they want to tell, and the visual story as evidence: Young people, research authority and research purposes in the education and health domains. *Visual Studies* 25 (3), 280–291.

Yin, R. (2009) *Case Study Research: Design and Methods* (4th edn). Thousand Oaks, CA: Sage.

9 Educating Refugees through 'Citizenship Classes and Tests': Integration by Coercion or Autonomous Agency?

Amadu Khan

This chapter examines refugee-background individuals' perceived benefits and limitations of the UK policy on 'citizenship classes and tests', and considers how these perceptions compare with the intentions (implicit and explicit) of policymakers. Additionally, it considers how such individuals compare their experiences of the policy with their own goals and efforts toward integration into the host society. Ultimately, it is argued that refugee-background individuals' experiences of and responses to integration differ from what is prescribed by the state. The chapter also describes how the English language classes self-organized by refugee-background community members inform the integration agenda of citizenship classes and tests. As the United Kingdom pursues the process of exiting from the European Union (EU) and attracting international talent, the chapter calls for attending to refugees and asylum seekers' cultural, linguistic and educational assets, which 'Brexiteers' argue are needed to compete in a global economy.

This chapter examines refugee-background individuals' perceptions of the benefits and limitations of the UK policy on citizenship classes and tests. Moreover, it considers how these perceptions compare with the implicit and explicit assumptions of policymakers. The 'citizenship classes and tests' policy (henceforth 'the policy') mandates that in addition to taking an oath at a citizenship ceremony, aspiring UK citizens must successfully complete culture and language classes and tests, which are provided through UK-accredited partnerships with local authorities, schools, universities and private organizations. The reasoning behind this policy, which will be discussed in greater detail later on, is that citizenship education will enable the cultural integration of refugee-background newcomers and other immigrants. In this chapter, I show how newcomers' conceptions of and efforts toward integration differ from those put forth by the British state – a mismatch evidenced most clearly in newcomers' responses to the aforementioned policy. I also consider how additional English language classes self-organized by the individuals in this study might inform the UK's integrationist agenda. This study therefore provides an empirical window into how a policy for citizenship education compares to refugee-background newcomers' practical interventions to enable their own integration into the host society.

In this chapter, I first briefly explore how symbolic politics underlie the citizenship classes and tests, explaining as well why I focus in this study on individuals with refugee backgrounds. Next, I provide an outline of the citizenship classes and tests policy, discussing its intersection with the symbolic politics of asylum-seeking migration in the United Kingdom. I then present methods, findings and implications, concluding with key lessons that can inform policy and practice in refugee citizenship education and integration.

The Symbolic Politics of Citizenship Education and Brexit

Symbolic politics, meaning the use of political gestures or actions to distract from political reality, has been a recurrent feature of migration and asylum policymaking in Western democracies (Faist, 1994). Interventions that might be intended or perceived primarily as political symbols may transmit into substantive policy, which can have a tangible impact on the policy's intended target (Edelman, 1985; Elder & Cobb, 1983). This is the case with the UK's 'citizenship classes and tests' policy, as will be discussed later in the chapter.

Some scholars have argued that citizenship education in the United Kingdom is informed by concerns about the perceived failure of a 'multiculturalist' approach to integration, attempting to resolve community tensions related to ethnic diversity through an agenda of cultural assimilation (Brubaker, 1992; Kofman, 2005). In so doing, citizenship education draws attention away from the historical and political dynamics surrounding migration to the United Kingdom, including the role that foreign policies in Africa and the Middle East might have played in creating the conditions that led to mass exodus. Discussions about citizenship education may also overlook structural inequalities, such as exclusion from many welfare services, which may create additional barriers to integration (Sales, 2007). While these dynamics are present for many immigrant groups, they are particularly relevant to refugees and asylum seekers, whose increased numbers in recent years have exacerbated concerns about social cohesion and the preservation of 'British' cultural values (Lentin & Titley, 2011;

Modood & Ahmad, 2007). This dynamic was also evident in the pro-Brexit campaign: then UKIP leader Nigel Farage, a key Brexiteer, used a campaign poster depicting a lengthy queue of asylum seekers arriving at UK borders, and expressing consternation over immigrants' inability to speak English. This poster communicated the message that the immigrant 'outsider' is a threat to UK sovereignty and nationhood, and that the UK's membership in the EU is to blame for enabling this threat. Yet, even in a post-Brexit United Kingdom, the requirements of international law may constrain efforts to limit the number of newcomer refugees and asylum seekers (see Adamo, 2008). Supporters of Brexit claimed that leaving the EU would provide an opportunity for the United Kingdom to become more outward looking, which would suggest an even greater role for the country in responding to migration crises.

Discussions about citizenship education also often overlook the 'autonomous agency' of individuals with refugee backgrounds – i.e. their ability to shape their lives through considered choices that are consistent with their own beliefs and values (Mackenzie *et al.*, 2007). This notion of agency also includes the capacity among newcomers to generate knowledge and contribute to social change that betters their community. These agentive choices can have a significant, positive impact on the social, economic, political and cultural integration of refugee-background populations (Brannan *et al.*, 2006; Cheong *et al.*, 2007; Forrest & Kearns, 2001).

Many critics have called for more research into the perspectives of individuals with refugee backgrounds who are aspiring UK citizens (Graham & McDermott, 2005; Miller-Idriss, 2006; Nagel, 2009). A few researchers have taken up this call: Some recent work has shown how asylum seekers and refugee-background populations contest some of the narratives about UK citizenship (e.g. Byrne, 2016). However, most of the critique of citizenship education policies has been from theorists, rather than empirical researchers (e.g. Adamo, 2008; Kiwan, 2008; Wright, 2008). Therefore, much needs to be learned about the views of asylum seekers and refugee-background individuals at various stages of the naturalization process. Moreover, while some scholars have examined the concept of agency within refugee resettlement communities (e.g. Feuerherm & Ramanathan, 2015), few have examined the link between agency and integration – particularly as it relates to voluntary efforts at educational intervention and societal integration by newcomers themselves (Eshach, 2007; Hoppers, 2006).

Background: Citizenship Education and the UK Policy

As noted, the policy on citizenship classes and tests introduced in 2002 requires aspiring UK citizens to complete citizenship and language classes and tests. The policy constitutes an expansion of the citizenship education present in the general school curriculum, to target immigrants outside of formal education (Kiwan, 2008). It provides two alternative routes to UK citizenship: (1) knowledge of language and (2) knowledge of life in the United Kingdom. The language route requires aspiring UK citizens to have speaking and listening proficiency in English, up to English speakers of other language (ESOL) Entry Level 3 in England, Wales and Northern Ireland. For those in Scotland, the (ESOL) level required is Intermediate Level 1' Immigrants in Scotland and Wales can choose Gaelic and Welsh, respectively, in place of English. The language route (commonly referred to as 'the ESOL route') is designed for immigrants whose knowledge of English is below ESOL Entry Level 3 or Intermediate Level 1. At the time of data collection, students taking the ESOL route were required to complete a language course that had embedded citizenship content. Satisfactory progress in this course could be used as evidence of meeting the cultural and language requirements of citizenship, thereby precluding the need to sit for the 'life in the UK' test.

The knowledge of life in the UK (citizenship test) route, in contrast, involves a stand-alone citizenship test. It must be successfully completed by everyone between 18 and 64 years of age who has not followed the ESOL route or has been deemed as below ESOL Level 3 or Intermediate Level 1. The cost of the citizenship test is £50 (UK Government, 2017). Some low-income or unemployed immigrants are entitled to free courses, but those who do not receive tuition waivers in England have to pay over £100 for ESOL (citizenship) classes (Advance Training Academy, 2017).

The citizenship content in both routes consists of UK history, politics, geography and civic life in the territories where it is administered (England, Scotland, Wales and Northern Ireland). In 2013, the curriculum was amended to replace practical information, such as how to access welfare services, with more content on British history and accomplishments. This change was a response to the long-held belief among many political elites that this sort of knowledge would help to instill 'British patriotism' in aspiring citizens (Jones, 2011).

The history of this policy serves as a reminder of how symbolic politics can influence substantive policy. The policy was first proposed by politicians in 2001 in the wake of racial riots in the North of England, and the perceived rise of segregated living between ethnic minority and the majority White populations (McGhee, 2009; Tyler, 2010; Waite, 2012). The then Labor government argued that knowledge of English and British cultural values would equip immigrants with linguistic and cultural capital to enable their integration (Byrne, 2007; Home Office, 2001). Critics argued that citizenship classes and tests were aimed at assuaging public apprehension over asylum-seeking migrants, particularly from Muslim countries, seen as a threat to British cultural values and an imagined sense of 'Britishness' (Fortier, 2010; Lentin & Titley, 2011;

Turner, 2006). The 2013 curriculum reform, with its increased focus on historical facts, was therefore a symbolic gesture, intended to quell these public anxieties, as the numbers of asylum seekers continued to rise. The policy therefore reflects and perhaps reinforces historically held negative stereotypes of ethnic minority immigrants – particularly Muslims – as a source of community tension (Gifford, 2004; Khan, 2012; Rothe & Muzzatti, 2004).

Politics around immigrant citizenship education in Scotland, however, are less fraught, and Scotland has been more generous in its implementation of the policy. This is in part because of Scotland's perception of itself as a compassionate and socially just nation (Henderson & McEwen, 2005; Scott & Mooney, 2009; Scottish Executive, 2004). For example, Scotland has always provided free English classes to asylum seekers without their having to meet a six-month residency requirement, as is required in England. In contrast to England, Scotland currently has comprehensive ESOL strategies that map out policy objectives and assessment measures. Additionally, refused asylum seekers in Scotland receive fee waivers for non-advanced part-time courses for further education, which has not always been the case in England. This policy divergence reflects Scotland's view that integration is a process that starts from the first day that asylum seekers arrive. Nevertheless, many policies for immigration and citizenship are the prerogative of the UK Parliament, and therefore, the dynamics around immigrant integration in Scotland are still shaped significantly by the broader UK policy.

Methodology

To explore how immigrants respond to and contest citizenship education, I draw from qualitative interviews I conducted with 23 asylum seekers and other immigrants with refugee backgrounds, residing in Scotland – 12 males and 11 females between the ages of 26 and 65. I used snowballing and convenience techniques to generate the sample of participants, who were selected for ease of access and ability to speak English.[1] I used a variety of networks for recruitment, including attending public and private meetings, social functions and other activities organized by agencies that work with refugee populations. Recognizing that my own refugee background might have an influence, I attempted to refrain from influencing participants' responses as much as possible, using an approach similar to Kezar (2005). However, my having been a refugee seemed to make participants willing to talk to me in a more candid way. In addition, my personal history enabled me to elicit feedback and cross-check with participants about issues that I perceived to be unclear, in order to ensure the accuracy of participants' information (Arthur & Nazroo, 2003).

The data for this analysis were generated from a larger study on refugees' citizenship formations and the perceived role of the UK media in this process. As part of that study, participants were asked about their perceptions of the English and citizenship classes and tests. These perceptions were compared with the explicit and implicit intentions of the policy. Thematic codes were identified inductively from the data, as well as drawn from existing literature on immigrant integration and agency. The list of codes was later reduced (Silverman, 2005), resulting in the themes presented below.

Findings: Benefits of Citizenship Classes and Tests

All but one participant were aware of the UK policy and its required English classes and tests. Among those who knew about the policy, 12 had either completed or were preparing for the English and/or citizenship tests through the ESOL route. None had taken the stand-alone citizenship test of the knowledge of life in the United Kingdom. Here, I focus on two of the participants' perceived benefits of the classes – learning English and gaining knowledge about rights – because these were the most commonly discussed themes relevant to issues of refugee agency and integration.

English as a lingua franca and facilitator of employment

All 23 participants viewed the ESOL classes as an important opportunity to learn English, in order to communicate with other residents, both native born and immigrant background. For example:

> How are you going to communicate with others? I think it is important for survival for someone to speak the language, for their own benefit. (Hael, female, Muslim, Somali)
>
> ...the language was a barrier, so, I was busy studying English. Once I found myself able to speak English I involved in the community ... It is better than staying at home. You know, if we stay at home, we have no family here, if we don't do that we don't keep busy. We will be mad... It was horrible time if you stay at home just thinking or feel isolated, it is a horrible feeling. (Marie, female, Muslim, Algerian)

Marie and Hael highly valued learning English as a language of communication with their neighbors and the wider society. Another participant observed that learning to speak English made it possible to 'interact' with people who were not just Bajuni and Swahili speakers like herself, but were from other linguistic communities (Jahi, female, Muslim, Somali). Notably, for these participants, the motivation for speaking English was never to assimilate into the cultural homogeneity of an imagined 'Britishness', but to integrate into a culturally diverse society (see Ager & Strang, 2004; Putnam, 2001).

Social interaction was valued in particular among female participants with pre-school-aged children. These women said learning English helped them overcome isolation and emotional trauma. Indeed, Marie (above) reported that being able to communicate through English helped her maintain her emotional and mental health. Here, participants' experiences align somewhat with policymakers' beliefs that the policy provides opportunities for social integration (e.g. Kofman, 2005).

Learning English was also linked to employment, as noted below:

> The English will help for work. If you don't know English, how can you work? You can't do business; you can't do everything to .... to make yourself more integrated. You can own your own business. For example, I think in future, I would like to own my own business, a shop, a cash and carry. (Taji, male, Muslim, Eritrean)

Other participants made a link between gaining employment and their ability to integrate, suggesting a pragmatic, economic orientation to integration, rather than a focus on cultural assimilation *per se*:

> Integration means you can participate in full activities not limited: you can be able to gain employment; you can go to school and your children can go to school; you can able to get all the necessary benefit in housing and things like that. That's what integration is all about. (Rob, male, Christian, Cameroonian)
> Job brings me into contact and interact with the wider public. (Chad, male, Christian, Congolese)
> I will say to them, allow us to work so that we can integrate more. They can learn the culture of this country. Let them not give boundaries, people are human beings. People know how to fit their lives in any way they can. So let them give freedom to people. (Pris, female, Christian, Nigerian)

These comments suggest that participants see integration as a result of – rather than a precursor to – employment, education and housing. Some participants in fact called for politicians to prioritize refugee integration from the outset of seeking asylum in the United Kingdom by creating opportunities for employment and access to other services:

> I think integration should begin at the very first process; when people come and seek asylum, they should be given the necessary support. This means access to education, health, with everything and that in itself have consequences, long term effect in the way people see the whole concept of citizenship. (Rob, male, Christian, Cameroonian)

In essence, participants considered *inclusion* – rather than assimilation – as crucial to integration. This conception is in sync with the devolved Scottish government's conception of refugee integration as a process that commences from the first day of refugee arrival. However, these views are out of sync with England's approach, which excludes asylum seekers from employment, ESOL courses and other resources until they have achieved a six-month residency status. Participants' reservations echo those of critics who say that behind the political symbolism of citizenship classes and tests is the reality that historically, the UK's citizenship policies have been exclusionary toward certain groups (Tyler, 2010).

Learning about 'basic rights' for citizenship

Participants were also asked whether they perceived any benefits from the cultural and historical content of the ESOL courses. Overall, there was a perception that the citizenship content helped participants gain knowledge about some of the 'basic rights' of being British citizens (Pat, male, Christian, Burundian). Marie described the content of the classes as a 'protocol of life' that enabled newcomers to know about 'what they should do and haven't to do' if they were to attain UK citizenship. They also felt that having knowledge of their rights improves their access to welfare services:

> … and most of the service providers or the Home Office, if you can't express yourself they take advantage of you. But if they know that you know your rights and you know the language they quickly provide you the services you've asked for. (Nie, female, Christian, Zambian)

The above extract is significant, because Nie suggests a strong relationship between having knowledge of English and the ability to advocate for her rights. However, participants also had some reservations about the content's focus on UK culture and history. As Leo (male, Christian, Rwandan) explained, the curriculum facilitated 'understanding some custom[s], some traditions, [and] some history' about the United Kingdom. However, Leo's use of the qualifier 'some' is a reminder that classes alone are insufficient for acquiring cultural and historical knowledge of the host country. This limitation was one of the concerns that participants raised about the potential of the citizenship classes and tests to facilitate their integration into the United Kingdom, as I discuss next.

Shortcomings of the citizenship classes

Participants raised questions about the format of the ESOL classes, their intended target and the intentions of policymakers. Participants also questioned the financial costs of participating in the classes and tests, for some individuals. Concerns about coercion and economic hardship were in part the rationale that some participants gave for organizing other, voluntary English classes for refugee-background newcomers.

Policy coercion

Many said that 'being forced' (Bag, male, Christian, Cameroonian) into taking tests on English language proficiency and British 'norms of living' (Sifo, female, Christian, Zimbabwean) is an ineffective approach to integration. As Leo (male, Christian, Rwandan) explained,

> ... my criticism is it is like a school system. So you could take a book today and study it for the whole night and tomorrow you are done. You pass it and you are done and that's not really a good way to get people to get to learn about a country.

This suggests that for some participants, the tests – rather than the classes – are a source of greater concern. This comment echoes the majority of participants, who said that they value the learning of English and cultural knowledge, but feel that the test itself was not a useful measure of their learning. The testing policy may in fact serve a function of alienation, rather than integration, as Sifo elaborated in a further exchange:

Amadu: So you are opposed to testing then...?
Sifo: You will learn about other people, their culture... by interacting with people. Not by doing the test. Because I did that test, but ask me any question now and I can't remember... I just did it because it was forced on me to do it.
Amadu: So to interact with your community helps you to learn about the culture and not by doing the classes and tests?
Sifo: I think the way you interact with the community, you will learn more.... by doing something you are enjoying. You know you don't have any other thoughts like oh, this is an exam I have to do.

Here, Sifo constructs the acquisition of the language and of knowledge about life in the United Kingdom – particularly its cultural values – as a process that best takes place through participants' own volition, rather than through the regurgitation of designed content or curriculum. This belief echoes scholars who have found that the 'micro-politics of day-to-day social interaction' play a major role in the integration process (Nagel, 2009: 404). The participants' views of integration, therefore, conflict with the approach assumed by policymakers. In other words, the top-down mandate for citizenship classes and tests takes on symbolic significance as a political gesture to promote cultural and linguistic homogeneity, while participants, in contrast, see integration as a long-term, ongoing process that is best facilitated through economic, social and educational opportunities (McGhee, 2009; Tyler, 2010; Waite, 2012).

Financial implications

All participants reported that the financial costs of participating in the citizenship classes and tests were too high for many refugee-background individuals who 'are already destitute' (Bag, male, Christian, Cameroonian). Some felt that the policy was driven by financial motives of the UK government, as it was 'another way of getting money' (Hael, female, Muslim, Somali). Many participants felt that the non-literate and the elderly would be most disadvantaged by the policy, as Hael explained further: '… some people went to college, went to school so they can read. But there are some people who cannot read. They are older people and to be forced to do that test is just unfair and stressful…'. Hael's perception of 'elderly' might be culturally constructed, since those older than 64 are not required to complete the test. Yet, her comments highlight that the age of exemption is arbitrary, and may therefore be a source of concern. While it might be countered that ESOL classes are free in Scotland, and passing the citizenship test is only mandatory for those applying for UK citizenship, people with refugee backgrounds in Scotland could still find it difficult to meet the financial costs of the test, including test-prep materials and testing fees. Again, participants' concerns echo those of critics, who have said that citizenship classes in the United Kingdom are part of a state apparatus that consigns the most vulnerable refugee-background individuals to 'failed citizenship' (Tyler, 2010). However, as the next section discusses, individuals with refugee backgrounds exhibit autonomous agency in organizing their own, voluntary English classes, which have played a role in the adjustment and integration processes for some participants.

Agency in language learning

As stated earlier, one of my goals in this project has been to understand individuals' perceptions of the policy's contribution, if any, to societal integration. However, participants were also keen to talk about their involvement in providing English classes to other refugee-background community members. This is partly because participants wanted to underscore their opposition to the mandatory nature of the tests, which they felt detracted from their sense of agency as language learners. It was also a way of raising questions about whether formal institutional settings are the only means of educating aspiring citizens, especially given the perceived shortcomings outlined above. More importantly, these comments provided an opportunity for participants to demonstrate agency in contrast to the institutional mandates, and to resist negative public perceptions of refugees.

Several participants spoke about voluntary activities that helped them to learn English and access other services that might enable integration. For example, there are classes organized by community members, which take place within their neighborhoods and draw participants from co-ethnic networks. The individuals who teach these classes have neither training in language teaching nor native-like English proficiency. Teachers and learners usually have a shared language, either a mother tongue or another lingua franca, such as French. The shared language is used to mediate the learning process. The *ad hoc* nature of these classes is therefore in stark contrast to the formalized structure of classes offered through government providers. As explained by Nie:

> I was dispersed to Glasgow in 2001 and they put me in this accommodation.... Well I realized that there were very few people who could speak English. So I used to have knocks on my door by people needing help – help like filling forms, from the Home Office or school forms for their children. ... Some people came to my door if they needed an ambulance. ... So I would phone the ambulance for them. So one day a lady called Koba [pseudonym], she came up to my house and asked me if we could do something to continue helping people. She asked me: 'Can we form an organization?' ... And em, the pastor also said: 'Nie, put up an English class, so that you can teach some basic English'. ... That's how we started. (Nie, female, Christian, Zambian)

Here, Nie recounts how she and others organized literacy classes to help newcomers to access vital services, and therefore played a role in the empowerment and social inclusion of members of their community. This is in contrast to some Brexiteers' fears that linguistic diversity poses a threat to integration. It also highlights agency among those with refugee backgrounds to learn English, beyond the compulsion to do so by the state or through formal structures (see Wodak, 2012). In fact, some participants proposed that a better assessment of qualification for citizenship would be a portfolio of activities such as community service, paid work and social networking, as indicators of integration:

> ...for me personally I think what I would like to see, well my dream, is for everyone to be given a certain period, like a year, where you can use your experience, your social interaction in the society, like em a recommendation from what you have done, right, which can make you a citizen (Mick, male, Christian, Zimbabwean)

Integration is therefore constructed as a learning process that includes agentive action, which should be prioritized over formalized citizenship classes. These comments contradict the deficit perspective that constructs refugees in marginalized social roles, and as passive victims who are recipients rather than providers of social services (Bowes *et al.*, 2009; Feuerherm & Ramanathan, 2015).

Implications for Educators and Policymakers

In conclusion, in contrast to the prevalent assumptions made by policymakers and right-wing Brexiteers, participants in this study were not opposed to learning English or to learning about the host society, for the purposes of integration. Many, in fact, enjoyed certain aspects of the language classes. Furthermore, refugee-background individuals understood the value of learning the language and of knowing the rights of UK citizenship for their full participation in all aspects of the host society (see Isin & Turner, 2007). However, they contested being forced to take citizenship classes, and in particular to the use of formal exams as a measure of integration. They also constructed the host society as a culturally diverse one into which they desire to integrate, in contrast to the prevalent notion of cultural assimilation into a homogeneous 'British' society, which underlies much of the rationale for the mandatory classes and tests.

Some key lessons can be extrapolated from this study to inform policy and practice. First, participants' experiences suggest that the citizenship and ESOL classes on their own may not be sufficient in facilitating newcomers' social and cultural integration, a concern that has been discussed in prior research as well (Brannan *et al.*, 2006; Cheong *et al.*, 2007; Kiwan, 2008). While participants claimed that attendance in classes and ability to speak English alleviated their isolation and supported their mental health, the mandatory nature of the classes and the costs associated with preparing for the citizenship tests compounded a sense of marginalization. Given that asylum seekers and others with refugee backgrounds often face unemployment and poverty, even after a protracted period of residency, policymakers should consider the provision of free and non-compulsory classes. Scotland, in particular, may be in a better position to do so than other parts of the United Kingdom, given its track record of formulating more progressive policies. At a time when the focus is on EU immigrants' residency status in a post-Brexit United Kingdom, fee waivers for citizenship classes and tests would enable a pathway to integration (and eventual naturalization) of individuals with refugee backgrounds, consistent with Scotland's values.

Participants also questioned whether written tests are a reliable measure of integration – another point raised in other studies (cf. Adamo, 2008; Wright, 2008). This finding suggests the need to reconsider how to gauge integration in a way that prioritizes newcomers' agency. Using a portfolio of activities, as was mentioned earlier, is an alternative worth exploring. In addition, recent adjustments to the content of the curriculum, leading to the removal of practical information (e.g. seeking medical help and other services), are at odds with the everyday needs of refugee-background individuals and families. Such a change may in fact exacerbate a sense of marginalization, since the majority of newcomers want to learn English to enable access to information and services that improve their social circumstances. Findings from this study also suggest that the state must play a role in expanding opportunities for employment, education and housing, since these opportunities are seen by participants as essential to integration. An expansion of these services and resources would help eradicate structural inequalities, and would enable fuller participation of individuals with refugee backgrounds in the life and well-being of their neighborhoods, and of UK society in general.

Finally, this study suggests that educators and policymakers should explore ways of developing curricula to tap into the diverse linguistic, cultural and social resources within communities of individuals with refugee backgrounds. For instance, the self-organized English classes described here could form the basis for collaborative educational programs, in which the resources and agency of communities can be integrated into formal school sectors. This would be a fitting response to calls for grassroots involvement in policy development (e.g. Graham & McDermott, 2005; Miller-Idriss, 2006). As the United Kingdom anticipates exiting from the EU and attracting international talent, individuals with refugee backgrounds who are already here provide the very cultural, linguistic and educational assets that 'Brexiteers' argue are needed to compete in a global economy. Attending more closely to these assets would help transform a post-Brexit United Kingdom into a place where the rhetoric of a global society becomes reality.

Note

(1) Admittedly, these criteria influenced the type of participants who took part in the study. It is therefore worth bearing in mind that even from this relatively advantaged position of knowing English, participants had concerns about the policy's ability to enable integration.

References

Adamo, S. (2008) Northern exposure: The new Danish model of citizenship tests. *International Journal of Multicultural Studies* 10 (1), 10–28.

Advance Training Academy (2017) ESOL for IRL & citizenship. See http://www.advancetraininguk.com/content.php?link=life (accessed 9 January 2018).

Ager, A. and Strang, A. (2004) *The Experience of Integration: A Qualitative Study of Refugee Integration in the Local Communities of Pollockshaws and Islington*. London: Home Office.

Arthur, S. and Nazroo, J. (2003) Designing fieldwork strategies and materials. In J. Ritchie and J. Lewis (eds) *Qualitative Research Practice: A Guide for Social Science Students and Researchers* (pp. 109–137). London: Sage.

Bowes, A., Ferguson, I. and Sim, D. (2009) Asylum policy and asylum experiences: Interactions in a Scottish context. *Ethnic and Racial Studies* 32 (1), 23–43.

Brannan, T., John, P. and Stoker, G. (2006) Active citizenship and effective public services and programmes: How can we know what really works? *Urban Studies* 43 (5–6), 993–1008.

Brubaker, R. (1992) *Citizenship and Nationhood in France and Germany*. Cambridge: Cambridge University Press.

Byrne, B. (2007) England – whose England? Narratives of nostalgia, emptiness and evasion in imaginations of national identity. *The Sociological Review* 55 (3), 509–530.

Byrne, B. (2016) Testing times: The place of the citizenship test in the UK immigration regime and new citizens' responses to it. *Sociology* 51 (2), 323–338.

Cheong, P.H., Edwards, R., Goulbourne, H. and Solomos, J. (2007) Immigration, social cohesion and social capital: A critical review. *Critical Social Policy* 27 (1), 24–49.

Edelman, M. (1985) *The Symbolic Uses of Politics*. Chicago, IL: University of Illinois Press.

Elder, C.E. and Cobb, R.W. (1983) *The Political Uses of Symbols*. New York: Longman Publishing Group.

Eshach, H. (2007) Bridging in-school and out-of-school learning: Formal, non-formal, and informal education. *Journal of Science Education and Technology* 16 (2), 171–190.

Faist, T. (1994) How to define a foreigner? The symbolic politics of immigration in German partisan discourse, 1978–1992. *West European Politics* 17 (2), 50–71.

Feuerherm, E. and Ramanathan, V. (2015) *Refugee Resettlement in the United States: Language, Policies, Pedagogies*. Bristol: Multilingual Matters.

Forrest, R. and Kearns, A. (2001) Social cohesion, social capital and the neighbourhood. *Urban Studies* 38 (12), 2125–2143.

Fortier, A. (2010) Proximity by design? Affective citizenship and the management of unease. *Citizenship Studies* 14 (1), 17–30.

Gifford, C. (2004) National and post-national dimensions of citizenship education in the UK. *Citizenship Studies* 8 (2), 145–158.

Graham, H. and McDermott, E. (2005) Qualitative research and the evidence base of policy: Insights from studies of teenage mothers in the UK. *Journal of Social Policy* 35 (1), 21–37.

Henderson, A. and McEwen, N. (2005) Do shared values underpin national identity? Examining the role of values in national identity in Canada and the United Kingdom. *National Identities* 7 (2), 173–199.

Home Office (2001) *Secure Borders, Safe Haven: Integration with Diversity in Modern Britain*. London: Her Majesty's Stationery Office (HMSO).

Hoppers, W. (2006) Non-formal education and basic education reform: A conceptual review. International Institute for Educational Planning (IIEP) UNESCO. See https://eric.ed.gov/?id=ED495405 (accessed 9 January 2018).

Isin, E.F. and Turner, B.S. (2007) Investigating citizenship: An agenda for citizenship studies. *Citizenship Studies* 11 (1), 5–17.

Jones, J. (2011, Dec.) How Britain got its patriotism back. *The Guardian*. See https://www.theguardian.com/culture/2011/dec/17/jonathan-jones-britain-new-patriotism (accessed 9 January 2018).

Kezar, A. (2005) Consequences of radical change in governance: A grounded theory approach. *The Journal of Higher Education* 76 (6), 634–668.

Khan, A.W. (2012) Asylum-seeking migration, identity-building and social cohesion: Policy-making vs. social action for cultural recognition. *Contemporary Social Science: Journal of the Academy of Social Sciences* 9 (3), 285–297.

Kiwan, D. (2008) A journey to citizenship in the UK. *International Journal of Multicultural Studies* 10 (1), 60–75.

Kofman, E. (2005) Citizenship, migration and the reassertion of national identity. *Citizenship Studies* 9 (5), 453–467.

Lentin, A. and Titley, G. (2011) *The Crises of Multiculturalism: Racism in a Neoliberal Age*. London: Zed Books.

Mackenzie, C., Christopher, D. and Pittaway, E. (2007) Beyond 'do no harm': The challenge of constructing ethical relationships in refugee research. *Journal of Refugee Studies* 20 (2), 299–319.

McGhee, D. (2009) The paths to citizenship: A critical examination of immigration policy in Britain since 2001. *Patterns of Prejudice* 43 (1), 41–64.

Miller-Idriss, C. (2006) Everyday understandings of citizenship in Germany. *Citizenship Studies* 10 (5), 541–570.

Modood, T. and Ahmad, F. (2007) British Muslim perspectives on multiculturalism. *Theory, Culture & Society* 24 (2), 187–213.

Nagel, C.R. (2009) Rethinking geographies of assimilation. *The Professional Geographer* 61 (3), 400–407.

Putnam, R. (2001) *Bowling Alone: The Collapse and Revival of American Community*. New York: Simon & Schuster.

Rothe, D. and Muzzatti, S.L. (2004) Enemies everywhere: Terrorism, moral panic, and US civil society. *Critical Criminology* 12 (3), 327–350.

Sales, R. (2007) *Understanding Immigration and Refugee Policy*. Bristol: Policy Press.

Scott, G. and Mooney, G. (2009) Poverty and social justice in the devolved Scotland: Neoliberalism meets social democracy. *Social Policy and Society* 3 (4), 379–389.

Scottish Executive (2004) *A Curriculum for Excellence: The Curriculum Review Group*. Edinburgh: Scottish Executive.

Silverman, D. (2005) *Doing Qualitative Research: A Practical Handbook*. (2nd edn). London: Sage Publications.

Turner, B.S. (2006) Citizenship and the crisis of multiculturalism. *Citizenship Studies* 10 (5), 607–618.

Tyler, I. (2010) Designed to fail: A biopolitics of British citizenship. *Citizenship Studies* 14 (1), 61–74.

UK Government (2017) Life in the UK test. See https://www.gov.uk/life-in-the-uk-test. (accessed 9 January 2018).

Waite, L. (2012) Neo-assimilationist citizenship and belonging policies in Britain: Meanings for transnational migrants in northern England. *Geoforum* 43 (2), 353–361.

Wodak, R. (2012) Language, power and identity. *Language Teaching* 45 (2), 215–233.

Wright, S. (2008) Citizenship tests in Europe – editorial introduction. *International Journal of Multicultural Studies* 10 (1), 1–9.

10 Using Photovoice with Cambodian and Guatemalan Youth to Uncover Community Cultural Wealth and Influence Policy Change

Erin L. Papa

This chapter examines the community cultural wealth (Yosso, 2005) displayed by Cambodian and Guatemalan refugee-background youth in an urban public school district in the northeastern United States. The data derive from a youth participatory action research (YPAR) study that used photovoice (Wang, 2006; Wang & Burris, 1997) methodology to analyze the home and community linguistic and social practices of the Cambodian and Guatemalan youth co-researchers, considering how such practices compared to those promoted in school. Through the use of photography and critical reflection, the youth developed policy recommendations for Eagle City Public Schools (ECPS) – a pseudonym – to improve learning experiences in school. Recommendations include providing language education that reflects the demographics of the community; offering greater access to information in students' home languages for parents and grandparents; and considering school location, in order to allow a better balance between school and work. Through this project, both groups of co-researchers demonstrated aspirational, familial, linguistic, social and navigational capital, and the Cambodian youth also demonstrated resistant capital, likely due to their participation in a youth-led community organization and their level of comfort with the researcher. Implications for other educational settings and possibilities for future research are also considered in the analysis.

This chapter explores the community cultural wealth (Yosso, 2005) displayed by Cambodian and Guatemalan refugee-background youth in

ECPS, an urban school district in New England. The data derive from a YPAR dissertation study using photovoice methodology (Wang, 2006; Wang & Burris, 1997) to examine the relationships and tensions among the home, community and school linguistic and social practices of the youth co-researchers. By positioning them as co-researchers, rather than subjects, and focusing on their community cultural wealth, I aim to challenge the deficit discourse about emergent bilingual refugee-background youth (Shapiro, 2014), and to stress that English-medium, Eurocentric education is insufficient for the development of bilingualism and biliteracy. The analysis demonstrates that the Cambodian and Guatemalan communities possess often unrecognized cultural wealth that could be used to transform educational practice.

Background and Literature Review

Although Cambodians and Guatemalans have a similar history of forced migration to the United States, leaving their home countries to escape genocide, poverty, starvation and violence (Menjívar, 2008; Smith-Hefner, 1993), the US government has treated them differently – granting refugee status to Cambodians, but not, by and large, to Guatemalans (Feuerherm & Ramanathan, 2016). Cambodian and Guatemalan youth make up a significant portion of the ECPS population; however, as a result of the essentializing of these groups into the broad racial categories of Asian and Hispanic or Latino, respectively (Ladson-Billings, 1998), the particularities of the voices and experiences of these youth often go unheard and unrecognized in educational contexts. Research suggests that both Cambodian- and Guatemalan-background youth tend to be criminalized as gang members (Chhuon, 2014; Chhuon & Hudley, 2010; Ngo & Lee, 2007) or as 'illegal' immigrants (Feuerherm & Ramanathan, 2016; United Nations High Commissioner for Refugees [UNHCR], 2014), and are otherized based on phenotype, name or language (Chhuon, 2014; Ngo & Lee, 2007). These youth are minoritized not only racially, but also linguistically. High-stakes testing in the current US education system, conducted predominantly in English, further marginalizes languages other than English and legitimizes a deficit view of bilingualism, although there is great demand for multilingual skills from both the public and the private sectors (Committee on Economic Development, 2006; Klein & Rice, 2012). In the scholarly literature on emergent bilingual urban youth (e.g. Cammarota, 2004; Huber & Cueva, 2012; Irizarry, 2011), little has been written on the experience of these two groups of youth in general, and specifically, there is a lack of research on their linguistic and social practices.

A common focus of qualitative studies on Latina/o youth more broadly is on changing the discourse about these oppressed and marginalized groups by drawing forth what are called counterstories, *testimonios*, and counternarratives in critical race theory (CRT) (Huber & Cueva, 2012; Yosso, 2005) and by using a critical ethnographic approach (Cammarota, 2004; Irizarry, 2011; Paris, 2011). Such studies aim to promote a humanizing stance in work with urban youth, as well as a deeper analysis of their struggles in and responses to the educational system (Huber & Cueva, 2012; Irizarry, 2011; Paris, 2011), yet typically lack a specific political advocacy component. Seeking to extend these examinations of students' language practices, in particular those by Irizarry and his youth co-researcher Nieves (Irizarry & Nieves, 2011) and Paris (2011), I used the photovoice approach for this study. Photovoice was developed by Wang and Burris (1997) for use with women in rural Yunnan, China, to (1) document and reflect on the strengths and concerns of the community; (2) engage in critical discussion of the photos; and (3) develop a political advocacy response.

In this study, I engaged Cambodian and Guatemalan youth as co-researchers using photography and discussion to critically examine their linguistic and social practices in the home and community and to make education policy recommendations to create more valuable learning experiences in school. Specifically, we sought to address the following research questions:

(1) What are the home and community linguistic and social practices of Cambodian and Guatemalan youth, and how are they related to, or in tension with, school practices?
(2) What stories do these youth tell using photovoice about their experience as bilingual individuals at home, in the community and at school?
(3) What recommendations do youth make based on their school learning experiences, and how might their recommendations be put into practice?

I conducted these as two parallel studies in an after-school program in Eagle City: one with second-generation Cambodian American youth (born in the United States to refugee parents) in a youth-led community organization, and the other with Guatemalan youth, who arrived in the United States as part of the wave of unaccompanied youth escaping Central America in 2014 (UNHCR, 2014) and/or reuniting with family. After the studies concluded, both groups held a joint photo gallery walk at City Hall, presenting their photos and educational recommendations to the mayor, education officials and the public.

Theoretical Framework: Critical Race Theory

CRT challenges dominant educational and social ideologies by building on the knowledge of marginalized communities to deconstruct oppressive conditions, thus potentially empowering these communities to advocate for social justice. CRT is often used by researchers conducting participatory action research (PAR) projects to analyze power relations through the intersection of race and racism with gender, class, language, sexuality, immigration status and other forms of subordination (Cammarota & Fine, 2008). Using Yosso's (2005) CRT-inspired framework of community cultural wealth, this study aims to make visible students' wealth of home, community and school linguistic and social practices. Community cultural wealth is a challenge to Bourdieusian (Bourdieu, 1986) interpretations of cultural capital that privilege the knowledge of the dominant class, instead foregrounding the cultural knowledge, skills, abilities and networks of people of color. This extends what Moll *et al.* (1992) call 'funds of knowledge' to include resistance to racism and other forms of oppression (Yosso & García, 2007). Yosso (2005) identified six forms of capital possessed and used by communities of color: aspirational, navigational, social, linguistic, familial and resistant.

The benefits of using CRT include creating methodologies that enable rich, descriptive analyses of marginalized individuals that can be used to counter the dominant discourse. By using photovoice as a form of resistance and empowerment, the youth in my study demonstrate community cultural wealth and show how educational practices might be transformed for these and other marginalized groups. Using the forms of community cultural wealth as a structure for data analysis, I illuminate the strengths of these two communities.

Methodology

Research context

ECPS is an urban, northeastern US district serving 23,867 students in the 2015–2016 academic year, 79% of whom were eligible for subsidized lunch. It has a racial distribution of 64% Hispanic, 17% African American, 9% White, 5% Asian, 4% multiracial and 1% Native American.[1] While ECPS does not report data by ethnicity, the US Census Bureau's 2006–2010 American Community Survey shows that 1,859 Cambodians and 4,607 Guatemalans aged three years or older were enrolled in school levels pre-kindergarten through graduate school (PK-20), with the majority in both groups below high school age (US Census Bureau, 2006–2010). An alarming 28.6% of Cambodian Americans between ages 18 and 24 in the state have not completed high school (or equivalent). This statistic is supported by data from a local Southeast Asian Youth Survey, in which 33.1% of respondents (Cambodian, Laotian and Hmong youth aged 18–24 residing in Eagle City) reported having opted out of school.[2] The data on high school completion by Guatemalan Americans in this age bracket are also a cause for concern with 57.5% statewide without a high school diploma or equivalent (US Census Bureau, 2006–2010). Of those enrolled in school, 63.3% of Cambodians and 60.5% of Guatemalans age three and older in the state reside in Eagle City.

Research design

This YPAR study engaged five Cambodian and seven Guatemalan youth between the ages of 14 and 21 who attend or had attended ECPS for a minimum of one semester, in a photovoice process (Wang, 2006; Wang & Burris, 1997), in order to develop educational recommendations distributed to policymakers in a photo gallery walk at City Hall, as noted. Following Nygreen (2009–2010), I sought to establish myself as an ally to both groups by spending time as a participant volunteer in both locations for six months to one year before the start of the study, being cognizant of the privilege I carry as a White, middle-class woman from the suburbs (Herr & Anderson, 2015). The Cambodian youth are members of a youth-led community organization; the Guatemalan youth are students in a program for students with interrupted formal education (SIFE) at one of the Eagle City high schools. After receiving institutional review board (IRB) approval at my university, I recruited youth (see Table 10.1) from both settings, using purposeful sampling (Patton, 2002). The Cambodian co-researchers included one ninth grader, two tenth graders, one eleventh grader and one 21-year-old who had been forced to drop out of high school and had since completed a general equivalency diploma (GED; an alternative to the high school diploma). All are dominant and highly proficient in English, with some degree of oral proficiency in Khmer. The Guatemalan co-researchers ranged in age from 15 to 18 and had been placed in ninth grade in the SIFE program, where they had been for about a year. All but one are multilingual in K'iche' (a Mayan language spoken prevalently in the department of El Quiché) and Spanish (with literacy in Spanish but not K'iche'), and are now learning English.

Table 10.1 Youth co-researchers' demographic information

Pseudonym	Sex	Age	Primary language	Secondary language	Third language
Linda	F	15	English	Khmer	Spanish
Foster K.	F	15	English	Khmer	Spanish
Drake	M	16	English	Khmer	French
Reptar	M	21	English	Khmer	
Ace	F	14	English	Khmer	Spanish
Alex	M	17	Spanish	K'iche'	English
Luis	M	17	Spanish	K'iche'	English
Marta	F	15	Spanish	K'iche'	English
Mileydi	F	15	Spanish	K'iche'	English
Oscar	M	18	Spanish	K'iche'	English
Silvestre	M	17	Spanish	English	
Elder Yobany	M	18	Spanish	K'iche'	English

I met weekly for one to two hours with each group separately for about 14 weeks, following Wang's (2006) photovoice strategy, which I modified based on the focus on linguistic and social practices. To focus our work and to help frame the photovoice process, I added a language use survey before implementing the steps in Wang's (2006) strategy, which we used as a discussion and reflection tool. The modified schedule we used was: (1) administer/take the language use survey and discuss responses; (2) introduce photovoice methodology and facilitate a discussion about the use of cameras, the power of the photographer and the ethics of taking and sharing photographs; (3) youth take photos of situations of primary language use in the home and community, then write about and discuss them using these guiding questions following Wang's SHOWED mnemonic:

(a) What do we **see** here?
(b) What is really **happening** here?
(c) How does it relate to **our** lives?
(d) **Why** does this situation, concern or strength **exist**?
(e) What can we **do** about it? (Wang, 2006: 151; emphasis in original);

(4) Repeat Step 3 for secondary language use and again for other language use or to create clarifying photos; (5) determine the audience for the photo gallery walk; (6) discuss themes identified in the photos and identify priorities for policy recommendations; and (7) distribute policy document at gallery walk. I recorded each of our group discussions using the iPhone voice memos application, and later transcribed them. After each session, I wrote field notes that included my general impressions, what took place, reasons for any changes in procedures and feelings about the session.

Data analysis and interpretation

After my work with the youth co-researchers, I coded the data using as codes the forms of capital articulated in Yosso's (2005) concept of community cultural wealth. Data sources included language use questionnaires, transcripts of group discussion, photographs, youth writings about the photos and my field notes. After reading through all the data to gain a general sense, I reread, coding for the youths' forms of capital and identifying systemic forces (economic, educational, etc.) that appeared to impede these forms of capital. Due to time constraints (i.e. the end of the school year, other commitments), the youth were not part of the coding process, but I shared a draft of my findings with the youth co-researchers, giving them time to respond, in a form of member checking.

Findings: Community Cultural Wealth of Guatemalan and Cambodian Youth

This section explores the community cultural wealth that the Cambodian and Guatemalan youth co-researchers identified in their photos, written responses and discussions. The data confirm the overlapping, dynamic nature of various forms of capital. In the following sections, I present illustrative excerpts from the data that most closely represent the forms of capital that emerged in the photos and discussions of the linguistic and social practices of my co-researchers. Due to space limitations, I include more salient examples from the Guatemalan co-researchers in some sections and from the Cambodian co-researchers in others. While both groups exhibited most forms of capital, they differed in that the Cambodian youth more strongly exhibited resistant capital.

'Porque es mi familia': Aspirational and familial capital

Aspirational capital is 'the ability to maintain hopes and dreams for the future, even in the face of real and perceived barriers' (Yosso, 2005: 77). Yosso (2005: 78) explains that aspirational capital is nurtured and passed on through social and familial networks via a storytelling tradition that allows marginalized people to 'nurture a culture of possibility'. Familial capital 'refers to those cultural knowledges nurtured among *familia* (kin) that carry a sense of community history, memory, and cultural intuition' (Yosso, 2005: 79). This form of community cultural wealth involves a commitment to community well-being and involves expanding the concept of family to include friends and community members outside of one's biological family, in contrast to many 'traditional' Euro-American individualized, classed and heterosexualized concepts of family. This commitment was stated clearly by Luis, a 17-year-old K'iché–Spanish bilingual co-researcher from the Guatemalan department of El Quiché, who, when asked why he must send money home, said with conviction, '*porque es mi familia* [because it's my family]' (Group discussion transcript). This commitment to family and community emerged in the stories and photos that both the Cambodian and Guatemalan youth shared and was interconnected with aspirational capital, although there were differences between the groups, probably as a result of their contrasting life experiences and structural barriers.

Aspiring to increase family status

Most of the Guatemalan youth had been separated from one or both parent(s) for most of their lives, as most parents had left Guatemala for the United States between 12 and 16 years previously, typically leaving the children in the care of family members. This separation was the result of what Foxen (2007) calls a 'family strategy' to send one member at a

166 Part 2: Access and Equity

time to the United States until enough financial stability was gained to support another trip. The youth reported that none of their parents had gone to school. Alex, a 15-year-old K'iche'–Spanish bilingual also from El Quiché, explained that the only thing their parents did before coming to the United States was '*sembrar milpa, buscar leña* [plant corn, search for firewood]', to feed the family. Despite their limited prior experience with formal education, the Guatemalan youth expressed plans to pursue higher education, whether to become a lawyer, teacher, doctor, mechanic or politician. Because of their uncertain immigration status, they also spoke about plans to work hard to send money and resources back to Guatemala, where they eventually hope to settle and possibly start businesses. The youth explained that they send packages of clothing and shoes to family about once a year (Figure 10.1).

Marta, a 14-year-old K'iche'–Spanish bilingual from El Quiché, explained, 'shoes, jacket is beautiful here', and Luis stated, 'they want to use what we [have] here'. Such packages seem to stand for more than assistance for family back home, functioning here as a sort of symbolic aspirational capital, in that the clothing symbolizes the extended family's connection to those in the United States and to a hope for a better future. This type of 'public display of wealth and status in the home', according to Foxen (2007: 133), is 'also an indication of belonging to the select group who have been *listo* (clever) enough to cross two borders, survive in distant [Eagle City], and send home the goods to prove it'.

Figure 10.1 Sending clothes to family in Guatemala

Aspiring to (re)claim Khmer

In contrast to the Guatemalan youth, the Cambodian youth, having lived their whole lives in the United States, spoke extensively about aspirations to reclaim their language, which they felt had been lost through their largely English-only education. Some youth have difficulties communicating with their parents and all with grandparents as a result of this loss of the Khmer language. Most youth have served as linguistic and cultural brokers (Orellana *et al.*, 2003) for family and community members throughout their lives, helping them to navigate complex bureaucratic processes, but now feel that their Khmer skills are lacking. They all expressed a deep and urgent longing to speak and read Khmer, which Ace, a 14-year-old Cambodian-Guatemalan American, who identifies more as Cambodian, demonstrates in her photo in Figure 10.2.

In discussing the photograph, Ace explained that she had always wanted to read and write in Khmer because of the beauty of the script and its connection to her culture, but since she has never had the opportunity, she is unsure of how to write even her own name. The Cambodian youth

Figure 10.2 Ace's attempt to write her name in Khmer

believe that to stop this language loss and remove this intergenerational language barrier for future generations, they have a responsibility to learn the language and to pass it on to their future children. This desire to gain Khmer language literacy and the ability to use Khmer orally to navigate various systems, demonstrates an overlap between aspirational and linguistic capital; I explore the latter with examples from the Guatemalan co-researchers in the following section.

Linguistic capital

Linguistic capital 'includes the intellectual and social skills attained through communication in multiple languages and/or linguistic styles' (Yosso & García, 2007: 160). The co-researchers exhibited linguistic capital in interpreting for one another, negotiating meaning using multiple languages, altering their speech for different audiences and contexts and identifying linguistic challenges in their respective communities. The US educational system tends to see these youth as lacking English language proficiency and neglects to recognize their wealth of linguistic assets (Gándara & Hopkins, 2010; García, 2009). For example, most of the Guatemalan youth entering ECPS in recent years are bilingual, but not highly (bi)literate, in Spanish and a Mayan language – typically K'iche' – upon arrival, as are six of the seven co-researchers in this study. However, they were placed in a SIFE program separate from the mainstream academic program where Spanish is used mainly as a crutch through translation of instructions and readings, rather than as a tool for academic language and literacy development.

Despite the lack of emphasis on K'iche' and Spanish in school, and the Guatemalan youths' focus on learning English for survival purposes, they demonstrated a keen understanding of the importance of maintaining (or developing) proficiency in their home languages, similarly to Ace above. When I asked why they thought that K'iche' was not taught in their schools in Guatemala, Luis answered, *'Porque hay unos que hablan, que hablan solamente K'iche'. No puedan hablar en español y por eso es necesario que las maestras enseñan bien español para que los niños saben bien el español'.* [Because there are some who speak, who only speak K'iche'. They cannot speak Spanish; therefore, it is necessary that teachers teach Spanish well, so that the children know Spanish well.] (Group discussion transcript). He went on to compare the power of Spanish in Guatemala to that of English in the United States, a point which Oscar elaborated upon by asserting that these are also the languages of business in their respective contexts. On the other hand, when I asked if they thought it was important to continue to speak K'iche', both Luis and Oscar saw the social and familial importance of maintaining oral proficiency in K'iche'.

Oscar: *Bueno, cuando uno habla en K'iche' de veras hay algunas personas que no pueden hablar español y tú dices puede ayudar, y ellos te dicen y tú les traducen. Como si era inglés, yo no puedo hablar inglés, bueno tengo compañero que habla, yo digo él y él se dice al otro.* [Well, when one speaks K'iche' there are some people who cannot speak Spanish and you say that you can help, and they speak to you and you translate for them. Like if it were English, and I cannot speak English, and I have a friend who can speak it, I speak to him and he says it to the other person.]

Luis: *Y, por ejemplo, tú no quiere ir a viajar en diferentes lugares, montañas, hay allí no hay mucho español, sólo K'iche', y se puede… Y si comunico uno, se puede comunicar.* [And, for example, you don't want to travel in different places, mountains, there is not much Spanish there, only K'iche', and you can… And if I can communicate in one, I can communicate.] (Group discussion transcript)

This exchange shows that both Oscar and Luis recognize the usefulness of K'iche' in communicating with elders and people in mountainous areas where Spanish is seldom spoken, and agree that it is their responsibility to help those who are monolingual in K'iche' to communicate with Spanish speakers. They also related this ability and responsibility to interpret for elders in Guatemala to how friends in the United States interpret English for them. Occasionally, their teacher asks Oscar to go to the office to interpret for a newly arrived student and parent who only spoke K'iche', so this skill has proven to be useful in Eagle City as well.

Social and navigational capital: Supports created by and for Guatemalans

Social capital in the CRT sense involves networks of people and community resources that can provide both instrumental and emotional support to respond to society's institutions (Yosso, 2005). Navigational capital can be understood as the skills necessary to maneuver through these social institutions that were not developed with communities of color in mind (Yosso, 2005). I have synthesized evidence of both social and navigational capital here, as these two forms of community cultural wealth were strongly interconnected in the data.

The Guatemalan co-researchers exhibited evidence of strong social networks and an acute ability to navigate through systems, including those created without their strengths and needs in mind and those created by and for their community. For example, all of them had navigated an extremely dangerous route through Guatemala and Mexico to reach the US border, where they were detained and eventually reunited with

Figure 10.3 A multiservice Guatemalan bakery in Eagle City

family in Eagle City. Locally, they all demonstrated knowledge of the local public transportation system. In terms of using social networks to access resources, their photos included many multiservice stores in the community, like the one in Figure 10.3, where Silvestre explained one can, *'cambiar cheques, pagar biles, pagar teléfono, comprar tarjetas para llamar a Guatemala, comprar desayuno'*. [cash checks, pay bills, pay for your phone, buy phone cards to call Guatemala, buy breakfast.] (Group discussion transcript).

Another shop had safety deposit boxes for rent, useful for people without access to a bank account. In addition, these shops provide space for the development of social and navigational capital by connecting youth with others in the community who may be able to advise on employment and educational opportunities, healthcare, immigration and legal processes.

Resistant capital

Yosso (2005: 80) describes resistant capital as 'those knowledges and skills fostered through oppositional behavior that challenges inequality' which she explains is 'grounded in the legacy of resistance to subordination exhibited by Communities of Color'. Through their involvement in a youth-led community organization, my Cambodian co-researchers developed resistant capital through what Ginwright and Cammarota (2007: 699) call 'critical civic practice, a process that develops critical consciousness and builds the capacity for young people to respond and change oppressive conditions in their environment'. They spoke about feeling overlooked and forgotten in school and the community, assumed to be non-American, associated with gang membership and profiled and harassed by the police, as demonstrated in the following exchanges.

In presenting his photo of police cars and emergency service vehicles parked in a lot awaiting service in their neighborhood, Reptar, a 21-year-old Cambodian American, explained, 'I took this photo because, Cambodians, they do not like police'. He elaborated, 'Because, um, we do not understand them. We understand that they're there for safety, but most of the time, it's not for our, our safety. It's for the safety of an American'. Foster K. responded in an annoyed tone in Khmer, and then explained in English, 'So, um, they're rude, and we don't like them'. Drake agreed with Foster K. Reptar added, 'No respect', and Ace said, 'Even though we're American'.

These youth seemed to associate the word 'American' with White people, although Ace did clarify that they are, in fact, American, so I asked, 'But when you say American, you mean people that look like me?' Drake responded, 'Haha, Erin', and the others laughed nervously. I continued, 'When you're talking about the police. No, I'm not offended. It's fine'. Reptar replied, 'Yeah, I'm not American to a police officer. When I, when I encounter police, they always ask me what country I came from'. I recognized the difference in treatment by the police in stating, 'Yeah, they would never ask me that'. Reptar explained that he would respond, 'Uh, America. I was born right here', to which Ace asked, 'What do they say, like, what are their reactions to that?' Reptar explained that sometimes the police would try to talk to him in Spanish, to which he would respond in an American accent, 'no habla es-pan-yol'. Other times, he explained, 'They ask me, um, what part of Cambodia I'm from, um, and when I tell them I'm not from Cambodia, then they're like, oh, you just look like you have been'. In these examples, the youth, while frustrated with the lack of police acknowledgment of their community strengths, demonstrated their resistant capital through their acute understanding of the structures and practices of racism.

In a later discussion, Reptar spoke about an encounter with the police in presenting his photo of the *ksai-see-ma* (Figure 10.4). Reptar explained:

> So, in English, it's pretty much a blessed string, brought to the evil spirits and whatnot. It's a little thing that we get taught early on. So it's, like, not really in education in America, but like, something you teach your kids about your religion.

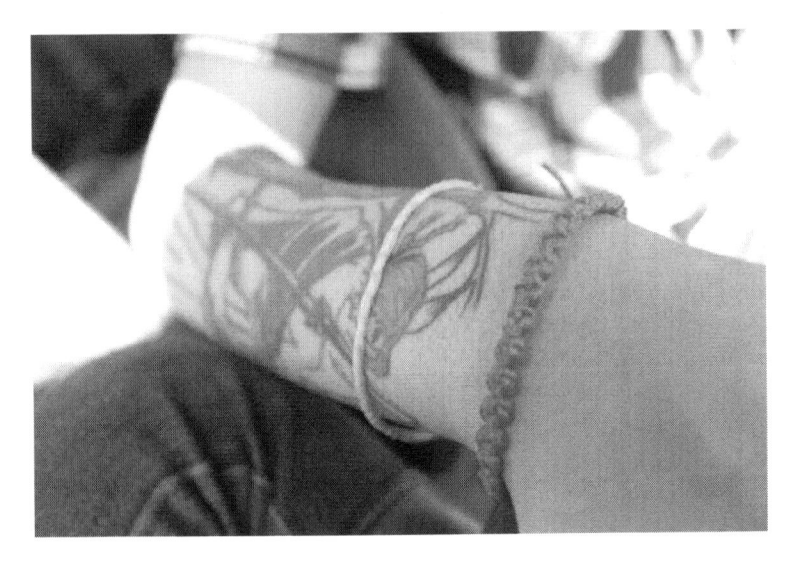

Figure 10.4 The *ksai-see-ma*

When I asked if Cambodians wore *ksai-see-ma* for their whole lives, they affirmed, although Reptar added, 'Mmhm, until you get arrested, then they cut it all off'. The others seemed surprised and offended that the police would cut it off and explained that the *ksai-see-ma* is an important cultural artifact. Reptar, using his resistant capital, explained, 'I was heated. I tried to use my, um, freedom of religion, and I was like, noooo', noting that law enforcement officials are culturally ignorant in cutting off the blessed string upon arrest: In the eyes of the police, the string is a potential weapon, but in the eyes of Cambodians, it is a religious object that offers protection and thus should not be removed. The youth explained the negative consequences of losing or removing one's *ksai-see-ma*. Foster K. explained, 'I get so scared whenever I lose my *ksai-see-ma*', to which Ace replied, 'This is a big deal. To Khmer folks it means a lot because without it you're open to evil spirits, like, messing with you'. Clearly, the *ksai-see-ma* provides a sense of hope and connection to a higher power, as well as to youth's cultural heritage. These exchanges exemplify the many criticisms that the youth had of their community, as well as their potential to promote cross-cultural understanding.

Youths' Recommendations and Implications for Educators

This analysis of the community cultural wealth demonstrated by the Guatemalan and Cambodian youth co-researchers in this study shows many untapped skills on the part of the youth that could be used to transform educational policy and practice to develop more appropriate learning experiences for these and other marginalized groups. Through this collaborative work, the youth co-researchers demonstrated the motivation, passion and commitment necessary to identify issues in their respective communities and to develop strategies for addressing those concerns, as will be discussed later. After our analysis and discussion of their photos, the youth developed recommendations for ECPS, as mentioned.

The Guatemalan co-researchers recommended that ECPS have more bilingual teachers in classes like biology and health; that class sizes be smaller to allow for more English practice; and that they attend a school closer to home to allow for better balance between school and work. These recommendations reflect their linguistic, aspirational, social and navigational capital. Rather than emphasizing that these youth lack formal education, the SIFE program could be transformed to reflect the various forms of capital that the youth developed through their rich life experience. Since most of these youth have around a third-grade level of Spanish proficiency, and typically no prior knowledge of the academic language and content of biology, in an English-only setting they find it difficult to access the content in a meaningful way.

Research has consistently shown that first language skills must be well developed in order to maximize academic and linguistic performance in the new language (Cummins, 1979). In order to expand their linguistic and content knowledge, the Guatemalan youth would benefit from a translanguaging (García, 2009) environment, in which educators (who may or may not be bilingual) bridge language practices with core content and language development standards (García et al., 2017). Specifically, teachers could encourage students to use multiple languages to preview, view and review tests (Freeman & Freeman, 2011). The biology teacher might provide an opportunity for the youth to preview the lesson content through discussion with peers in Spanish, for example, then facilitate the lesson using comprehensible input (García, 2009) in English, and finally have students review by summarizing in Spanish.

In the longer term, the SIFE program could be transformed into a bilingual program, where newcomers and proficient English speakers learn side by side. The English speakers could be heritage speakers of Spanish or those who have learned some Spanish in school and would like to develop their academic language and literacy skills. Such a program may also include a social justice component (García et al., 2017). It thus could provide a space for teachers and students to use their social and navigational capital to develop critical civic praxis (Ginwright & Cammarota, 2007), perhaps by investigating issues of concern in the community, including a deep exploration of the history of Guatemala and the causes of migration.

The Cambodian co-researchers called for Khmer language education and classes that provide space for a study of Cambodian history and migration to the United States, building on their aspirational, familial, linguistic, spiritual, social, navigational and resistant capital. All demonstrated deep longing and aspirations to learn their home language, culture and history for the betterment of their community (familial capital), and insisted that these opportunities be provided as credit-bearing classes during the school day (social/navigational capital). Since most are nearing the end of high school, it may be difficult to meet the needs of this group, but for younger students, introducing Khmer language and history classes at the high school level would be a first step at reclaiming their language and mending intergenerational communication struggles. Youth recommended that ECPS could work with the monks at local temples and with the Cambodian Society to develop curricula and to prepare Cambodian teachers, a proposal reflective of their social and navigational capital.

To avoid detrimental language loss among younger children (Gándara & Hopkins, 2010), as well as to foster Khmer and English skills simultaneously, ECPS could collaborate with other Cambodian communities across the country to develop heritage language programs in Khmer, or a two-way immersion program that could grow slowly starting with a kindergarten class, adding to an established K-5 Spanish dual language program that Guatemalan families can select for their children. This could attract English speakers to this program, in addition to promoting the cognitive, social, emotional and academic benefits of bilingual education (García, 2009). Lastly, youths' critical civic praxis could be fostered in the classroom, incorporating their linguistic capital in Khmer and English, social networks and navigational capital to identify, research and develop solutions for issues affecting the community.

Notes

(1) Data source not included to maintain the anonymity of the site.
(2) Data source not included to maintain the anonymity of the site.

References

Bourdieu, P. (1986) The forms of capital. In J. Richardson (ed.) *Handbook of Theory and Research for the Sociology of Education* (pp. 241–258). Westport, CT: Greenwood.
Cammarota, J. (2004) The gendered and racialized pathways of Latina and Latino youth: Different struggles, different resistances in the urban context. *Anthropology & Education Quarterly* 35 (1), 53–74.
Cammarota, J. and Fine, M. (eds) (2008) *Revolutionizing Education: Youth Participatory Action Research in Motion*. New York: Routledge.
Chhuon, V. (2014) 'I'm Khmer and I'm not a gangster!': The problematization of Cambodian male youth in US schools. *International Journal of Qualitative Studies in Education* 27 (2), 233–250.
Chhuon, V. and Hudley, C. (2010) Asian American ethnic options: How Cambodian students negotiate ethnic identities in a U.S. urban school. *Anthropology & Education Quarterly* 41 (4), 341–359.

Committee on Economic Development (2006) *Education for Global Leadership: The Importance of International Studies and Foreign Language Education for U.S. Economic and National Security.* Washington, DC: Author.

Cummins, J. (1979) Linguistic interdependence and the educational development of bilingual children. *Review of Educational Research* 49 (2), 222–251.

Feuerherm, E.M. and Ramanathan, V. (eds) (2016) *Refugee Resettlement in the United States: Language, Policy, Pedagogy.* Bristol: Multilingual Matters.

Foxen, P. (2007) *In Search of Providence: Transnational Mayan Identities.* Nashville, TN: Vanderbilt University Press.

Freeman, D. and Freeman, Y. (2011) *Between Worlds: Access to Second Language Acquisition* (3rd edn). Portsmouth, NH: Heinemann.

Gándara, P. and Hopkins, M. (2010) *Forbidden Language: English Learners and Restrictive Language Policies.* New York: Teachers College Press.

García, O. (2009) *Bilingual Education in the 21st Century: A Global Perspective.* Malden, MA: Wiley-Blackwell.

García, O., Johnson, S.I. and Seltzer, K. (2017) *The Translanguaging Classroom: Leveraging Student Bilingualism for Learning.* Philadelphia, PA: Caslon.

Ginwright, S. and Cammarota, J. (2007) Youth activism in the urban community: Learning critical civic praxis within community organizations. *International Journal of Qualitative Studies in Education* 20 (6), 693–710.

Herr, K. and Anderson, G. (2015) *The Action Research Dissertation: A Guide for Students and Faculty* (2nd edn). Thousand Oaks, CA: Sage.

Huber, L.P. and Cueva, B.M. (2012) Chicana/Latina testimonios on effects and responses to microaggressions. *Equity & Excellence in Education* 45 (3), 392–410.

Irizarry, J. (2011) *The Latinization of U.S. Schools: Successful Teaching and Learning in Shifting Cultural Contexts.* Boulder, CO: Paradigm Publishers.

Irizarry, J. and Nieves, K. (2011) The 'Language Police': Teachers' responses to diverse language practices. In J. Irizarry (ed.) *The Latinization of U.S. Schools: Successful Teaching and Learning in Shifting Cultural Contexts* (pp. 87–105). Boulder, CO: Paradigm Publishers.

Klein, J.I. and Rice, C. (2012) *U.S. Education Reform and National Security: Independent Task Force Report No. 68.* New York: Council on Foreign Relations Press. See http://www.cfr.org/united-states/us-education-reform-national-security/p27618?co=C007301.

Ladson-Billings, G. (1998) Just what is critical race theory and what's it doing in a nice field like education? *International Journal of Qualitative Studies in Education* 11 (1), 7–24.

Menjívar, C. (2008) Educational hopes, documented dreams: Guatemalan and Salvadoran immigrants' legality and educational prospects. *Annals of the American Academy of Political and Social Science* 620 (1), 177–193.

Moll, L.C., Amanti, C., Neff, D. and Gonzalez, N. (1992) Funds of knowledge for teaching: Using a qualitative approach to connect homes and classrooms. *Theory Into Practices* 31 (2), 132–141.

Ngo, B. and Lee, S.J. (2007) Complicating the image of model minority success: A review of Southeast Asian American education. *Review of Educational Research* 77 (4), 415–453.

Nygreen, K. (2009–2010) Critical dilemmas in PAR: Toward a new theory of engaged research for social change. *Social Justice* 36 (4), 14–35.

Orellana, M.F., Dorner, L. and Pulido, L. (2003) Accessing assets, immigrant youth as family interpreters. *Social Problems* 50 (5), 505–524.

Paris, D. (2011) *Language across Difference: Ethnicity, Communication, and Youth Identities in Changing Urban Schools.* New York: Cambridge University Press.

Patton, M.Q. (2002) *Qualitative Research and Evaluation Methods* (3rd edn). Thousand Oaks, CA: Sage.

Shapiro, S. (2014) 'Words that you said got bigger': English language learners' lived experiences of deficit discourse. *Research in the Teaching of English* 48 (4), 386–406.

Smith-Hefner, N.J. (1993) Education, gender, and generational conflict among Khmer refugees. *Anthropology & Education Quarterly* 24 (2), 135–158.

United Nations High Commissioner for Refugees (2014) Children on the run: Unaccompanied children leaving Central America and Mexico and the need for international protection. See http://www.unhcr.org/56fc266f4.html (accessed 30 January 2018).

US Census Bureau (2006–2010) American Community Survey. See https://www.census.gov/programs-surveys/acs/.

Wang, C. (2006) Youth participation in Photovoice as a strategy for community change. *Journal of Community Practice* 14 (1/2), 147–161.

Wang, C. and Burris, M.A. (1997) Photovoice: Concept, methodology, and use for participatory needs assessment. *Health Education & Behavior* 24 (3), 369–387.

Yosso, T.J. (2005) Whose culture has capital? A critical race theory discussion of community cultural wealth. *Race, Ethnicity and Education* 8 (1), 69–91.

Yosso, T.J. and García, D.G. (2007) 'This is no slum!': A critical race theory analysis of community cultural wealth in culture clash's Chavez Ravine. *Aztlán: A Journal of Chicano Studies* 32 (1), 145–180.

11 Swedish Teachers' Understandings of Post-Traumatic Stress Disorder among Adult Refugee-background Learners

Eva Holmkvist, Kirk P.H. Sullivan and Asbjørg Westum

Many refugees and asylum seekers have been exposed to traumatic events prior to resettlement. This study examines Swedish language teachers' understandings of post-traumatic stress disorder (PTSD) among adult students with refugee backgrounds, who need to learn the societal language to restart their lives. This study is based in the introductory Swedish language class, where communication between student and teacher – including about learning challenges that may be related to PTSD – may be limited. Using focus groups, teachers discussed their understandings of PTSD, how it manifests itself in the classroom and how they have changed their teaching to accommodate refugee-background students with PTSD. The focus group discussions revealed that many teachers were unsure how PTSD manifests, and that they felt insecure in their teaching approaches. Nevertheless, the teachers worked hard to provide a safe place for all students to learn and applied teaching and learning approaches that they felt were appropriate for adult learners. These results suggest that teachers' self-confidence in their abilities to support adult refugee-background students could be increased through formal training on PTSD, as well as other supports that improve teacher–student communication.

> We have so many students who don't feel well.
> - Teacher of Swedish as a second language to adults with refugee backgrounds

In 2013, 54,259 persons applied for asylum in Sweden (The Swedish Migration Agency, 2014), and by 2015 the number had risen to 162,877 persons (The Swedish Migration Agency, 2016), primarily because of armed conflicts in the Middle East. As is the case with war veterans (e.g. de Rond & Lok, 2016; Tanielian & Jaycox, 2008; US Department of Veteran Affairs, 2015), the prevalence of serious mental disorders, including PTSD, is higher for refugees than for the general population (Fazel *et al.*, 2005). It is estimated that around 30% of refugees arriving in Sweden have PTSD (Wretling, 2006). This is not unexpected, since, as de Rond and Lok (2016: 1965) write, 'War can be deeply traumatizing, even for those not in the firing line, for it tears at the fabric of what it is to be human'. Ehntholt *et al.* (2005: 236) point out that living in a host country as a refugee can create further ongoing stressors, including 'financial hardship, frequent accommodation changes with resulting changes in schools, uncertainties over asylum applications, as well as the challenges of adapting to a different culture and learning a new language'.

This chapter considers the views of teachers working with adult refugee-background students who are learning Swedish as a second language during their initial period in Sweden, often while they await confirmation or denial of refugee status and a residence permit. More specifically, this chapter examines these teachers' perceptions of PTSD as a factor in their work with adult refugee-background students. Psychological research has found that PTSD often manifests itself as flashbacks, anxiety and anger attacks, tiredness and inability to concentrate (American Psychiatric Association [APA], 2013), and teachers of students with PTSD must try to help students engage actively in learning while they deal with such symptoms (Alisic, 2012; Ko *et al.*, 2008). Hence, teachers' perceptions of PTSD are likely to affect their approaches to teaching. Our focus on teachers' perceptions finds support in the work of Alisic (2012: 57), which indicates that 'a largely understudied topic [is] teachers' perspectives on supporting children who have been exposed to trauma'. The same holds true for teachers of adult learners.

Using focus groups with teachers working with adult refugee-background students in Swedish as a second language classes during students' initial period in Sweden, we explore how these teachers conceptualize PTSD, a condition that emerges from a socially constructed and culture-specific diagnosis (Johnson & Thompson, 2008).[1] During the focus groups, teachers were asked how they experience the impact of what they perceive as PTSD on their teaching and on student learning. This study reveals that while teachers have some preconceptions about PTSD and its effects on their students, teachers feel that they are ill-prepared and require more specific professional development and training to identify symptoms of PTSD and support students experiencing those symptoms.

PTSD and Language Learning

Experiencing, witnessing or otherwise being 'confronted with an event that involved actual or threatened death, serious injury, or threat to physical integrity' and reacting to this event with 'intense fear, helplessness, or horror' (Barlow, 2007: 65) are requisites for a PTSD diagnosis (see also APA, 2013). It is in these ways that PTSD differs from the majority of psychiatric diagnoses: PTSD requires the affected person to have experienced trauma. Its diagnosis and treatment are complex, as evidenced by the range of practical guidelines for effective assessment and treatment (Foa *et al.*, 2008).

PTSD in educational settings

PTSD has been widely researched among school-age youth in educational settings, with a focus on intervention and treatments to help students suffering from PTSD to better access their education. Generally, these students suffer from poor concentration and intrusive thoughts; thus, educational interventions have been tested in these areas. Research has shown that teachers can be trained to identify and help students who might need additional supports (e.g. O'Shea *et al.*, 2000). A 2011 review and meta-analysis of school-based intervention programs for PTSD symptoms by Rolfsnes and Idsoe (2011: 163) found that 'school professionals [including teachers] ... can be successfully utilized in providing intervention to children and adolescents following traumatic events'. This point is corroborated by Kataoka *et al.* (2012) who present an overview of the 'evidence-informed model' known as Listen, Protect, Connect (LPC), developed by Schreiber *et al.* (2008). Kataoka *et al.* (2012) posit that when early intervention is school based, students' well-being, concentration and academic achievements improve – a position supported by Cossu *et al.* (2015) as well.

However, few prior studies have examined teachers' perspectives on the influence of trauma, including PTSD, on classroom teaching and learning. Alisic (2012) reports that teachers need better professional training in how best to support children suffering from PTSD and how to balance these students' learning and support needs with those of other children in their classes. Since 2012, some research has examined schoolteachers' perspectives on PTSD more closely (e.g. Toros & Tiirik, 2016). However, this is still an understudied topic, and teachers' perspectives in relation to adult refugee-background students exposed to trauma are even less represented. Thus, teachers of these students have particular experiences and understandings that have to date not been fully explored.

Methodology

The aim of the present study is to gain an understanding of teachers' perspectives on the teaching and support of adult refugee-background students perceived to be suffering from PTSD. We designed a qualitative study with semi-structured focus groups to address the following three research questions:

(1) What do teachers of Swedish as a second language for adult refugee-background students know about PTSD?
(2) How do these teachers think PTSD affects these adults' learning of Swedish?
(3) How do these teachers adapt their teaching for students they perceive as suffering from PTSD, including building on these students' resilience and other resources?

Context of the study

The context for the study is a northern Swedish town of approximately 50,000 people, 90 miles south of the Arctic Circle. At the time of the study, there were 475 adults with refugee backgrounds enrolled in Swedish language courses. Most refugees arriving in Sweden are escaping war, and it is likely that many experienced traumatic events before and during their forced migration. Their classes were taught by 25 qualified female teachers of Swedish as a second language; the number of students in their classes fluctuated widely. Teachers were supported by two assistants – one who speaks Dari and the other Arabic.

Participants and data collection

We set a minimum of five years of experience teaching adult refugee-background students as a selection criterion to involve teachers as participants in the study. This minimum was set to ensure that the teachers' perceptions were based on their experiences working with many students from a variety of backgrounds. All participants had attended a half-day Red Cross information lecture on refugees and mental health issues as well, which we hoped would provide them with vocabulary to express their perceptions.

The eight teachers who agreed to participate in the focus groups were randomly placed into two groups. Following established ethical guidelines (e.g. Swedish Research Council, 2011), participants gave their informed consent. To further preserve anonymity, we do not report the participants' ages. When reporting focus group discussions, participants are coded according to focus group, FGA and FGB, and numbered 1–4.

The discussions were conducted in Swedish, using a semi-structured interview protocol. Two example questions (translated here into English) used to engage participants were: (1) I wonder what you think of when you hear the term 'post-traumatic stress disorder' or 'PTSD'? and (2) Turning to your classroom teaching experiences, which ones have been positive and you would repeat, develop or encourage a colleague to use with students who may be suffering from PTSD?

We allowed discussions to develop naturally, with the protocol primarily used to ensure that main topics were covered. Both focus groups were led by the first author (Eva Holmkvist), and lasted around an hour. Eva teaches at the college where the study was conducted. Eva is, therefore, an insider practitioner-researcher studying her colleagues' perceptions and understandings. Thus, Eva's position needs to be considered when interpreting the results and conclusions presented in this chapter, as discussed below.

Data analysis

Focus group discussions were recorded and transcribed verbatim, with identifying information removed. Each member of the research team independently read the transcriptions, and recursively grouped selected passages of the transcriptions. These groupings were then discussed, adapted, thematically coded (e.g. 'defining PTSD', 'what is seen in the classroom', 'classroom disruptions' and 'teachers' needs') and ultimately aligned to the three research questions by the research team collectively. The outsider perspective represented by the second and third authors balances the insider perspective of the first author. The data were translated into English after we had selected the quotes to illustrate the themes.

Findings

The answers to the three research questions provide a picture of how Swedish teachers categorize adult refugee-background students with perceived PTSD, what aspects of the students' behaviors trigger the teachers' categorization and how the teachers' perception affects their language and literacy instruction with students. In this section, we foreground the teachers' perspectives by using English translations of their voices. We consider each research question in turn.

Limited understandings of PTSD

One theme derived from the findings was the core issue that many teachers are unaware of whether students have PTSD:

> ...but we can't know if anyone has a diagnosis or if they want to let us know about it. How are we to know? (FGA1)

Apparently few students tell their teachers if they have a diagnosis of PTSD. The teachers expressed frustration at not knowing, as they thought such knowledge might explain aspects of classroom behavior and lead to more appropriate lesson planning, in order to make better use of the students' assets and experiences.

A second theme is that some teachers are not sure what PTSD means, nor how it may intersect with other possible diagnoses. One participant sees the term being used most frequently to describe students' behaviors but points out that many other terms are used as well, such as anxiety disorder, acute stress disorder, obsessive-compulsive disorder, schizophrenia, Asperger's, attention deficit hyperactivity disorder (ADHD) and substance-related disorders: 'Sometimes they [diagnoses] can look the same; you just don't remember' (FGA2).

Although the participants see a range of unclear boundaries, the one to which participants refer the most is that between learning challenges due to PTSD and challenges facing any adult learner – particularly regarding issues of concentration or memory. This concern is clearly expressed in the following extract:

> I wonder how you really define PTSD as what we often see is when people have concentration and memory [problems]… when stuck [in their studies], but then you also hear stories when they have flashbacks and relive the dramatic experience again and their bodies freeze and so on. (FGA2)

Yet, when defining PTSD, the teachers described students as having a bad memory and forgetting everything; being unable to think clearly and focus on their studies; and displaying emotional problems by getting angry, expressing dissatisfaction or showing fear. The teachers commented on students' occasional flashbacks, coupled with inappropriate behavior. Thus, we see that the teachers' understanding of PTSD is incomplete and at times seems rather restrictive. Earlier research has suggested that teachers are able to identify psychologically disturbed refugee-background students in need of mental health support based solely on their classroom experience (e.g. Ehntholt *et al.*, 2005), yet teachers' understanding of specific diagnoses, such as PTSD has not, to our knowledge, been examined.

Participants' conceptions of PTSD correspond somewhat with the diffuse symptoms outlined by the medical profession (e.g. APA, 2013). The wide range of symptoms that can be associated with PTSD seems to confuse many teachers, and resulted in a challenge when the teachers were asked to consider how PTSD affects refugee-background adults' learning of Swedish.

Perceived physical and cognitive effects of PTSD

One theme in response to the second research question was, 'of course it [PTSD] affects their learning of Swedish!'. However, precisely *how* PTSD affects language learning is far from clear in the teachers' discussions. The teachers do, however, relate their understanding of PTSD to their understanding of what can make learning difficult. One of the focus groups discussed emotional issues and listed factors they thought would affect students' ability to learn. We coded these as *anger, dissatisfaction, sadness, emotional distance* and *fear* – emotions that shift students' focus away from the classroom and their learning of Swedish. For example, one teacher discussed how mentally re-experiencing an event or context can make it difficult to be cognitively present in the classroom (i.e. causing dissociation) and to participate in learning: 'Imagine that you are stuck in something, inside your head. Difficult to focus, difficult to be present' (FGA1).

Another theme derived in response to the second research question was that PTSD overlaps with other factors that affect their learning. The PTSD symptoms that participants mentioned knowing about included depression, headaches, stomach aches, chest pains and feelings of dizziness. One teacher, FGB1, talked about how useful it had been to learn about PTSD during the Red Cross training session, as it helped her realize that students who fell asleep at their desks may not have a general behavioral problem or have been out too late at night, but rather, may not be feeling emotionally well and could be taking sleeping pills or other medicines whose side effects make them drowsy in class.

In sum, many teachers think that PTSD affects students' experiences in the Swedish as a second or other language classroom, and that learning is made more difficult and complex because of PTSD by itself or in combination with other factors. Teachers' observations of student behaviors in their classrooms inform how they might adapt their teaching for their refugee-background students, including building on the resources and resilience that students bring with them, as we discuss next.

Pedagogical responses to perceived PTSD

One theme derived in response to the third research question was the importance of helping refugee-background students generally. Within this theme of general help, many suggestions made in the focus groups for working with students who have PTSD are good classroom support techniques for all students. For example, in one focus group the importance of creating a calm, safe environment was mentioned, as was the importance of presenting the structure of the day on the whiteboard. These are aspects of standard good classroom management that we recognize from other classrooms in Swedish schools from Grade 1 upwards. Hence, in keeping with the concept of Universal Design for Learning (e.g. Rose & Meyer, 2006), what is seen as good pedagogy for students with PTSD or other challenges is, in many cases, good for all students.

A broad second theme was the importance of creating a feeling of safety in the classroom through play, and by using everyday Swedish in class in engaging ways (e.g. pair work and participatory dialogues) to reduce the authoritative role of the teacher. Although structure and egalitarianism can appear to be contradictory goals, the structure is a macro-frame that allows less authoritative micro-management in the classroom (Oral, 2013; Reeve & Tseng, 2011). One teacher describes her teaching techniques to reduce stress and increase learning for adult refugee-background students as follows:

> But I use my tricks like this. And then there was this time we were studying verbs when I did my thing, that is a typical drama exercise that is done like this: one group stands in a line, then someone from the other group comes and asks: Hi, what are you doing? And so starts the drama exercise [stands up and demonstrates]. Oh, you're jumping. Yes. And then you change places. And this can sound silly but it is really useful and there are many who [say], 'Ah so useful! What we have learnt!' (FGB1)

This teacher finds that by being silly in this way, she develops a fun environment for teaching and learning, which reduces the perception of her as a humorless authority figure and reveals her humanity and individuality. At the same time, the students have a feeling that they have learned a greater range of useful verbs than they might have gained from more traditional, non-participatory methods. Thus, teachers feel that this playful, dramatic approach, in which teaching includes aspects of total physical response (e.g. Asher, 2009), helps the students relax and encourages better learning.

Another example of using language play and structure to create an activity that is safe but useful was given by teacher FGB2. She discussed a class she offers for women, many of whom feel insecure about coming to class, and who may encounter difficulties in getting away from home to attend class. She has found that using language play – rhymes, in this case – motivates these students to come to class:

> There's a lot of, er, language awareness. That is not so such vocabulary training but it is actually… well, rhyming words and that sort of thing. So they get a little, umm, 'sun, bun, fun' [example changed to English rhymes] and this how we work. Then we write, and they write a little. We only write so that words are recognized, and to see what is the same and different. Find words that begin with the same letter, same sound. That

type of writing. Then they sit there and write. But that is the level they are at, at the moment. But this feels right for these women who are blocked [in their learning]. Actually it does. (FGB2)

A third theme was supporting students in overcoming the concentration problems that may be a result of PTSD. The teachers employ means such as computers, tablets and mobile phone apps to support language play, to enable working longer with each topic and to create personalized learning opportunities. This approach allows students to work at their own pace and in line with their concentration abilities. Creating individualized learning opportunities allows students with PTSD to experience less external stress, as it reduces the feeling of needing to keep up. The teachers also point out that it is necessary to teach the same thing many times, to use many short pauses to maintain the students' concentration levels and to work with the same topic over an extended period of time. Indeed, FGA discussed the importance of not rushing things:

FGA3: And I think that is it important that you don't rush things.
FGA4: And it is important when everything is new, before they start doing other new things, that you may have learned these four sounds and so on. Practice them for a while.
FGA1: Practice them and at the same time add a few extra new things, you can't only... you have to use pictures and do this practically.

Repetition and recycling of previously learned material is seen as another way to overcome the learning limitations created by the concentration challenges of some of the students suffering from PTSD. One teacher pointed out the need for short teaching and learning sequences and individualized solutions to reduce the impact on memory and concentration issues – again, approaches that benefit all students and are examples of Universal Design for Learning (e.g. Rose & Meyer, 2006) for adult learners:

What I've done when people have told me that they have this type of problem is to find individualized solutions as the person may only have the ability to work for a short period of time or says so. If it is a good day they may be able to work well for 20 minutes and they can need their own solutions that differ from the others in the group or workplace. (FGB4)

A final theme mentioned by a number of teachers was avoiding materials that might trigger bad memories. However, some participants pointed out that it is impossible to guess what will trigger negative memories, since using what is seen as universally appropriate – for example, discussion of topics immediate to the students such as family, children, home and work – may also trigger bad memories and flashbacks. This tension between trying to avoid and accidently triggering bad memories occupied some of the teachers' thoughts.

Hence, although all of the teachers have only a vague idea of what PTSD is and how it impacts learning, they have many suggestions for how to work in the classroom to support students they suspect have PTSD. These ideas are based on what they have learned from the Red Cross training about PTSD, their understanding of the most common symptoms and their years of experience teaching adult refugee-background students. These teachers use a variety of approaches to respond to issues over which they have little or no control. The common aspects of their approaches are the practical and the individual, using short teaching blocks and employing student-centered activities. In the focus groups, there was a feeling of always attempting to find common ground with the students in the classroom, and incorporating topics that do not create trauma. In these ways, the teachers are continually negotiating with students and formatively assessing the class to find the most appropriate topics and contexts to teach. They are in essence following the tenets of trauma-informed teaching (e.g. Carello & Butler, 2014; Montero, this volume; Morgan *et al.*, 2015) as they attempt to keep the possibilities for retraumatization to a minimum, by creating safe, structured environments for learning. It was apparent that participating teachers were looking for support and a deeper understanding of PTSD.

Teachers also referenced building upon their students' resources and resilience. The female students discussed above, for example, show resilience in how they juggle their desire to learn Swedish and integrate into society with the demands of their co-ethnic community, working together with the teacher to create a safe, all-female learning environment. In class, the students may at times be blocked in their learning, yet they have resources such as oral language abilities that allow them to discuss learning challenges together and with classroom support translators, when available. Students also have listening and narrative skills from their first or multiple languages, and are willing to invest in classroom learning activities that help create a safe classroom for all.

Discussion

From the focus group discussions, we saw that the teachers see their role as not to be authoritative, but rather to provide a safe place for all students to learn. The teachers blended teaching approaches that they believe reduce stress and create this safe environment, in keeping with trauma-informed pedagogy. However, it is also clear that the teachers feel insecure at times about what they are doing. As discussed earlier, teachers do not know if a student has a diagnosis, or whether he or she wants to let the teachers know about his or her diagnosis, suggesting that teachers need assistance and training in learning to discuss these issues with their adult refugee-background students. Teachers also need guidance on when to refer students to appropriate professionals. In terms of efficacy, though teachers are putting much effort into adapting their classrooms, they have little evidence to show whether these approaches actually reduce students' stress and create conditions for language learning.

Implications

The key implication that became clear from this research is that a formal and continuous training program that helps language teachers learn to distinguish illnesses, including PTSD, would allow them to identify students in need of support and resources, and to consider how their instructional design might best meet students' needs. Training would also allow teachers to better understand students' classroom behaviors.

Notably, language teachers working with newly arrived students with no knowledge of written or spoken Swedish, in comparison with subject teachers working with students after they have achieved a basic level of Swedish, often have the additional challenge of not being able to communicate extensively with their students. That is, unlike most teachers, language teachers may not have the possibility of communicating directly with a newcomer suffering from PTSD about his or her experiences, because they do not usually share the language of the student. As communication is a central part of distinguishing illnesses, including PTSD, it was surprising to us how little the teachers referred to interpreters and other language support assistants as a resource for the classroom. Any formal and continuous training program that helps language teachers to identify and support students with PTSD might usefully include training about how best to integrate interpreters and other language support assistants into classroom instruction. When teachers experience a rise in self-confidence regarding their ability to support adult refugee-background students with PTSD and to work together with interpreters and other language support assistants, it is likely that the quality of language teaching and the amount of student learning will also rise.

Limitations and Future Research

One limitation of this research is that the number of participants in our study was low, and we captured only one point in time. Moreover, the familiarity of one author with the participants and their institution might have influenced participant responses. The use of focus groups brings with it limitations as well: While the data collected from focus groups are highly detailed, there is a risk that participants might overly influence one another's responses and/or that one participant could dominate the group. Although we did not observe this latter phenomenon, we have kept these issues in focus during our analysis, and these aspects should be considered when interpreting our findings.

Future research could usefully investigate the role of the interpreter and other language assistants in the language classroom for newly arrived, adult refugee-background students. It is often assumed that these staff members can act as cultural brokers, helping the teachers to understand cultural issues that may impact student learning, thereby improving the classroom climate and learner uptake. Moreover, when difficult moments occur in the classroom, language assistants might be able to work with individual students, gathering more information about their experiences and helping the students return more quickly to the safe language classroom environment. Future research could examine these various functions and identify best practices, so that interpreters and language assistants could contribute maximally to student learning.

Another line of research could investigate how various forms of ongoing support may affect teachers' self-confidence in their ability to support adult refugee-background students with PTSD. For example, if language and literacy teachers were offered regular opportunities to discuss their teaching experiences with healthcare professionals and senior teachers, would this strengthen their knowledge about PTSD – in particular their ability to build on the assets and resilience of adult refugee-background students in the language learning classroom?

Finally, the research presented in this chapter has primarily focused on teacher perspectives, and could be complemented with first-hand perspectives from refugee-background students in language/literacy courses. Accessing these student perspectives would afford insights into how students and communities develop strategies and resources for responding to the challenges of trauma and PTSD, potentially turning these challenges into assets and opportunities.

Note

(1) Indeed, historical studies show that many diseases and psychological conditions are socially contextualized and interpreted (see e.g. Bhugra & Gupta, 2011; Harper, 2016; Langum, 2016; Westum & Langum, 2015).

References

Alisic, E. (2012) Teachers' perspective on providing support to children after trauma: A qualitative study. *School Psychology Quarterly* 27 (1), 51–59.

American Psychiatric Association (APA) (2013) *Diagnostic and Statistical Manual of Mental Disorders* (5th edn). Arlington, VA: American Psychiatric Publishing.

Asher, J.J. (2009) *Learning Another Language Through Actions* (7th edn). Los Gatos, CA: Sky Oak Productions.

Barlow, D.H. (2007) *Clinical Handbook of Psychological Disorders: A Step-by-Step Treatment Manual* (4th edn). New York: Guilford Press.

Bhugra, D. and Gupta, S. (eds) (2011) *Migration and Mental Health*. Cambridge: Cambridge University Press.

Carello, J. and Butler, L.D. (2014) Potentially perilous pedagogies: Teaching trauma is not the same as trauma-informed teaching. *Journal of Trauma and Dissociation* 15 (2), 153–168.

Cossu, G., Cantone, E., Pintus, M., Cadoni, M., Pisano, A., Otten, R., Kuijpers, R., Pintus, E., Sancassiani, F., Moro, M.F., Holzinger, A., Mereu, A., Preti, A. and Carta, M.G. (2015) Integrating children with psychiatric disorders in the classroom: A systematic review. *Clinical Practice and Epidemiology in Mental Health* 11 (1), 41–57.

de Rond, M. and Lok, J. (2016) Some things can never be unseen: The role of context in psychological injury at war. *Academy of Management Journal* 59 (6), 1965–1993.

Ehntholt, K.A., Smith, P.A. and Yule, W. (2005) School-based cognitive-behavioural therapy group intervention for refugee children who have experienced war-related trauma. *Clinical Child Psychology and Psychiatry* 10 (2), 235–250.

Fazel, M., Wheeler, J. and Danesh, J. (2005) Prevalence of serious mental disorder in 7000 refugees resettled in western countries: A systematic review. *The Lancet* 365 (9467), 1309–1314.

Foa, E.B., Keane, T.M., Friedman, M.J. and Cohen, J.A. (eds) (2008) *Effective Treatments for PTSD: Practice Guidelines from the International Society for Traumatic Stress Studies*. New York: Guilford Press.

Harper, M. (ed.) (2016) *Migration and Mental Health: Past and Present*. Basingstoke: Palgrave Macmillan.

Johnson, H. and Thompson, A. (2008) The development and maintenance of post-traumatic stress disorder (PTSD) in civilian adult survivors of war trauma and torture: A review. *Clinical Psychology Review* 28 (1), 36–47.

Kataoka, S., Langley, A., Wong, M., Baweja, S. and Stein, B. (2012) Responding to students with PTSD in schools. *Child and Adolescent Psychiatric Clinics of North America* 21 (1), 119–133.

Ko, S.J., Ford, J.D., Kassam-Adams, N., Berkowitz, S.J., Wilson, C., Wong, M., Brymer, M.L. and Layne, C.M. (2008) Creating trauma-informed systems: Child welfare, education, first responders, health care, juvenile justice. *Professional Psychology: Research and Practice* 39 (4), 396–404.

Langum, V. (2016) *Medicine and the Seven Deadly Sins in Late Medieval Literature and Culture*. New York: Palgrave Macmillan.

Morgan, A., Pendergast, D., Brown, R. and Heck, D. (2015) Relational ways of being an educator: Trauma-informed practice supporting disenfranchised young people. *International Journal of Inclusive Education* 19 (10), 1037–1051.

Oral, Y. (2013) 'The right things are what I expect them to do': Negotiation of power relations in an English classroom. *Journal of Language, Identity, and Education* 12 (2), 96–115.

O'Shea, B., Hodes, M., Down, G. and Bramley, J. (2000) A school-based mental health service for refugee children. *Clinical Child Psychology and Psychiatry* 5 (2), 189–201.

Reeve, J. and Tseng, C.M. (2011) Agency as a fourth aspect of students' engagement during learning activities. *Contemporary Educational Psychology* 36 (4), 257–267.

Rolfsnes, E.S. and Idsoe, T. (2011) School-based intervention programs for PTSD symptoms: A review and meta-analysis. *Journal of Traumatic Stress* 24 (2), 155–165.

Rose, D.H. and Meyer, A. (2006) *A Practical Reader in Universal Design for Learning*. Cambridge, MA: Harvard Education Publishing Group.

Schreiber, M., Gurwitch, R. and Wong, M. (2008) *Listen, Protect, Connect – Model & Teach: Psychological First Aid (PFA) for Students and Teachers*. Folsom, CA: US Department of Education, Readiness and Emergency Management for Schools (REMS) Technical Assistance Center.

Swedish Research Council (2011) *God forskningssed* [*Good Research Practice*]. Stockholm: Vetenskapsrådet.
Tanielian, T. and Jaycox, L. (eds) (2008) *Invisible Wounds of War: Psychological and Cognitive Injuries, Their Consequences, and Services to Assist Recovery*. Santa Monica, CA: RAND Corporation.
The Swedish Migration Agency (2014) *Inkomna ansökningar om asyl, 2013* [Applications for asylum received, 2013]. See https://www.migrationsverket.se/download/18.7c00d8 e6143101d166ddae/1485556207418/Inkomna+ans%C3%B6kningar+om+asyl+2013+-+Applications+for+asylum+received+2013.pdf (accessed 4 January 2018).
The Swedish Migration Agency (2016) *Inkomna ansökningar om asyl, 2015* [Applications for asylum received, 2015]. See https://www.migrationsverket.se/download/18.7c00d8e61 43101d166d1aab/1485556214938/Inkomna+ans%C3%B6kningar+om+asyl+2015+-+Applications+for+asylum+received+2015.pdf (accessed 4 January 2018).
Toros, K. and Tiirik, R. (2016) Preschool teachers' perceptions about and experience with child abuse and neglect. *Early Childhood Education Journal* 44 (1), 21–30.
US Department of Veteran Affairs (2015) Analysis of VA health care utilization among Operation Enduring Freedom (OEF), Operation Iraqi Freedom (OIF), and Operation New Dawn (OND) veterans. See http://www.publichealth.va.gov/docs/epidemiology/healthcare-utilization-report-fy2015-qtr1.pdf (accessed 4 January 2018).
Westum, A. and Langum, V. (2015) I människan själv, eller utanför?: Föreställningar om pestens orsaker i lärda skrifter och folktro [Within or outside? Perceptions of the causes of the plague in scholarly texts and popular belief]. *Kulturella Perspektiv* 2015, 11–19.
Wretling, O. (2006) Studerande med posttraumatiskt stressyndrom och andra stressutlösta ångestsyndrom [Students with post-traumatic stress and other stress-induced anxiety disorders]. In Myndigheten för Skolutveckling (ed.) *Stöd- och referensmaterial om vuxnas lärande – Del 3 Specialpedagogik i vuxenperspektiv* [*Support and Reference Materials about Adult Learning – Part 3 Special Education Adult Perspective*] (pp. 43–55). Stockholm: Myndigheten för Skolutveckling.

12 Education of Refugee-background Youth in Germany: Systemic Barriers to Equitable Participation in the Vocational Education System

Annette Korntheuer, Maren Gag, Phillip Anderson and Joachim Schroeder

Germany received around 300,000 refugee newcomers ages 16–25 in 2015. Educational participation is a key process for the integration of these young people. This is especially true for the German vocational education and training (VET) system that provides opportunities for a fast and successful transition into the labor market. The few extant studies on migrant students in Germany have shown considerable problems in achieving educational equity. Based on the theoretical assumption that systemic discrimination creates important barriers to educational equity, we investigate how institutional and systemic factors influence the educational participation of refugee-background youth and how these youth cope with such barriers. Using a two-case study in the cities of Hamburg and Munich, we performed a meta-analysis of research reports, complemented by secondary analysis of primary data. Results show institutional barriers in both the education and asylum systems, and that youth cope with these barriers through high educational aspirations.

Germany, with a population of 82 million people, has become a major recipient of asylum applications, with 202,834 claimants in 2014 and 476,649 in 2015 (Bundesamt für Migration und Flüchtlinge [BAMF], 2016). The age group of youth and young adults (16–25 years) accounted for about 29% of asylum applicants in 2015. An estimated 300,000 newcomers between the ages of 16 and 25 registered as asylum seekers in Germany in 2015.

The vast majority of youth with refugee backgrounds start their educational paths as asylum seekers. During this time, their living conditions are influenced by restrictive policies, such as the obligation to live in a refugee shelter for the term of their asylum process (Müller *et al.*, 2014). Only recently has Germany made efforts to establish a small national resettlement program. However, the numbers of resettled refugees are marginal (BAMF, 2016). Therefore, in referring to youth with refugee backgrounds, our focus in this chapter is on asylum claimants and accepted or denied asylum seekers from 16 to 25 years old. In some sections, we compare their situation to immigrant students, meaning to all young people that are either first- or second-generation immigrants to Germany.

Educational participation is a key process for the integration of refugee-background youth, but it has only very recently received attention from political stakeholders and the academic community (Deutsches Institut für Wirtschaft Berlin, 2016). Available information has mostly been restricted to municipal reports (Anderson, 2016; Gag & Schroeder, 2012) and a limited number of studies focusing on specific subgroups of refugee-background youth based on their nationality and legal status (Müller *et al.*, 2014). For those in the age group 16–25, access to education has generally been limited to preparatory classes at vocational schools (Korntheuer, 2016; Müller *et al.*, 2014). Research on immigrant students in Germany more broadly finds considerable problems in achieving educational equity within the German schooling systems and vocational education (Autorengruppe Bildungsberichterstattung, 2016; Diehl *et al.*, 2016; Organization for Economic Cooperation and Development [OECD], 2014). Studies show that unequal educational outcomes for immigrant youth tend to be linked to systemic barriers and institutional structures (Fereidooni, 2011; Gomolla & Radtke, 2009). To extend this research, this chapter synthesizes data from prior studies, to answer these questions:

(1) How do institutional and systemic factors influence the educational participation of refugee-background youth (aged 16–25) in the vocational education system?
(2) How do these youth perceive and cope with these factors?

As Germany is a federal state, the educational policies of the 16 states (Laender) are independent, so there are different rules for the education of youth with refugee backgrounds from one state to another. These differences can be shown with the example of two big cities: Munich, the capital of Bavaria, traditionally a conservative state, and Hamburg, an independent city state with comparatively liberal educational policies. Both Munich and Hamburg are large, multicultural, urban areas with a high percentage of refugee-background youth (Freie und Hansestadt

Hamburg, 2015; Regierung von Oberbayern, 2016), and are the focus of our analysis.

We begin this chapter by describing the main structures of secondary and vocational education systems in Germany as important context for this study. We draw on current educational research to highlight the existing systemic barriers for immigrant students overall in Germany, since specific research on youth with refugee backgrounds is not available. Our theoretical framework, drawn from Feagin and Feagin (1978/1989) and Gomolla and Radtke (2009) focuses on institutional and structural discrimination as important barriers to equitable educational participation. In the findings from our meta-analysis, we point out institutional barriers in the education system and asylum policies that create systemic barriers. In addition, we identify youths' important coping strategies, such as having high educational aspirations and motivation, and propose directions for future research and policymaking.

Background and Literature Review

The educational participation of young refugee students is shaped through a segregated secondary schooling system and unequal access of immigrant students to the different programs of the German VET system.

Access to secondary schooling

The educational paths for youth with refugee backgrounds are restricted throughout the educational structures in Germany. As the federal states are responsible for the school systems, there are considerable differences in the school structures within Germany (von Maurice & Roßbach, 2017). Primary school includes the first four or five years, after which secondary schooling takes place in two or three school tracks: (1) Gymnasium (Grades 5 to 12/13), which provides the basis for tertiary education; (2) Realschule (Grades 5 to 10), the intermediate level that enables transition into a broad range of vocational education programs; and (3) Haupt- or Mittelschule (Grades 5 to 9/10), the lowest level of secondary schooling, which leads mainly to one of the different programs existing within the VET system (Hoeckel & Schwarz, 2010). In some federal states, the second and third tracks (above) are combined, which leads to different school leaving certificates and often to entering the vocational education system (Secretariat of the Standing Conference of the Ministers of Education and Cultural Affairs of the Länder in the Federal Republic of Germany, 2015). Support for learning German as a new language is mostly provided at the lowest level of secondary school. Haupt- or Mittelschule offers schooling for students younger than age 16. For refugee students, these structures present barriers to the higher types of secondary school and exclude them from secondary school after age 16

(Barth & Meneses, 2012; Müller *et al.*, 2014). For students arriving after age 15, access is mainly limited to language learning and preparatory classes within the VET transition programs at vocational schools. These classes are focused on learning German, mathematics and other school subjects needed for the lowest, formal school leaving certificate. Refugee-background youth can also undertake longer internships in companies to qualify them for employment. The ultimate goal is their preparation for vocational education programs (Gag & Schroeder, 2012).

The VET system in Germany

Germany's dual apprenticeship programs are globally known to comprise a very successful system, combining work-based learning in companies with school-based learning in part-time VET schools. Approximately 350 different trades can be studied through dual apprenticeship programs. These apprenticeship options are appealing not only for students with the intermediate or lowest school leaving certificate. In fact, 21% of new apprentices had a university entry qualification in 2015 (Autorengruppe Bildungsberichterstattung, 2016). For specific labor market sectors such as the food and construction industry, there is a significant lack of new apprentices, whereas for the business sector, new media and information, the demand is very high, and entrance is almost exclusively offered to students with university entry qualifications and intermediate secondary certificates (Autorengruppe Bildungsberichterstattung, 2016).

Besides the dual apprenticeship program, the German VET system offers training through full-time VET schools and VET transition programs. The VET transition programs have been shown to be problematic, however, because of low rates of successful transition into the regular VET system (Hoeckel & Schwarz, 2010).

Unequal access to vocational education in Germany

A number of studies have shown unequal access for immigrant students (including refugees and asylum seekers) to the dual apprenticeship system and full-time VET schools (Hunkler, 2016). In 2014, 46% of German students with the intermediate school leaving certificate were able to transition successfully into the dual apprenticeship program, whereas this was the case for only 28% of the students without German nationality but with equal certifications (Bundesministerium für Berufsbildung, 2016). Furthermore, immigrant youth are mostly limited to lower demand sectors, such as food service and construction. Participation rates in the transition VET programs, in contrast, are twice as high for immigrant students as for students with German nationality (Autorengruppe Bildungsberichterstattung, 2016). Twice as many immigrant students leave secondary school without any form of school leaving certificate, compared with German nationals. On the other hand, German students are three times as likely to obtain a university entry qualification as immigrant students. Moreover, not surprisingly, language skills and socioeconomic status are significantly lower for immigrant students overall (Autorengruppe Bildungsberichterstattung, 2016).

In a literature review, Hunkler (2016) points out two possible reasons for the lack of equity for immigrant students in the vocational system: (1) unequal human capital (language skills, school leaving certificates, socioeconomic status) of immigrant students compared with native-born students at the transition moment; and (2) discrimination against immigrant students by employers within the dual system. Understanding equity as offering not only equal access but also support for students with diverse skills, we would add a third possible reason: insufficient language support and intercultural sensitivity in the VET system (Anderson, 2016; Gag & Schroeder, 2012). Although newcomer immigrant students enter the educational system with limited language skills, language support is often lacking in schools (Hunkler, 2016). The same applies to vocational training schools. Thus, German schools and the VET system are usually monolingual, in German (Fereidooni, 2011). Language support is mostly limited to specialized programs in the VET transition and is still lacking in the dual apprenticeship programs (Anderson, 2016).

Theoretical Framework

Our understanding of equity is based on Flitner's (1987) discussion of institutional justice in schools. While Flitner (1987) demands equal access for all students, he also states that distinctive support must be provided for students with differences in ability, interests and socioeconomic background. A study by Gomolla and Radtke (2009) on institutional discrimination provides an influential explanation model for the lack of equity of immigrant students within German educational systems.

Some scholars differentiate between direct and indirect institutional discrimination. *Direct institutional discrimination* usually involves regular actions based on policies or organizational routines (Feagin & Feagin, 1978/1986; Gomolla & Radtke, 2009). *Indirect institutional discrimination*, on the other hand, is not intentional but is carried out through norms and procedures that appear superficially appropriate, but have a negative and differentiating effect on certain social groups (Feagin & Feagin, 1978/1986). Hormel (2007) distinguishes between interactional, institutional and structural discrimination. Citizenship creates a state-regulated basis for selective access to organizations and functional systems. It essentially determines the modes of exclusion and inclusion in law, the economy, healthcare and education. Few studies to date (e.g. Behrensen & Westphal, 2009) have indicated the importance of the concept of institutional and structural discrimination for the educational participation of refugee-background youth in Germany (Gag & Schroeder, 2012). Therefore, educational participation of refugee-background youth in the German VET system, as we are able to show in our study, is hindered by both direct and indirect institutional and structural discrimination.

Research Methodology

In this study, we analyzed educational participation in a 'two-case' study using multiple sources of empirical evidence (Yin, 2009). In 2015, we brought together a multidisciplinary research team of academic and practitioner partners in Munich and Hamburg. As researchers and practitioners in the field of forced migration, we are committed to social justice and anti-oppressive frameworks, and aim to enforce the integration of research and frontline practice.

Site identification and data collection

The cities of Munich and Hamburg were chosen for this study. While both are multicultural urban areas characterized by a significant presence of refugee-background youth, they differ markedly in terms of educational systems, reflecting different dimensions of educational structures in Germany. For both cities, a broad range of research reports and primary interview data were accessible, allowing the research team to include multiple sources for each case. Table 12.1 shows the site profiles, including the sources and the main characteristics of the case study database.

Interviews with refugee-background youth and other key informants were conducted in German and English using semi-structured protocols. All interviews were recorded, summarized and partly transcribed. Focus groups were used to deepen the analysis. Throughout the research process, consideration was given to the fact that these youth often live under unstable and insecure living conditions. Protection of the interview participants was considered a top priority; therefore, demographic data collected were limited to gender, age and continent of origin. In the

Table 12.1 Research reports

Case 1: Hamburg	Case 2: Munich
Municipal report on refugee monitoring (Gag & Schroeder, 2012) City report (Gag, 2013) Country report I (Gag, 2015) Country report II (Gag & Schroeder, 2015) Explorative study about education experiences in companies (Meyer, 2014)	Evaluation report on vocational schooling of refugee-background youth (Anderson, 2016) PhD dissertation on educational participation of refugee-background youth in Munich and Toronto (Korntheuer, 2016)

original data set, a total of 36 refugee-background youth (Munich: $n = 20$; Hamburg: $n = 16$) and 63 other informants (Munich: $n = 33$; Hamburg: $n = 30$) were interviewed.

Data analysis

A qualitative meta-analysis (Timulak, 2009) was implemented using research reports in both cities, resulting in categories for the cross-case comparison. Our research questions were closely linked to the focus of the original reports (refugee-background youth/educational participation/ institutional structures) but were more focused on aspects of structural and institutional discrimination. Through meta-analysis, we achieved a more comprehensive and differentiated description (Timulak, 2009) of the participation of refugee-background youth in the vocational education system in urban areas in Germany.

As a second step, categories or themes were explored in-depth through secondary analysis of the primary data from the published reports, which enabled the categories of the cross-case comparison to be (re)grounded in empirical data. Therefore, we could minimize the loss of contextualization of data and research procedures, which is a common critique of qualitative meta-analysis (Paterson et al., 2001).

Findings

To contextualize our findings we start with a short description of the two cities. Subsequently, we identify and describe three main themes that resulted from our analysis.

Case 1: Hamburg: Long-standing tradition in VET programs for refugee-background youth

The city-state of Hamburg has witnessed an enormous rise in immigrant numbers since 2014. As a result of the increased inflow, refugees stay much too long in mass accommodation without privacy, often in unacceptable hygienic conditions. A decrease in the quality of staff has been noted, which is particularly serious for the situation of unaccompanied underage refugees, who are cared for by various organizations within the framework of children's aid society programs (Landesbetrieb Erziehung & Beratung, 2015).

In Hamburg, 'refugee courses' were established at vocational schools in 1996. By the end of 2015, more than 2,000 students were taught in 135 classes at 27 vocational training schools. Although the Hamburg authorities have been providing funds since 2002 to prepare refugees for the employment market, it was only from 2013 onwards that this group was included in the Hamburg Integration Concept. Since then, this integration support has been an interdisciplinary task for all of Hamburg's departments and political bodies (Freie und Hansestadt Hamburg, 2013).

Case 2: Munich: Strong recent investments in VET programs for refugee-background youth

Despite being the capital of one of the most restrictive states, the policy of the city of Munich has been driven by a humanitarian approach toward refugees and asylum seekers, focusing on their integration needs (Crage, 2009). In February 2016, the Bavarian government stated that 15,313 refugee claimants were living in shelters in Munich, with approximately 4,500 youth estimated within this group. In 2016, Munich was accommodating 5,119 unaccompanied minors with refugee backgrounds, in programs of the childrens' aid society (Regierung von Oberbayern, 2016).

'Refugee courses' have been provided as part of VET transition programs since 2011. In February 2016, more than 1,500 refugee-background youth were being taught in this type of model at vocational schools. An additional 500 spaces were offered through specialized schooling programs for these youth. These programs are carried out by non-governmental organizations (NGOs) but are financially supported by Munich, where numbers of available study places have more than doubled since 2013 (Anderson, 2016).

School structures are implemented on a state level. Language support is almost exclusively offered in the lowest level of secondary schooling in Bavaria. Policies still focus on creating a homogeneous student body in the three different types of secondary school. Vocational training is the main educational option for refugee-background youth, due to their exclusion from the higher levels of secondary schooling. This trend is reinforced by the existing needs of the German labor market and the desire for refugee youth to stabilize their legal status through vocational qualification (Korntheuer, 2016).

Cross-case analysis

The following main themes were identified in our analysis across these two cases: (1) institutional barriers to accessing secondary school options and within the vocational education system; (2) insecure legal status, which creates additional individual and institutional barriers; and (3) high educational aspirations as an important resource for coping with systemic barriers.

Institutional barriers in secondary schooling and VET system

Our analysis shows as a first important result the existence of institutional barriers through segregated schooling of refugee-background youth in the VET transition programs. Specialized programs face important challenges in providing appropriate institutional support structures. Furthermore, young refugee students who succeed in moving on to the dual apprenticeship program are confronted with insufficient institutional language support at school as well as in the workplace. Educational policies that lead to segregated schooling in specialized programs represent sources of direct and indirect mechanisms of institutional discrimination, having a negative effect on the access of refugee-background youth to education in Germany (Gomolla & Radtke, 2009).

Segregated schooling in VET system

Structures for refugee-background youth in both cases focus on vocational training. As a result, youth with high educational aspirations may perceive these structures as exclusion from higher secondary schools and therefore a form of systemic discrimination, as the following quote from a refugee student in Munich reveals:

> I told him [a social worker], I cannot stay in this language course; I want to go to school. I want to learn. We said, 'We are human beings as well, we have equal rights to go to school like German youth'. And he told me there is no school for foreign youth. (…). (Korntheuer, 2016)

A research report from Hamburg (Gag & Schroeder, 2012) shows that these specialized programs are facing further challenges. Refugee courses in the VET transition programs receive less funding than comparable courses for young Germans. The curricular concept is inconsistent and inflexible, and examination regulations are inappropriate for newcomer students. The age limit of 18 excludes those older from basic education, a major disadvantage in the case of Hamburg (Gag & Schroeder, 2012).

The Munich reports echo these findings, even though the policy grants access to vocational school until age 25 (Anderson, 2016). With the large inflows of asylum seekers, the limited spaces are generally made accessible to younger students, rather than to older students. The two-year preparatory courses face a number of major challenges: (1) staff need to improve intercultural skills; (2) the schools need to develop culturally sensitive curricula; (3) greater collaboration is needed with ethnic communities as potential employers in small and medium-sized enterprises; and (4) teachers and social workers need to develop a holistic support approach to keep the young apprentices on board while they are earning a low wage (Anderson, 2016).

The comparison of cases shows commonalities related to the lack of an inclusive schooling approach and the lack of intercultural sensitivity, both present in the current model of schooling. A major challenge in both cities is the exclusion of older youth and the lack of support for transitioning into the dual apprenticeship programs. Differences in the federal educational systems lead to different types of access to secondary school certificates. In Hamburg, refugee classes at vocational schools provide access to the examination of low and intermediate leaving certificates, while in Munich usually only the certificate for the lowest level of secondary schooling can be obtained.

Lack of language support

Refugee students in Munich (Anderson, 2016) often referred to the challenge of learning specialized language related to the trades they were studying. One aspect of this is the difficulty of grasping the abstraction of technical terms in textbooks. Another challenge is the variety of the spoken dialect. Participants pointed out the difficulty of understanding teachers or work supervisors who speak a broad Bavarian dialect. Moreover, there is the challenge of mastering different registers of spoken German – for example, the slang of the workplace is different from the academic language of the classroom (Anderson, 2016). These differences can be hard for young people who have grown up in a very different sociocultural environment to cope with, as stated by a garage supervisor in Hamburg:

> You know it is always very, very hard to explain things to him [trainee Omar, refugee background] and work together. Not so much when he is doing hands on, because, this I can say is working well. His colleagues, they are used to him and understand his accent. They manage to do that. But during theoretical training, classes or writing tasks, this is really difficult. (Meyer, 2014)

Despite the supposed differences in 'school culture' in Hamburg and Munich, lack of language support in the VET system emerged as a common theme in both cases.

Insecure legal status as an individual and institutional barrier

Modes of inclusion and exclusion in the German VET system are strongly influenced by the lack of a secure legal status, which causes direct exclusion from institutional support systems, serving as a form of structural discrimination. Furthermore, emotional insecurity acts as an important individual barrier for accessing education.

Direct mechanisms of structural discrimination

Our empirical data show that young asylum claimants transitioning into vocational education or the workplace are typically subject to huge disadvantages as a result of legal regulations. Approvals are required from the local Foreigners' Registration Office and the Jobs Agency for both the vocational preparation programs and vocational training in the dual system. These complicated bureaucratic procedures prevent many companies from training refugee-background youth (Gag & Schroeder, 2012; Meyer, 2014). For example, companies cannot be sure that the skilled personnel they train, and urgently need, will be available at a later date, because of difficulties in getting work permits. Some youth are therefore excluded from vocational education for long periods of time, as described by Arash, a young man in Hamburg: 'The best moment of all was when I got my work permit at the beginning of the year, to work eight hours a day. That was the first time for ten years I was allowed to do real work. I have kept that document' (Gag, 2013: 161).

Youth also face uncertainty in how to cover their costs of living, because of long waiting periods for financial support under the Vocational Training Funding Act. Many interviewees claimed not to receive social benefits, for example, to make up for low pay during training, to buy necessary tools or work clothes, or to compensate for gaps in schooling due to interruptions in their education (Gag, 2013). Lack of financial resources is a particular barrier for refugees who have come to Germany without their families; they are often unable to afford the transportation fares to attend school or engage in leisure activities. Those who cannot show identity papers are likely to be excluded from getting a driving license or setting up a bank account – requirements for certain jobs and to receive payments from the company that is training them (Gag, 2015). Our study has identified further disadvantages for individuals with serious mental or physical impairments, who are denied access to financial support systems in the first 15 months after arrival because of their legal status (Gag & Schroeder, 2015). In sum, structural discrimination through the federal asylum system acts as a systemic barrier across both city cases.

Emotional insecurity through insecure legal status

Policies such as the obligatory stay of refugees in mass shelters create institutional structures that oppress asylum claimants, making them feel powerless. Legal uncertainty can have negative effects on refugees' mental and physical well-being, as well as their performance in training and education (Gag, 2013, 2015; Gag & Schroeder, 2012). This situation can in turn affect the private realm, as shown by Hassan's experience in a refugee mass shelter:

> **Hassan:** Ok it was just young people, hanging around listening to music, no problem. But you know then the most terrible thing, what I cannot understand until nowadays, why did they do that to us. In the middle of the night, no matter what time it is, people coming into your room, not matter if you locked it up with a key, they have another key [speaking very loud] they just come into your room and tell you 'Give me your passport!'

> Interviewer: And this happened a few times to you?
> Hassan: A few times? No, every night! While I was in the [shelter] you cannot imagine this (...) this was horrible shit. Why did they do that? (Korntheuer, 2016: 311)

While this case may have been extreme, the same dynamic applies to other daily life situations. Young refugee claimants depend on the extension of residence and working permits to be allowed to stay and work in Germany. The insecurity of their legal status can decrease educational aspirations, cause them to abandon training and to feel that pursuing education is useless.

High educational aspirations as proactive coping strategy

The refugee-background youth in our study have high educational aspirations and are motivated to work hard to succeed in the educational system. Indeed, the experience of forced migration can lead to proactive coping strategies and a high value for education (Korntheuer, 2016). Interviews indicate that refugee-background youth can develop exceptional educational paths despite structural barriers. For example, Lilly, a young woman from a country in South Central Asia, arrived in Munich in 2008, at the age of 16 and with 12 years of schooling in her country of origin. Because of her age, she was excluded from regular secondary school and went to a schooling program for refugee-background youth instead. Lilly's high educational aspirations are closely related to her life history, including her father's death:

> For me, myself, why I didn't give up on it, for example why I didn't let them decide over me and intimidate me, this is just ... my father, even when my mom was still alive I was really close to him I loved him very much and still love him. I even don't like to talk in past tense about him. Yes, but it was his dream, he knew me as somebody that was going to study at the university. (Korntheuer, 2016)

When Lilly demanded access to the Gymnasium, it was denied by her legal guardian and the social worker from the youth shelter she was living in. This was a crucial moment on Lilly's educational path. Relying on herself and the support of a teacher from her schooling program, she was able to change schools. By 2016, after doing an apprenticeship as a medical assistant, she was studying for a bachelor's degree in physics at a university in Munich.

High educational aspirations and motivation on the part of refugee-background youth were confirmed by virtually all key informants as well. They described a desire to learn, to get good jobs and to succeed in a new life as ubiquitous among these young people, regardless of their educational and socioeconomic background. As a coordinating teacher for the refugee classes at vocational schools in Munich commented, 'Finally people realize the potential of this group [refugee students]. It is like that. We have known that for a long time, but now more people realize it' (Korntheuer, 2016: 266).

To maintain high motivation and aspiration, students need support from social and institutional networks, as well as meaningful relationships with adults and peers (Korntheuer, 2016). Familial, religious and ethnic communities play an important part in supporting these goals. The high degree of motivation to learn is related to the fact that refugee students know that they need to get remunerative employment for the sake of their families. On the other hand, economic and familial responsibilities can lead youth to drop out and take low-paying jobs (Anderson, 2016). As one youth in Munich noted: 'I do have too my stress in Africa, like this one needs me, this one needs me ... yeah to send money back. Bring the money' (Korntheuer, 2016: 306).

Some programs have changed their policies and practices in order to increase students' opportunities to achieve their educational goals. A reform in the educational program in Hamburg since 2014 aimed to tailor instruction more effectively to the target group, and to the needs of the individual, to improve refugee-background students' chances of attaining school leaving certificates and accessing vocational education. Integration support staff employed by external organizations with experience in transition management have been appointed to work in schools and companies. These individuals work with teaching staff inside a company, to coach the youth in language and subject matter and, at the same time, to improve the methodological skills of the company's training staff (Bürgerschaft, 2015a, 2015b). The result has been greater awareness and receptiveness of companies and public authorities to the specific needs of asylum seekers (Gag & Voges, 2014). Youth with refugee backgrounds perceive these structures as supportive – not only to accomplish their educational aspirations but also to stabilize their legal status. As stated by Arash:

> My dream was always to become an architect. But when I got the offer to take the training course in reinforced concrete construction, I said 'yes' straight away. The fact that EQUAL [an organization] secured my right to stay gave me the security that I would not be deported for at least a year. At last a year of opportunity to show what I can do. (Gag, 2013: 161)

Mentoring programs are another promising practice, providing youth with meaningful relationships with adults, as described by a project mentor in Hamburg:

> The focus of our cooperation was on support work at the vocational school and at the restaurant, in family matters and in his contacts with the authorities. Apart from improvements in [the youth's] performance at

vocational school, the primary goal of our mentor–mentee relationship is to keep his traineeship going. (Gag, 2013: 175)

The evaluation report in Munich shows that more and more companies are willing to accept refugees and asylum seekers as trainees. They have recognized the potential of the young people and see their high level of motivation and multiple language skills as an advantage (Anderson, 2016). A skills shortage and an aging demographic are forcing businesses to be more open to employing these individuals as a means of closing the gap. The chambers of handicraft and commerce in Germany have recently become more proactive, encouraging small businesses to view asylum seekers as a resource. Moreover, state employment agencies have tried to reduce red tape in order to provide financial support and skills-enhancing training for the target group once they start an apprenticeship (Anderson, 2016).

Discussion and Implications

We conclude from our study that legal and institutional frameworks lead to mechanisms of exclusion in the vocational educational systems for refugee students in Germany. In both Hamburg and Munich, participation in secondary schooling is strongly attached to age limits and language skills, which leads to disadvantages in the VET system. In addition, educational institutions in both cities lack the language support necessary for success in these programs. Finally, restrictive asylum policies exclude young refugee claimants from certain support systems and are resulting in emotional insecurity. There are some differences between the cases as well: In Hamburg, access to secondary schooling certificates is more flexible than in Munich, but the age limit for refugee courses at vocational schools is 18, while policies in Munich grant access until age 25.

Similar dynamics of institutional and structural discrimination have been found in other research (e.g. Fereidooni, 2011; Gomolla & Radtke, 2009; Hormel, 2007). In both cities, inequitable access can be assumed based on qualitative empirical evidence but there is a lack of quantitative data, suggesting a need for larger-scale studies in future research (Barth & Meneses, 2012; Gag & Schroeder, 2012; Korntheuer et al., in press; Müller et al., 2014). Moreover, because students with refugee backgrounds are an extremely diverse group, further qualitative and quantitative research is necessary to focus on subgroups, such as girls and young women, youth living in rural areas of Germany, youth arriving with disrupted schooling experiences and youth with special needs – all of whom may be especially vulnerable to systemic barriers. While these barriers can create significant challenges, our findings demonstrate that refugee-background youth are active, resilient and able to resist these institutional barriers – a trend that has been documented in other studies as well (Fernando & Ferrari, 2013; Seukwa, 2006; Shakya *et al.*, 2010).

We propose three immediate actions to build on the resilience and motivation of refugee-background students in Germany: (1) raise the age limit for attendance at vocational and general schools; (2) increase available supports, including language training, social workers, partnership with ethnic communities and mentoring programs; and (3) develop monitoring and evaluation approaches to expose institutional discrimination and document long-term outcomes. These actions could lead to a more equitable participation of refugee-background youth in the German VET system and hence have positive effects on the integration trajectories of youth and the broader social cohesion of German society.

References

Anderson, P. (2016) *'Lass mich endlich machen!' Eine Strategie zur Förderung in der beruflichen Bildung für junge berufsschulpflichtige Asylbewerber und Flüchtlinge (BAF)*. Report for the City of Munich.

Autorengruppe Bildungsberichterstattung. (2016) *Bildung in Deutschland 2016 Ein indikatorengestützter Bericht mit einer: Analyse zu Bildung und Migration*. Bielefeld: Bertelsmann.

Barth, S. and Meneses, G.V. (2012) *Zugang jugendlicher Asylsuchender zu formellen Bildungssystemen in Deutschland*. Frankfurt: Institut für Soziale Infrastruktur.

Behrensen, B. and Westphal, M. (2009) Junge Flüchtlinge- ein blinder Fleck in der Migrations- und Bildungsforschung. In L. Krappmann, A. Lob-Hüdepohl, S. Kurzke-Maasmeier and A. Bohmeyer (eds) *Bildung für junge Flüchtlinge - ein Menschenrecht. Erfahrungen, Grundlagen und Perspektiven* (pp. 45–55). Bielefeld: Bertelsmann.

Bundesamt für Migration und Flüchtlinge (BAMPF) (2016) *Das Bundesamt in Zahlen 2015. Asyl, Migration und Integration*. Nürnberg.

Bundesfachverband Unbegleitete minderjährige Flüchtlinge (2015) *Inobhutnahmen von unbegleiteten Minderjährigen im Jahr 2014*. Berlin.

Bundesministerium für Berufsbildung (2016) *Datenreport zum Berufsbildungsbericht 2015: Informationen und Analysen zur Entwicklung der beruflichen Bildung*. Bonn: BIBB Bundesministerium für Berufsbildung.

Bürgerschaft der Freien und Hansestadt Hamburg (2015a) *Gute Schule von Anfang an – Bildung für die nach Hamburg geflüchteten Kinder und Jugendlichen*. Hamburg. Drucksache 21/2193 vom 10.11.2015.

Bürgerschaft der Freien und Hansestadt Hamburg (2015b) *Bericht des Schulausschusses*. Hamburg. Drucksache 21/2663 vom 21.12.2015.

Crage, S.M. (2009) Ideological conflict and refugee aid policy development in Munich. *German Politics* 18 (1), 71–95.

Deutsches Institut für Wirtschaft Berlin (ed.) (2016) *DIW Wochenbericht: Vol. 35. Integration Geflüchteter*.

Diehl, C., Hunkler, C. and Kristen, C. (eds) (2016) *Ethnische Ungleichheiten im Bildungsverlauf: Mechanismen, Befunde, Debatten*. Wiesbaden: Springer VS.

Feagin, J.R. and Feagin, C.B. (1986) *Discrimination American Style: Institutional Racism and Sexism* (2nd augmented edn). Malabar, FL: R.E. Krieger Pub. Co. (Original work published 1978.)

Fereidooni, K. (2011) *Schule – Migration – Diskriminierung: Ursachen der Benachteiligung von Kindern mit Migrationshintergrund im deutschen Schulwesen*. Wiesbaden: VS Verlag für Sozialwissenschaften.

Fernando, C. and Ferrari, M. (eds) (2013) *Handbook of Resilience in Children of War*. New York: Springer.

Flitner, A. (1987) Gerechtigkeit als Problem der Schule. In A. Flitner (ed.) *Für das Leben – Oder für die Schule?* (pp. 15–44). Weinheim/Basel: Beltz.

Freie und Hansestadt Hamburg (2013) *Hamburger Integrationskonzept: Teilhabe, Interkulturelle Öffnung und Zusammenarbeit*. Hamburg: Behörde für Arbeit, Soziales, Familie und Integration.

Freie und Hansestadt Hamburg (2015) *Daten zur Zuwanderung*. See http://www.hamburg.de/fluechtlinge-daten-fakten/ (accessed 7 Jan 2018).

Gag, M. (2013) City report Hamburg. Vocational integration of refugees and asylum-seekers in Hamburg – roundabout routes from model to structure. In L.H. Seukwa (ed.) *Integration of Refugees into the European Education and Labour Market. Requirements for a Target Groups Oriented Approach* (pp. 143–193). Frankfurt am Main: Peter Lang Verlag.

Gag, M. (2015) Country report Germany – focus: Refugees and asylum seekers. In J. Schroeder, (ed.) *Breaking Down Barriers from Education to Employment. The Journey Towards Inclusion for Vulnerable Groups* (pp. 137–165). Sofia: Bulgarian Comparative Education Society.

Gag, M. and Schroeder, J. (2012) *Refugee Monitoring. Zur Situation junger Flüchtlinge im Hamburger Übergangssystem Schule/Beruf* [Berichterstattung]. Hamburg: Herausgegeben von der Passage gGmbH.

Gag, M. and Voges, F. (2014) *Inklusion auf Raten. Zur Teilhabe von Flüchtlingen an Ausbildung und Arbeit* (S. 15–28). Münster: Waxmann Verlag.

Gag, M. and Schroeder, J. (2015) Country report Germany – focus: Migrants with special needs. In J. Schroeder (ed.) *Breaking Down Barriers from Education to Employment. The Journey towards Inclusion for Vulnerable Groups* (pp. 167–202). Sofia: Bulgarian Comparative Education Society.

Gomolla, M. and Radtke, F.-O. (2009) *Institutionelle Diskriminierung* (3rd edn). Wiesbaden: VS Verlag für Sozialwissenschaften.

Hoeckel, K. and Schwarz, R. (2010) *Learning for Jobs: OECD Reviews of Vocational Education and Training Germany*. Paris: OECD Publishing.

Hormel, U. (2007) *Diskriminierung in der Einwanderungsgesellschaft: Begründungsprobleme pädagogischer Strategien und Konzepte*. Wiesbaden: VS Verlag für Sozialwissenschaften.

Hunkler, C. (2016) Ethnische Ungleichheiten beim Zugang zu beruflicher Ausbildung. In C. Diehl, C. Hunkler and C. Kristen (eds) *Ethnische Ungleichheiten im Bildungsverlauf. Mechanismen, Befunde, Debatten* (pp. 597–641). Wiesbaden: Springer.

Korntheuer, A. (2016) *Die Bildungsteilhabe junger Flüchtlinge. Faktoren von Inklusion und Exklusion in München und Toronto*. Bildung in Umbruchsgesellschaften Band 13. Münster: Waxmann.

Korntheuer, A., Korn, A. and Hynie, M. (in press) Education pathways: Policy implications for refugee youth in Germany and Canada. In S. Pashang, N. Khanlou and J. Clarke (eds) *Today's Youth and Mental Health: Hope, Power and Resilience*. New York: Springer.

Landesbetrieb Erziehung und Beratung (2015) *Unbegleitete, minderjährige Flüchtlinge. Inobhutnahme und Erstversorgung im Landesbetrieb Erziehung und Beratung*. Hamburg, Germany.

Meyer, F. (2014) *'Das ist für uns schon ein Experiment'. Erfahrungen von Ausbilderinnen und Ausbildern mit jungen Flüchtlingen in der dualen Ausbildung*. Hamburg: Passage gGmbH.

Müller, D., Nägele, B. and Petermann, F. (2014) *Jugendliche in unsicheren Aufenthaltsverhältnissen im Übergang Schule-Beruf*. Göttingen: Zoom Gesellschaft für prospektive Entwicklungen e.V.

Organization for Economic Cooperation and Development (2014) *Education at a Glance 2014: OECD Indicators*. Paris: OECD Publishing.

Paterson, B.L., Thorne, S.E., Canam, C. and Jillings, C. (2001) *Meta-Study of Qualitative Health Research: A Practical Guide to Meta-Analysis and Meta-Synthesis*. Thousand Oaks, CA: Sage.

Regierung von Oberbayern (2016) *Unterbringung von Asylbewerbern in Oberbayern. Stand 31.1.2016* (geändert 15.2.2016). Regierung von Oberbayern. Sachgebiet 14.1 Flüchtlingsunterbringung.

Secretariat of the Standing Conference of the Ministers of Education and Cultural Affairs of the Länder in the Federal Republic of Germany (2015) The education system in the federal republic of Germany 2013/2014. A description of the responsibilities, structures and developments in education policy for the exchange of information in Europe. Standing Conference of the Ministers of Education and Cultural Affairs, Bonn.

Seukwa, L.H. (2006) *Der Habitus der Überlebenskunst: Zum Verhältnis von Kompetenz und Migration im Spiegel von Flüchtlingsbiographien*. Münster: Waxmann.

Shakya, Y.B., Guruge, S., Hynie, M., Akbari, A., Malik, M., Htto, S. and Alley, S. (2010) Aspirations for higher education among newcomer refugee youth in Toronto: Expectations, challenges, and strategies. *Refuge* 27 (2), 65–78.

Timulak, L. (2009) Meta-analysis of qualitative studies: A tool for reviewing qualitative research findings in psychotherapy. *Psychotherapy Research* 19 (4–5), 591–600.

von Maurice, J. and Roßbach H.-G. (2017) The educational system in Germany. In A. Korntheuer, P. Pritchard and D. Maehler (eds) *Structural Context of Refugee Integration in Canada and Germany* (pp. 49–52). Cologne: GESIS Institute for the Social Sciences.

Yin, R.K. (2009) *Case Study Research: Design and Methods*. Los Angeles, CA: Sage.

13 Iraqi Refugee-background Adolescents' Experiences in Schools: Using the Ecological Theory of Development to Understand Discrimination

Amy Pucino

Islamophobia at the macro-level of public political discourse on refugee policy may influence interactions within micro-level environments, such as schools, leading to discrimination toward refugee newcomer students. Research is thus necessary to examine the ways that refugee youths experience, respond to and make meaning of discrimination in schools. The study presented in this chapter is framed by Bronfenbrenner's ecological theory of development and explores the experiences of discrimination felt by Muslim Iraqi refugee-background youths in US schools. Interviews with 17 youths (ages 14–20) in a mid-Atlantic metropolitan area reveal three main findings: (1) Most participants experienced discrimination in schools perpetrated by students and staff on the basis of language, faith or nationality. (2) Participant reactions to the discrimination ranged from passive (ignoring the discrimination) to active (confronting or seeking to educate) approaches. (3) Decisions of whether and how to respond to discrimination were related to participants' personal characteristics (shyness, perceived English language ability) or context (fear of personal safety, fear of punishment). Implications include ways in which schools can become safer spaces for newcomers.

The United States has been a leading country in refugee resettlement, resettling over 3 million refugees since 1975 (Igielnik & Krogstad, 2017). In fact, the United States raised the cap for annual refugee admissions from 70,000 in 2015 to 85,000 for 2016 (Zong & Batalova, 2015). However, at the time this chapter was written, an executive order had put a 90-day ban on migrants from seven largely Muslim countries – a list that initially included Iraq. The order also instated a 120-day ban on all refugee admission, and capped refugee annual admission at 50,000 (Executive Order No. 13769, 2017). The legality of the executive order is currently under review, and the ban has been temporarily lifted. Therefore, refugee policy, particularly for Muslim and/or Middle Eastern refugees, is currently tenuous. Yet, this debate is happening when an estimated 65.3 million people are forcibly displaced as refugees, asylees and internally displaced persons across the world (United Nations High Commissioner for Refugees [UNHCR], 2015); conflicts in the Middle East and Africa in particular have left people without sanctuary (Igielnik & Krogstad, 2017).

This is not the only time that the United States has sought to tighten security on Middle Eastern refugee admissions. The September 11, 2001 attacks motivated increased security standards, resulting in fewer refugees entering from the Middle East (Gibney, 2010; Haines, 2007). After mounting criticism from the global community, particularly after declaring war in Iraq in 2003, the United States began to take an increased responsibility for Iraqi refugee resettlement (Applebaum, 2010). In fact, Iraqi refugees were the largest group of refugees resettled in the United States between 2009 and 2014, totaling 98,000 (US Department of Health and Human Services, 2016). Moreover, since 2002, 32% of all refugees resettled have been Muslim, and in 2016 alone, 46% of new arrivals were Muslim (Conner, 2016), showing a notable growth in this demographic.

Many Muslim and/or Middle Eastern refugees face institutional and individual discrimination during resettlement in the United States (Byng, 2008; Esposito & Kalin, 2011; Wadud, 2011). Particularly since September 11, 2001, public political discourse and policy have been marked by Islamophobia and xenophobia (Nimer, 2011). Recently, with the rise of the Islamic State, media coverage of Islam has become less favorable (Kolmer & Schatz, 2015). Such representation, combined with unfriendly policies toward refugees and immigrants, can lead to anti-Muslim and anti-immigrant sentiment (Esposito & Kalin, 2011). In fact, favorable public sentiment toward Islam has declined over time, and Americans' attitudes toward Islam are more negative than those toward other religions (Pew Research Center, 2010, 2014). Prejudicial views have played out in acts of discrimination as well; the FBI reported that assaults and intimidation crimes on Muslims rose in 2015 (Kishi, 2016).

Research from the Council of American and Islamic Relations (CAIR) shows that Middle Eastern and Muslim youths, moreover, report experiencing discrimination in US schools, which may negatively impact their academic achievement and well-being (CAIR, 2014; McBrien, 2009). Notably, after globally publicized acts of terrorism, former US Secretaries of Education wrote a 'Dear Colleague' letter to school personnel:

We support your efforts to ensure that young people are not subjected to discrimination or harassment based on race, religion, or national origin, particularly at this time when fear and anger are heightened, and when public debate sometimes results in the dissemination of misinformation. (Duncan & King, 2015)

They also stated that the discrimination faced in schools may negatively impact student learning and well-being, showing their awareness of the relationship between macro-level discourse and the youth's experience of discrimination in schools. As US refugee policy shifts, and public debate continues, research is needed that explores the relationship of such discourse with the incidence of discrimination in schools.

The study presented in this chapter has several goals: (1) to document the experiences of discrimination felt by Iraqi refugee-background adolescents (ages 14–20) in a mid-Atlantic metropolitan area from interviews with youths; (2) to highlight how participants respond to discrimination within the microsystem of school interactions; (3) to consider the question of how such interactions may relate to the macrosystem of overall Islamophobic and xenophobic discourse; and (4) to suggest implications for creating an ecological environment that does not stigmatize refugee-background youth.

Literature Review

Research has documented that many immigrant and refugee-background students experience discrimination from teachers and the school as an institution, presenting a major obstacle to adapting to the United States (Brown, 2015; Portes & Rumbaut, 2001). For example, teachers may insult, exclude or misrepresent students or their families (McBrien, 2005, 2011). Furthermore, schools and teachers may perpetuate a deficit ideology by looking at youths' language and cultural differences as barriers to success rather than strengths (Crumpler *et al.*, 2011; Shapiro, 2014), which lowers teacher expectations (Ford & Grantham, 2003). Moreover, even well-intentioned educators may subtly discriminate. For example, Rah *et al.* (2009) problematized the use of 'helping' discourse among educators working with refugees, as this discourse positions refugees as being in need of charity rather than focusing on their agency.

Many (im)migrant youths face harassment from peers on the basis of their religion and language ability (Brown, 2015). Previous research with a focus on Middle Eastern, Arab-American or Muslim refugee-background individuals has looked at several dimensions of discrimination. Somali and Iranian mothers in McBrien's (2011) study reported that their children experienced discrimination at school related to language and race. Religion is also a focal point of discrimination: McBrien's (2009) study of adolescent (ages 12–19) refugee-background girls in the United States found that many Muslim students were ridiculed for wearing the hijab (headscarf), which sometimes led them to avoid school. In another notable study, Tabbah *et al.* (2012) found that more than half the students surveyed had faced discrimination or witnessed discrimination, with reports of being called 'terrorist' or having head coverings pulled off. Discrimination was negatively related to school competence, defined as students' perceptions of their intelligence and academic performance.

Discriminatory experiences have problematic educational effects. As noted previously, discrimination is associated with lower academic outcomes and motivation (Benner & Graham, 2011; Tabbah *et al.*, 2012), and higher levels of anxiety, depression and feelings of isolation in school (e.g. Ellis *et al.*, 2010; United Nations High Commissioner for Refugees, 2009). Moreover, discrimination unfairly places those experiencing discrimination in the position of having to decide whether and how to respond, which can absorb energy that might otherwise be invested in pursuing academic and social goals.

Immigrant students may exhibit a range of behaviors in response to discrimination, from a more passive withdrawal to active measures, such as seeking social support or confronting the perpetrator (Brown, 2015). Active rather than passive responses to discrimination tend to reduce stress and empower individuals (Swim & Thomas, 2006); such empowerment is better facilitated by safe, supportive school environments and strong ethnic identity on the part of youths (Brown, 2015). However, not all students feel safe responding to discrimination. A study carried out by CAIR (2014) of 621 American Muslim students (ages 11–18) found that students sometimes avoided reporting discrimination because they thought that school personnel would not believe them; they perceived the situation would worsen; they were afraid or embarrassed to talk about the issue; or they were reluctant, because the discrimination was presented in a joking tone.

As shown, previous literature offers insights into the experience and consequences of discrimination with a range of immigrant and refugee-background youths. The current qualitative study seeks to understand how Iraqi refugee-background youths, in particular, experience and respond to discrimination in the school environment and how this experience relates to the political and public discourse around Muslim refugees.

Theoretical Framework

The theory used to frame this research is Bronfenbrenner's (1979, 1986, 1994) ecological theory of development, which emphasizes the importance of interactions within ecological environments such as the home, school and broader society for development across the life course. The theory has two main propositions. First, development occurs through the *proximal process* (Bronfenbrenner, 1995), which is defined as ongoing and increasingly complex reciprocal relationships between the developing person and other people and things. Second, the impact of the proximal process depends on both the *characteristics* of the developing person as well as the *environment*.

The environment is made up of various systems (Bronfenbrenner, 1979, 1986, 1994). Those most relevant to this research are the *microsystem*, which is the immediate environment of the family or school, and the *macrosystem*, which comprises the larger patterns of society, including societal belief systems and opportunity structures. For refugee-background students, interactions within the microsystem of the school are shaped by the macrosystem of the social, cultural and political context (Hamilton & Moore, 2004) as well as the historical context.

Bronfenbrenner's theory has been used to frame the discussion of refugee adaptation in previous work, such as Hamilton and Moore's (2004) edited book, *Educational Interventions for Refugee Children: Theoretical Perspectives and Implementing Best Practice*, which describes how experiences at various stages of the migration process impact refugee-background students' development in their resettlement country. Additionally, McBrien's (2009) research on how refugee adolescent girls' encounters in US schools impact school motivation used Bronfenbrenner's model to understand the individual and environmental factors contributing to the girls' agency. In this chapter, Bronfenbrenner's theory is used to ground a discussion of Iraqi refugee-background youths' experiences of and responses to discrimination in the microsystem of school and its relationship to misinformation, xenophobia and Islamophobia, characteristic of the post-9/11 macrosystem. This theory, therefore, sheds light on the way that macro-level discourse may negatively impact the daily lives of Muslim refugee-background youths within the microsystem of the school.

Research Methods

I conducted in-depth, semi-structured, one-hour long interviews with 17 youths, ages 14–20. Participants had been resettled in a mid-Atlantic metropolitan area between 2008 and 2011. I used snowball sampling to find participants – an approach useful for researching small populations who may be marginalized or difficult to access, with 'multiple eligibility requirements' (Sadler *et al.*, 2010: 370). The eligibility requirements included Iraqi refugee background, adolescent age group and recent or current enrollment at a public high school. This study was approved by the institutional review board, and all participants (or their legal guardians) provided written consent to be interviewed.

The 17 participants represented about 20% of the population of Iraqi refugee-background students between the ages of 14 and 20 in the city.

The participant demographic information is shown in Table 13.1. To ensure confidentiality, the students chose pseudonyms, and pseudonyms were also used for their high schools. All participants had lived in the United States for three to five years at the time of the interview, and most were over the age of 17 (13) and male (11). All participants were Muslim. About half of the sample had graduated from high school in the previous year, and two were attending colleges.

Five high schools are represented in this study, with two city and two county schools in the same metropolitan area where participants were resettled. While a detailed analysis of these schools is beyond the scope of this chapter, it is useful to offer some background to set the stage as part of the participants' ecological environment. All of the high schools had relatively high (>50%) numbers of students eligible for free and reduced-priced meals (FARM), except for Adams School, which had 20% FARM eligibility. Not only were the majority of these schools populated by low-income students, but they also had lower standardized assessment scores and offered fewer advanced placement (AP) courses than the average for the state.

The constant comparative method (Glasser & Strauss, 1967; Roulston, 2010) was used to analyze the data. 'Open coding' (Neuman, 2003) was used during the initial read; then 'selective coding' was used to assess and revise codes. Codes were compared to ensure consistency, and then placed into categories such as 'responses to discrimination', which included codes for 'active' and 'passive' approaches. Interactions within the 'microsystem' and evidence of the impact of the 'macrosystem' were also coded.

Table 13.1 Interview participant characteristics

Name	Sex	Age	US arrival year	Educational attainment	School
Akram	Male	18	2010	H.S. graduate	Jackson
Ashley	Female	17	2009	H.S. graduate	Emerson
Chis	Male	19	2009	H.S. graduate	Madison
Dena	Female	17	2010	11th grade	Lincoln
Eric	Male	17	2010	12th grade	Emerson
Hussain	Male	14	2010	9th grade	Lincoln
Iraq	Male	17	2010	11th grade	Lincoln
Linda	Female	20	2009	College	Emerson
Mike	Male	17	2008	12th grade	Emerson
Mimi	Female	19	2010	H.S. graduate	Jackson
Reg	Male	17	2010	11th grade	Lincoln
Ronaldo	Male	20	2010	College	Lincoln
Shann	Male	16	2009	11th grade	Lincoln
Sara	Female	19	2010	H.S. graduate	Madison
Ted	Male	15	2008	10th grade	Adams
Warda	Female	17	2010	H.S. graduate	Madison
Zozo	Male	16	2010	11th grade	Madison

Reflexivity and positionality were important considerations in this research. Prior to this study, I had volunteered with an Iraqi refugee-background family for three years, beginning in 2009, visiting their home once per week to tutor the children. My previous involvement in the community meant that I needed to shift my role for this project from tutor and advocate to researcher. As an outsider, White, middle-class woman, I discussed this shift explicitly with the families that I had worked with, and also conveyed my desire not to 'other' the community.

Findings and Discussion

While not all of the participants felt that they had experienced discrimination, 12 of the 17 interviewees shared incidences of mistreatment by non-refugee students or school personnel. Participants had various reactions, including acquiescing to, ignoring, confronting or educating the perpetrator. In this section, I describe the findings in connection with the ecological theory of development.

Experiences of discrimination among Iraqi youths

Participants experienced mistreatment mostly from peers, but on occasion from school staff as well. Discrimination was directed at the participants' language, religion or Iraqi nationality, often through the perpetrators' misguided association of that nationality with September 11. These characteristics of language, faith and nationality can either be valued or devalued within the microsystem. When these characteristics are devalued, they reinforce a stigmatized status for students. Thus, respondents who experienced discrimination often linked that discrimination to a sense of stigmatization within the microsystem of school.

Participants described that elements of their culture, including language and faith, were often a focus of discrimination. For example, Iraq (age 17, pseudonym chosen by the student) described, 'Some people try to mess with my language. Like when I speak with an Arabic guy from my country, like trying to copy what I am saying'. Not only was the usage of Arabic mocked, but attempts to speak English were also a focal point of discrimination. Akram (age 18) described that he was afraid to speak English because people would 'bully' or 'laugh' at him. Dena (age 17) and Mimi (age 19) also mentioned that they felt that other students were 'mean' to them when they arrived in the United States because they could not speak English well. Therefore, participants' language minority status became stigmatized within the microsystem of the school, echoing the stigmatization from media and other sources of misinformation within the macrosystem.

In contrast, Mimi mostly described discrimination directed at her religion. She explained that when she first arrived in the United States, she was young and not yet wearing a headscarf. However, when she made the religious decision to begin wearing it, she noticed a difference in how she was treated, explaining that students would 'turn their face' or 'talk to each other' about her. More problematically, Mimi described that a staff person at the school asked her to remove her head covering, which is illegal: 'A man told me "You can't wear it" and to take it off. And I wasn't speak that good English, and I was crying. But I took it off'. After that incident, Mimi did not wear a headscarf for a while, because she was afraid of punishment. Effectively, she learned that the environment of the school proved to be an unsafe space for the public display of her faith.

Iraqi nationality was also a focal point of discrimination. Ashley (age 17) reported that once other students learned that she was from Iraq, they would ignore or avoid her:

> Like some of the people when I am talking to them, when I say to them like I am from Iraq and stuff like that, they are just saying, 'Oh my God! You're from Iraq? Oh my God' and they just walking away from me. They really mean with me.

Eric (age 17) also described that people discriminated based on his Iraqi nationality. He mentioned that on a few occasions, he had gotten into physical fights because US-born students 'treat [Iraqis] differently than they treat other students'. He felt the fights were caused by 'racism'. Reg (age 17), Shann (16), Chris (19) and Ronaldo (20) had all been called 'terrorist' or 'Osama bin Laden'. Reg said that after he told people where he was from, 'they say, "Go back to your country, Osama bin Laden"'. Shann also described a troublesome experience, which took place on the anniversary of September 11:

> My worst one was 9/11. That was my worst day. Every 9/11 people will look at me and ask if I have a bomb with me. I just smile because it's just so stupid. It is not me. We were here after it [September 11]. I mean and how many people die in it? A lot right, but one bomb in Iraq kill more people, and nobody think about that. There it happened every day and here it happened once. I am not saying it's the right thing.

Notably, Shann explained that this type of discrimination took place each September 11, suggesting continued experiences of discrimination. In fact, he described that on September 11 each year, he was reluctant to go to school.

The targeting of Iraqi nationality after September 11 shows that the interactions within the microsystem are impacted by the macrosystem. The participants' reports of discrimination are consistent with other research that suggests that refugee-background persons from the Middle East overall have faced increased prejudice and discrimination since 9/11 (e.g. Byng, 2008; Tabbah *et al.*, 2012). These participant responses suggest that the macrosystem of Islamophobia and xenophobia purported by the media post-9/11 have potentially impacted the microsystems, encouraging discrimination and stigmatization of Iraqi youths in schools. Hence, the theory helps to contextualize experiences described by the respondents as 'bullying' or 'meanness' within the larger ecosystem.

Reactions to discrimination

Problematically, discriminatory behavior forces those experiencing the discrimination to make difficult decisions about whether and how to respond. Here, the responses of participants to discrimination are explained in connection with the ecological theory. As mentioned, participant responses ranged from passive to active approaches. Whether or not participants responded actively was complicated by individual or contextual factors within the *proximal process* of the ecological system. For example, the students' sense of their English language ability (individual factor) or sense of safety within the context of school (contextual factor) impacted their response to the discrimination.

Ashley, Mimi, Dena and Hussain (age 14) described passive responses to mistreatment. Ashley expressed discomfort and confusion, explaining that she didn't know what to do when people would ignore her because of her nationality. Mimi also struggled with this: as described above, though she did not want to do so, she acquiesced by removing her head covering when she was asked by school staff because she was afraid of punishment. She had mentioned that she was 'shy' and had difficulty expressing feelings in English, and said that the discrimination made her 'afraid' and 'embarrassed'. Dena explained that students were 'mean' to her because she initially did not speak English. The experience made her cry and feel limited in her ability to respond otherwise. However, as she began to learn English, she felt better able to speak up for herself.

Hussain sometimes used a passive approach and other times a more active one. When he was asked if he experienced discrimination often, he responded:

> Not really, because I was friendly. People may say things that they misunderstand because they don't know; they may think you are from Afghanistan like Osama bin Ladin. I just ignore them or tell them the truth. Not everybody is like that. Sometimes I ignore them, sometimes talk to them... They talk about my country, and how bad it was. Most

of the time I ignore them, but if they talk bad about my family, I can't ignore them.

Here, Hussain makes the decision on whether to inform people that Osama bin Laden was not from Iraq or simply to ignore them. He also decides whether to respond based on how important the issue is to him, his family being the most important factor. Also notable is that he initially mentions being friendly as a means of avoiding discrimination. This suggests that while some groups might experience societal privilege and therefore avoid discrimination without having to be friendly, others may learn that, within the proximal process of daily interactions with peers, coming across as friendly helps to avoid ongoing experiences of discrimination.

Chris actively responded to discrimination but mentioned thinking that the interaction was funny. After Osama bin Laden was captured and killed, Chris was told, 'We caught your leader'. In response, he would say, 'I don't care; he [Osama bin Laden] doesn't represent me'. Like Hussain, Chris wanted to explain to his peers the difference between himself and bin Laden. When asked if this interaction bothered him, Chris said 'It didn't bother me that much. And they weren't serious. They were just joking... I thought it was funny, because I knew they were so ignorant'. Though I did not probe much further about the meaning behind his belief that the scenario was funny nor about his labeling the comment as a joke, it is worth noting that humor is sometimes used to mitigate or soften a negative situation. Belief that discriminatory comments are meant in gest is, as was referenced earlier, one reason many students do not report mistreatment (CAIR, 2014).

Linda also laughed in response to comments made by her peers, and she explained that she tried not to be 'mean' when confronting other students. In response to a peer thinking that she could 'make a bomb' because she was from Iraq, Linda, who stopped short of describing the comment as a form of discrimination, reacted:

> I started laughing and said 'If you don't know how [to make a bomb], I don't know how. Really, you think I know how to make bombs?' Maybe she really did think I could make one [a bomb]. I didn't think of it as discrimination because a lot of people have just the wrong idea so you have to correct them... I try not to be mean with them because if you want to be mean with them, you are just showing them that you're worst than them. So if they are just asking me, then I just answer rather than being silent or avoiding them.

Linda presented as confident in her response and ultimate choice to educate her peer rather than being silent. She did not seem distressed by this situation; however, like Hussain, who prioritized being 'friendly', she seemed to prioritize not presenting as worse than her peers, making an effort not to be 'mean'.

Shann also responded to his peers actively by educating them. When peers would ask, 'Why don't you go back to your country?' Shann educated them about the forced migration he experienced, explaining: 'I would go back if you all [the United States] leave our country [Iraq]. I mean it wasn't a choice. I always tell them if I had a choice I wouldn't leave [Iraq]'. Reg also described that when peers would say 'You terrorist, go back to Iraq' or 'Go back to your country, Osama bin Laden', he would tell them:

> Not everybody is the same in every way. So when I came here, there was a lot of black people in my class, so I told them that a lot of people told me that black people are dangerous and gangsters but when I came here, I found it differently. Not everybody is the same.

Here, Reg explained that judging all Iraqis as terrorists was unfair and similar to stereotyping all Black people as dangerous. Ronaldo, similarly, tried to help his peers empathize with being wrongly accused of something. When another student called him a 'terrorist', he told the student:

> Hold on a second. Like the [US] army, when they came to Iraq, and killed my uncle and killed my best friend. And they killed this and that person. Were you included in that? ... No, you don't have anything to do with that. I was like, 'me too'.

However, Ronaldo explained that he would only speak up if a teacher was in the room. He described, 'Sometimes it [discrimination] happens in the cafeteria and then the teachers aren't there and I just cannot go there and like talk to them [the students]'. This scenario shows that whether or not he was able to speak up was influenced by his sense of safety within the context. The proximal process of the respondents' ongoing relationships with teachers and students within particular contexts within the school microsystem communicated to students whether or not they were safe enough to challenge the discrimination.

During interviews with participants who chose to actively respond to discrimination, one theme that continued to arise was that discrimination might come from a place of ignorance or being misinformed. Participants recognized that the students who discriminated were not just being 'mean' or 'bullying', but had in fact absorbed the prejudicial ideologies of the macrosystem disseminated by the media. Seven of the respondents mentioned that American students received inaccurate and negative information about Iraq from the media and other institutions. As Shann described:

I think the way Americans picture the world is on TV and they are the best and everyone else don't have nothing. They live in the desert. It makes me sad because in my country, we study about America and the whole world, but here, they only study themselves.

Notably, Shann perceives that students in the United States are not taught to be aware of the rest of the world. This shows his sense that there are different standards applied to people from Iraq versus people from the United States, and this contrast upsets him. Ashley echoed this point; when asked why discrimination occurs, she said, 'The things they hear about Iraq... But um if they go to Iraq and see then they may know better things than how they are here'. Ashley explained that she would try to tell peers about the positive things about Iraq; however, she said, 'they [students] don't believe me. They just say, "we see and hear it different than you see it"'. Such recognition of their peers' misinformation revealed that participants were aware of the influence of macro-level messaging presented through institutions like the media on the belief systems of their peers. Particularly noteworthy was that respondents who recognized this felt more agency to confront the discriminator.

Implications and Conclusion

In summary, this research has made methodological and theoretical contributions by conducting qualitative interviews with Iraqi refugee-background youths about their experiences of discrimination, using Bronfenbrenner's ecological theory of development to highlight how those experiences, and students' responses, are informed by macro-level factors. This study showcases several key findings about the discrimination experienced by Iraqi refugee-background youths. First is that discrimination is prevalent, and is perpetrated mainly by peers, but in some cases by school staff as well. Discrimination was directed at participants' language, faith or nationality, a finding consistent with previous research on Muslim youths (e.g. CAIR, 2014; McBrien, 2009; Tabbah *et al.*, 2012). Participants described that misinformation from the media – a macro-level factor – influenced their peers' prejudicial beliefs and actions.

In responding to the discrimination, participants used a variety of approaches including passive techniques, such as ignoring the discrimination, and active approaches, such as confronting or educating the perpetrator. Participants' active approaches add to the body of literature showing the resilience and agency of refugees from other regions (e.g. Bash & Zezlina-Phillips, 2006; Montgomery, 2010). Additionally, active responses have shown to be sources of empowerment and stress reduction

(Swim & Thomas, 2006), helping students navigate the complexities of the microsystem of the school environment.

However, this study shows that participants did not always feel that active responses would reduce stress; in fact, findings reveal the complexity involved in maneuvering discriminatory interactions. Participants' personal characteristics such as feeling shy, embarrassed or unable to fully communicate in English made them feel unable or unsure of how to respond. Elements of the context, such as fear for their personal safety or fear of punishment, also shaped students' responses. These findings are again consistent with other research (CAIR, 2014). Furthermore, two youths alluded to their belief in the importance of being friendly, avoiding meanness, essentially managing their impression to prevent or mitigate discrimination. Within the ecological development theory's proximal process, the characteristics of the individual influence development. These characteristics of friendliness and impression management, therefore, may have also played a role in how respondents engaged in the microsystem. Such characteristics may not have been necessary if not for the influence of the xenophobia and Islamophobia of the public, political discourse.

This study reveals key principles, grounded in the ecological theory of development (Bronfenbrenner, 1979, 1986, 1994), which inform implications. First, this study suggests that the macrosystem of societal belief systems, including Islamophobia and xenophobia, influenced by a post-September 11 society, can lead to prejudicial viewpoints and discrimination within the microsystem of the classroom. While this research shows that refugee-background youths experienced some agency in maneuvering challenging situations, it also suggests the failure of their context to fully protect them from discrimination. Putting the onus to correct discrimination on the young Iraqi refugee-background English language learner who is experiencing the discrimination is unfair, given that students whose language, faith or nationality is *not* stigmatized are free from such responsibility, and thus able to engage more fully in school.

There are three main implications of this research. First, school systems in refugee resettlement communities should ensure that personnel are trained to prevent, recognize and respond to discrimination in schools, in order to better create safe spaces for students. Also, since strong family and community support can shield against the negative impact of discrimination (e.g. Greene *et al.*, 2006; McBrien, 2009), efforts should be made to include and support refugee-background families and communities in school programs. These efforts might show refugee-background youths and families their value to the school, and could help communicate this value to the larger community, lessening stigma. Such efforts in the microsystem could offer a counterpoint to the macro-level discourse. Finally, this research shows agency among former refugees, and therefore suggests that refugee-background students and their families should be involved in making school-based changes. For example, refugee-background youths could educate school personnel on how to create safer environments. Additionally, participants had clever ideas of how to educate their peers about Islam, the Middle East and the implications of US foreign policies; this knowledge base should therefore be recognized and utilized in the classroom. Participants also mentioned their peers' getting false perceptions from the media, which suggests that creating a curriculum focused on media critique would be an important element in addressing problems of discrimination. In this way, the curriculum might help students understand how broader public discourse and ideologies (macrosystem) make their way into the school setting (microsystem).

A limitation of this study was its single data source. The study would have benefitted from classroom observations and other types of data collection to triangulate findings and expand my understanding of the microsystem of the classroom. Also, future research could explore how school and community characteristics impact student experiences of discrimination. Exploring the impact of other parts of the ecological system might also be beneficial: researchers might, for example, examine the *mesosystem*, which includes the relationships between elements of the microsystem (e.g. school, home and neighborhood); they might also consider the *chronosystem*, which includes the impact of time or transitions in life. Through additional research, as well as adaptations to school programming and training, educational researchers and policymakers must commit to ensuring that schools are not environments where refugee-background individuals' languages, religions or nationalities are stigmatized. Unless the ecological environment of the school is adapted to limit stigmatization, young people who come to the United States to seek safety, bringing with them their strengths and agency, will continue to find themselves discriminated against in schools.

References

Applebaum, A. (2010) The Iraqi refugee crisis: Examining the admission of Iraqi refugees into the United States since 2003. *The Roosevelt Review* 4 (1), 7–27.

Bash, L. and Zezlina-Phillips, E. (2006) Identity, boundary and schooling: Perspectives on the experiences and perceptions of refugee children. *Intercultural Education* 17 (1), 113–128.

Benner, A. and Graham, S. (2011) Latino adolescents' experiences of discrimination across the first two years of high school: Correlates and influences on educational outcomes. *Child Development* 82 (2), 508–519.

Bronfenbrenner, U. (1979) *The Ecology of Human Development: Experiments by Nature and Design*. Cambridge, MA: Harvard University Press.

Bronfenbrenner, U. (1986) Ecology of the family as a context for human development: Research perspectives. *Developmental Psychology* 22 (6), 723–742.
Bronfenbrenner, U. (1994) Ecological models of human development. In T. Husen and T.N. Postlethwaite (eds) *International Encyclopedia of Education* (Vol. 3; 2nd edn; pp. 1643–1647). Oxford: Elsevier.
Bronfenbrenner, U. (1995) Developmental ecology through space and time: A future perspective. In P. Moen, G. Elder Jr. and K. Lüscher (eds) *Examining Lives in Context: Perspectives on the Ecology of Human Development* (pp. 619–647). Washington, DC: American Psychological Association.
Brown, C.S. (2015) *The Educational, Psychological, and Social Impact of Discrimination on the Immigrant Child*. Washington, DC: Migration Policy Institute.
Byng, M.D. (2008) Complex inequalities: The case of Muslim Americans after 9/11. *American Behavioral Scientist* 51 (5), 659–674.
Conner, P. (2016) U.S. admits record number of Muslim refugees in 2016. Fact Tank News in the Numbers. Washington, DC: Pew Research Center. See http://www.pewresearch.org/fact-tank/2016/10/05/u-s-admits-record-number-of-muslim-refugees-in-2016/ (accessed 11 January 2018).
Council of American and Islamic Relations (2014) Mislabeled: The impact of school bullying and discrimination on California Muslim students. Santa Clara, CA. See https://ca.cair.com/sfba/wp-content/uploads/2015/10/CAIR-CA-2015-Bullying-Report-Web.pdf (accessed 11 January 2018).
Crumpler, T.P., Handsfield, L.J. and Dean, T.R. (2011) Constructing difference differently in language and literacy professional development. *Research in the Teaching of English* 46, 55–91.
Duncan, A. and King, J. (2015, Dec. 31) Dear colleague letter. US Department of Education, Office for Civil Rights, Washington, DC.
Ellis, H., MacDonald, H., Klunk-Gillis, J., Lincoln, A., Strunin, L. and Cabral, H. (2010) Discrimination and mental health among Somali refugee adolescents: The role of acculturation and gender. *American Journal of Orthopsychiatry* 80 (4), 564–575.
Esposito, J. and Kalin, I. (2011) *Islamophobia: The Challenge of Pluralism in the 21st Century*. New York: Oxford University Press.
Executive Order No. 13769, 82 C.F.R. 8977 (2017).
Ford, D.Y. and Grantham, T.C. (2003) Providing access for culturally diverse gifted students: From deficit to dynamic thinking. *Theory into Practice* 42 (3), 217–225.
Glasser, B.G. and Strauss, A.L. (1967) *The Discovery of Grounded Theory: Strategies for Qualitative Research*. Chicago, IL: Aldine Publishing Company.
Greene, M., Way, N. and Pahl, K. (2006) Trajectories of perceived adult and peer discrimination among Black, Latino, and Asian American adolescents: Patterns and psychological correlates. *Developmental Psychology* 42 (2), 218–236.
Gibney, M. (2010) *Global Refugee Crisis: A Reference Book* (2nd edn). Santa Barbara, CA: ABC CLIO.
Haines, D. (2007) Refugees. In M.C. Waters and R. Ueda (eds) *The New Americans: A Guide to Immigration Since 1965* (pp. 56–69). Cambridge, MA: Harvard University Press.
Hamilton, R. and Moore, D. (eds) (2004) *Educational Interventions for Refugee Children: Theoretical Perspectives and Implementing Best Practice*. New York: RoutledgeFalmer.
Igielnik, R. and Krogstad, J.M. (2017) Where refugees to the U.S. come from. Washington, DC: Pew Research Center. See http://www.pewresearch.org/fact-tank/2017/02/03/where-refugees-to-the-u-s-come-from/ (accessed 11 January 2018).
Kishi, K. (2016) Anti-Muslim assaults reach 9/11-era levels, FBI data show. Fact Tank News in the Numbers. Washington, DC: Pew Research Center. See http://www.pewresearch.

org/fact-tank/2016/11/21/anti-muslim-assaults-reach-911-era-levels-fbi-data-show/ (accessed 11 January 2018).

Kolmer, C. and Schatz, R. (2015) Annual Dialogue Report on Religion and Values. New York: Media Tenor. See https://www.mediatenor.cz/wp-content/uploads/2015/02/ADR_2015_LR_WEB_PREVIEW.pdf (accessed 11 January 2018).

McBrien, J.L. (2005) Educational needs and barriers for refugee students in the United States: A review of the literature. *Review of Educational Research* 75, 329–364.

McBrien, J.L. (2009) Beyond survival: School-related experiences of adolescent refugee girls and their relationship to motivation and academic success. In G. Wiggan and C. Hutchinson (eds) *Global Issues in Education: Pedagogy, Policy, School Practices and the Minority Experience* (pp. 294–330). Plymouth: Rowman & Littlefield.

McBrien, J.L. (2011) The importance of context: Vietnamese, Somali, and Iranian refugee mothers discuss their resettled lives and involvement in their children's education. *Compare* 41 (1), 75–90.

Montgomery, E. (2010) Trauma and resilience in young refugees: A 9-year follow-up study. *Development and Psychopathology* 22 (2), 477–489.

Neuman, W.L. (2003) *Social Research Methods: Qualitative and Quantitative Approaches* (5th edn). Boston, MA: Allyn and Bacon.

Nimer, M. (2011) Islamophobia and anti-Americanism: Measurements, dynamics and consequences. In J. Esposito and I. Kalin (eds) *Islamophobia: The Challenges of Pluralism in the 21st Century* (pp. 77–92). Oxford: Oxford University Press.

Pew Research Center (2010) Public remains conflicted over Islam. Washington, DC: Pew Research Center. See http://www.pewforum.org/2010/08/24/public-remains-conflicted-over-islam/ (accessed 11 January 2018).

Pew Research Center (2014) How Americans feel about religious groups. Washington, DC: Pew Research Center. See http://www.pewforum.org/2014/07/16/how-americans-feel-about-religious-groups/ (accessed 11 January 2018).

Portes, A. and Rumbaut, R.G. (2001) *Legacies: The Story of the Immigrant Second Generation*. Berkeley, CA: University of California Press.

Rah, Y., Choi, S. and Nguyen, T.S. (2009) Building bridges between refugee parents and schools. *International Journal of Leadership in Education* 12 (4), 347–365.

Roulston, K. (2010) *Reflective Interviewing: A Guide to Theory and Practice*. London: Sage.

Sadler, G., Lee, H., Lim, R. and Fullerton, J. (2010) Recruitment of hard-to-reach population subgroups via adaptations of the snowball sampling strategy. *Nursing and Health Science* 12 (3), 369–374.

Shapiro, S. (2014) 'Words that you said got bigger': English language learners' lived experiences of deficit discourse. *Research in the Teaching of English* 48 (4), 386–406.

Swim, J. and Thomas, M. (2006) Responding to everyday discrimination: A synthesis of research on goal-directed, self-regulatory coping behaviors. In S. Levin and C. van Laar (eds) *Stigma and Group Inequality: Social Psychological Perspectives* (pp. 105–128). Mahwah, NJ: Lawrence Erlbaum Associates.

Tabbah, R., Miranda, A.H. and Wheaton, J.E. (2012) Self-concept in Arab American adolescents: Implications of social support and experiences in the schools. *Psychology in the Schools* 49 (9), 817–827.

United Nations High Commissioner for Refugees (2009) UNHCR annual report shows 42 million people uprooted worldwide [press release]. See http://www.unhcr.org/4a2fd52412d.html (accessed 11 January 2018).

United Nations High Commissioner for Refugees (2015) Global trends: Forced displacement in 2015. See http://www.unhcr.org/576408cd7.pdf (accessed 11 January 2018).

US Department of Health and Human Services (2016) Office of Refugee Resettlement Annual Report to Congress, FY 2014. See https://www.acf.hhs.gov/sites/default/files/orr/orr_annual_report_to_congress_fy_2014_signed.pdf (accessed 11 January 2018).

Wadud, A. (2011) American by force, Muslim by choice. *Political Theology* 12 (5), 699–705.

Zong, J. and Batalova, J. (2015) *Refugees and asylees in the United States*. Washington, DC: Migration Policy Institute. See https://www.migrationpolicy.org/article/refugees-and-asylees-united-states-4 (accessed 11 January 2018).

14 Besides a Degree, What Do Refugee-background Students Gain from College?

Eliana Hirano

When refugee-background students come to college, they have often been through life experiences, including forced migration, that distinguish them from their peers. Because pursuing higher education often represents a challenge for this population, it is important to understand what practices in college may help them to achieve their personal goals. Using the concept of communities of practice as a heuristic (Lea, 2005), this chapter analyzes the experience of six refugee-background students, investigating their self-reported growth and accomplishments in college against the backdrop of their membership in various communities. Data collection included monthly interviews in the first year of college and an exit interview in the semester before graduation. Data analysis followed qualitative methods and was recursive and inductive. Findings indicate that these students felt particularly legitimized in communities of practice that were not part of their core academic requirements. Participation in these non-academic communities supported the construction of positive identities and the development of a sense of belonging and legitimacy, thus contributing to student persistence. This study has implications for mentors and advisors who work with refugee-background students in college.

Refugee-background students often face challenges in completing higher education, as a result of their life experiences, including forced migration and the resettlement process. It is important, therefore, to understand what practices may contribute to their persistence and success in college (Keddie, 2012). They also tend to come to college having had less academic preparation, for reasons such as interrupted or poor quality education, challenges with transition across languages and school systems and sometimes traumatic experiences that interfere with academic development.

The percentage of refugee-background students that completes a college degree in the United States is unknown, in part because there is no system that tracks their numbers from high school into higher education. Duff (2001) claims that refugee students tend to have limited access to college, which may help explain the scarcity of studies exploring their experience in this setting (see also Dryden-Peterson & Giles, 2010). Because pursuing higher education often represents a challenge for refugee-background students, it is important to understand what practices in college may help them to be successful (Vásquez, 2007).

Before engaging with the study at hand, it is necessary to clarify two ways that learning can be conceptualized in the higher education setting. Traditionally, institutions of higher education have operated under the assumption that learning is an individual process promoted by explicit teaching in academic disciplines (Hodgkinson-Williams *et al.*, 2008; Lea, 2005). The concepts of communities of practice and situated learning (Lave & Wenger, 1991; Wenger, 1998), in contrast, allow us to take 'learning out of the classroom' (Barton & Tusting, 2005: 3) and expand our view of higher education beyond disciplinary boundaries (Lea, 2005). From this perspective, institutions of higher education can be conceptualized as 'landscapes of practice consisting of a complex system of communities of practice' (Wenger-Trayner & Wenger-Trayner, 2015: 13). Learning can be reconfigured from the acquisition of knowledge to 'the becoming of a person who inhabits the landscape with an identity whose dynamic construction reflects [their] trajectory through that landscape' (Wenger-Trayner & Wenger-Trayner, 2015: 19). As Lave and Wenger (1991) explain, learning and a sense of identity are aspects of the same phenomenon. Each time a person participates in a new community, his or her identity is negotiated anew (Fenton-O'Creevy *et al.*, 2015). By viewing identity as a negotiated experience, 'we define who we are by the ways we experience our selves through participation as well as by the ways we and others reify our selves' (Wenger, 1998: 149).

Besides the construction of new identities, membership in different communities also promotes an increased sense of belonging (Hurtado & Carter, 1997; Mwangi, 2016; Strayhorn, 2012), which in turn, contributes to student persistence and retention (Hausmann *et al.*, 2007). Tinto (1993) claims, moreover, that membership in at least one supportive community, even at the margins of institutional life, may be sufficient to promote students' continued persistence.

Using the concept of communities of practice as a heuristic (Lea, 2005), this chapter analyzes refugee-background students' self-reported growth and accomplishments against the backdrop of their membership in various communities in college. It reveals the types of participation that promote these students' sense of belonging and legitimacy in the higher education space. More specifically, it addresses the following research questions:

(1) What do refugee-background students view as their major areas of growth during college?
(2) What do refugee-background students view as their major accomplishments in college?

Methodology

Research context

This study took place at Hope College,[1] a small, private, liberal arts college located in the southeastern United States. In fall 2009, when this study began, the college had about 2000 students, mostly at the undergraduate level, with international students representing less than 2% of the student body, and ethnic minorities in total a little over 10%. As a result, no services specifically dedicated to language minority students (e.g. English as a second language [ESL] classes) were offered. In its mission and purpose, the college affirms its commitment to be accessible to students from varied social and economic backgrounds. In line with its mission, the college admitted seven refugee-background students for the 2009–2010 academic year. Even though their scores in standardized tests were low, the college believed that these students had the necessary motivation to succeed, and thus offered them full scholarships including tuition, housing and meal plans. In return, the students agreed to work on campus a certain number of hours a year, reflecting the value that the college places on work experience.

Participants

The refugee-background students who took part in this study were chosen through purposive sampling (Merriam, 1998; Stake, 2000). I used to volunteer at a Saturday school program for refugee-background populations, where I heard of these students who had been admitted to Hope College.

Table 14.1 introduces the participants for this chapter. The information about students' age and length of residence in the United States was obtained in fall 2009. Tabasum's age is given as a range because she lacks a birth certificate, and there is conflict between her account and her immigration documents. The 'grades skipped' row refers to the school years that participants did not have access to education before being resettled in the United States.

Table 14.1 The participants

Pseudonym	Yar Zar	Arezo	Kayhan	Tabasum	Sabrina	Solange
Country	Burma	Afghanistan	Afghanistan	Afghanistan	Afghanistan	Rwanda
Sex	M	F	M	F	F	F
Age	19	19	18	19–21	18	19
Years in the United States	7	6	6	5	4	4
Starting grade in the United States	6th	End of 6th	7th	7th	9th	9th
Grades skipped	None	Most of 6th	5th and 6th	2nd–6th, 8th	6th–8th	4th and 5th
Major	International studies	Accounting	Psychology	Family studies	Accounting	Accounting

Data collection and analysis

This chapter uses the two research questions as lenses to explore data collected in a larger, qualitative, longitudinal, multiple-case study (Duff, 2008). The first part of the study was a year-long investigation of the academic literacy experiences of refugee-background students in college. Considering their histories of interrupted education and resettlement experience, I followed seven participants in their first year of college to document how they navigated tertiary reading and writing practices. I was interested in looking at the challenges they faced, as well as the resources and strategies they used to cope with these challenges. The main findings from the first year of investigation are reported in Hirano (2014, 2015).

After the seven participants had completed their first year of college, I kept in touch with them informally. They would tell me about their academic work, the progress they were making in their majors, their extracurricular activities and so on. In their final semester of college, I invited all seven participants for an exit interview. Six of them were able to meet with me, but the seventh mentioned that, even though he was interested, his schedule was too busy, and I ended up not being able to interview him. In the exit interview, besides following up on their academic literacies, I became interested in learning what college had meant for these students and what they felt that they were getting out of it, besides a degree. To this end, I inquired about their areas of growth and accomplishments, as well their plans for the future. This chapter uses data from both the first and the final year of college for participants.

The main sources of data used for this chapter are interviews and written documents. I interviewed each participant face to face and individually nine times: four times in fall 2009 (i.e. Interviews 1–4), four times in spring 2010 (i.e. Interviews 5–8) and once in their final semester of college (i.e. the exit interview), either in spring or fall 2013, depending on when each participant graduated. All of the interviews were semi-structured and transcribed.

Written documents obtained from the participants and their instructors include admissions material, course syllabi, writing and reading samples, quizzes, exams, assignment prompts and feedback on writing. I also use data from my research journal, including field notes from 13 classroom observations. I observed each participant in at least four different courses in their first year of college. These courses were those that participants considered the most challenging in terms of reading and/or writing. Several courses had more than one participant in them.

The analysis of the interviews was ongoing, recursive and inductive (Duff, 2008; Taylor & Bogdan, 1998). I initially analyzed all data through a grounded theory process of open coding, looking for excerpts relevant to my research questions, then examining data for 'emergent patterns and themes' (Mackey & Gass, 2005: 241). Findings from analysis of the interviews were complemented by insights based on the written documents.

Researcher positionality

As mentioned above, before the study, I used to volunteer at a Saturday school program for refugee-background students. I tutored three of my participants in this context. I was, and continue to be, an advocate for refugee-background populations. As Creswell (2003: 182) notes, 'the personal-self becomes inseparable from the researcher-self' in qualitative studies. Even though I never tutored the participants in college, I always cheered for their success, and, according to them, my interview questions made them more reflective and indirectly suggested coping strategies, such as when I asked whether they had sought professors' assistance. In this sense, I was not a neutral observer, if such a thing is even possible.

Research involving human participants always requires careful thought and consideration of ethical issues, which is even more the case when participants come from a refugee background (Hynes, 2003; McBrien, 2005; Ngo *et al.*, 2014). Besides complying with the rules for the protection of human subjects as dictated by the institutional review boards of my institution and Hope College, I tried to involve my participants in different parts of the project. They each received a transcription of their interviews to review and I invited each to meet with me so I could share my analysis and the profile I had written on each of them.

Findings: Besides a Degree

In this section, the findings are organized around the two research questions. For each question, I present the themes suggested by each participant's interview, followed by a longitudinal overview of one of the participants to illustrate key themes. These overviews provide contextual background to situate the participants' experience in college and offer an opportunity for the reader to glance 'at the full sweep of [these students'] journey across time' (Harklau, 2008: 26).

Besides a degree, many areas of growth

In the exit interviews, some participants wondered whether the growth area I was asking about had to be in an academic area. When I told them it could be anything, they all indicated personal growth, with recurring themes of self-esteem, self-confidence, maturity and independence. Table 14.2 summarizes their answers.

Table 14.2 Major areas of growth in college

Participant	Major areas of growth
Yar Zar	More mature, more Americanized
Arezo	More independent, more mature, able to live by herself
Kayhan	Not as shy anymore. Learned to be more sociable, to smile. Learned to be more independent
Tabasum	Self-esteem, communication and leadership skills
Sabrina	More independent, able to handle situations on her own
Solange	Self-confidence

These areas of growth all point to changes in these students' sense of identity, facilitated by engagement in different communities of practice, as I argue in the section titled 'Discussion'. For the longitudinal overview, I present Tabasum's story to illustrate the growth of a refugee-background student in college because, having accompanied her on her journey from admission to graduation, I was able to witness the remarkable changes she experienced, especially in her self-esteem and self-confidence.

Tabasum's profile

> I feel like I shouldn't be here, because I feel like I'm in the wrong place because I want to, like, participate like other students and I want to be involved and everything, but I don't know and lots of times I'm shy because when I start speaking, people look at me and [...] I have accent and I don't speak like formal English, so I don't feel like speaking [...] My self-esteem is very low [...] I'm not confident in anything because I know that I don't know and I'm shy and I always feel bad. (Interview 4, fall of first year)

Of all the participants, Tabasum had the most challenging history of literacy development, which likely affected her self-esteem and self-confidence in college. She was born in Afghanistan to uneducated parents and had attended school for a year before conflicts with the Taliban started. Her father was killed, so she fled to Pakistan, where she lived for six years. Because she helped her mother weave carpets to provide income for the family, she was unable to attend school. Upon arriving in the United States in her teenage years, and despite having only one year of formal education, Tabasum was placed in seventh grade. To make matters worse, she had to skip eighth grade in order to complete high school while she was 21, the maximum age allowed in the school district.

Considering that in total, Tabasum only had six years of schooling before starting college, it is not surprising that she faced a variety of challenges. To her credit, she worked extremely hard and made extensive use of institutional support systems such as the writing center. In her first year, she completed 24 credit hours, earning mostly Bs and Cs. She came to college aspiring to become a nurse, but the requirements for that major, including a minimum grade point average (GPA) of 3.0, discouraged her. She graduated in four and a half years with an interdisciplinary major in family studies and a minor in psychology.

As the above excerpt from Interview 4 reveals, Tabasum displayed low self-esteem and sense of belonging early on, and felt self-conscious about her English ability. In addition, she felt that she lacked content knowledge and socialization skills. In her words:

> Every time I like compare myself to other student, I don't know, I don't know English of course, but I don't know like the area subjects [...] like I should [...] 'cause I didn't go to school. Also, you know like when you are in a school you are socialized and you know people can communicate easily, but I have not been in a school, I've been at home like all the time like before I came to the US, and it's very hard to communicate with people and be socialized. (Interview 4, fall of first year)

Her behavior in the classroom paralleled her self-perception: she rarely spoke up, even when working in small groups, and she always sat at the back of the classroom.

Between the first phase of the study and the exit interview, in Tabasum's final semester, I occasionally ran into her on campus. I noticed that she was smiling more and overall seemed happier with her life. I was still surprised at the exit interview to realize how confidently she spoke, bearing no resemblance to the shy first-year student who spoke so reluctantly. When I asked her in what areas she felt that she had grown the most during college, she mentioned self-esteem, communication skills and leadership skills. She believed that her self-esteem had improved because, 'I know a lot of things, and uh, like when you know yourself better and you can – you have communication skills and people have respect for you, so it's just easy, you know, that you have confident' (Exit Interview). Her statement 'I know a lot of things' contrasted markedly to her first year, when she often highlighted what she did not know.

In the exit interview, Tabasum reported that courses in her major helped her in many ways, including helping her deal with personal struggles:

> The social science, what I majored [in], [...] it's not only about education, it's just helped me learn about my life, about myself, and about people around me. [...] I'm still in the grieving process [after having lost her father in Afghanistan and a brother soon after starting college]. It help me, you know, grow better and heal. [...] I'm learning that I'm not alone. There's a lot of people who are dealing with similar problems, and a lot of people struggle with life. (Exit Interview)

She explained that several of her courses, especially in the family studies program, helped her intentionally develop communication skills such as 'effective listening, effective giving feedback, and reassuring'. In class, students practiced these skills in groups, presented to the class, then received feedback. Hence, the community created within the courses in Tabasum's major helped to increase her sense of belonging and positive identity in college.

The final area that Tabasum mentioned was leadership skills. She co-created and was the president of the campus Muslim Heritage Group. Her work in this group was publicly recognized when she received the annual Multicultural and International Student Leadership Award, given to two Hope College students who promote understanding of the diverse needs of students at the college.

Tabasum's prior history of interrupted education makes her growth through college particularly remarkable. However, the other five participants showed admirable growth as well. My perceptions in the exit interviews matched theirs – that they were all more mature and self-confident, with good speaking skills.

Besides a degree, many accomplishments

When I asked participants about their biggest accomplishment in college, Sabrina and Yar Zar started off from a big picture perspective, mentioning that they were graduating 'when odds were against [them]' (Yar Zar, Exit Interview). They then named specific major events, which is how other participants answered the question. Table 14.3 summarizes their answers.

In this section, I elaborate on Solange's major accomplishments in college. As mentioned, participants were required to work on campus as part of their scholarship. In their first semester, they worked on the grounds,

Table 14.3 Major accomplishments in college

Participant	Major accomplishment
Yar Zar	Successfully graduating from college, co-starting the Muslim Heritage Group, captaining the club soccer team, being awarded resident assistant (RA) of the year, being a presidential ambassador
Arezo	Going from not being able to run half a mile to completing a half marathon
Kayhan	Giving the opening speech to a college-wide audience to introduce Warren St. John, author of *Outcasts United*, the first-year summer book
Tabasum	Co-creating and leading the Muslim Heritage Group, receiving the Multicultural and International Student Leadership Award and being featured as the Intern Spotlight for her summer internship with the International Rescue Committee
Sabrina	Graduating, friendships, relationships, service trip to Costa Rica, being a resident assistant
Solange	Being solely responsible for the Interlibrary Loan Services and supervising four student workers for almost a year

mowing lawns and washing windows, among other tasks. Participants then had jobs that involved increasing responsibility, eventually becoming resident assistants, research assistants and in Solange's case, head of the Interlibrary Loan Services.

Solange's profile

> I cannot change the fact that I lost my father at the age of six. I cannot change the fact that I do not know if my mother survived the war in Burundi. I cannot change the fact that the woman who raised me, my grandmother, is no longer with me. And I cannot change the fact that I am a refugee. Through it all, I have never used my life as an excuse. I have never once complained about the life I have lived. I have only used my past to make myself stronger. I can and will achieve everything I want, including a college education. (Excerpt from admissions essay)

Solange always seemed very mature. She was born in Burundi, to a Burundian mother and a Rwandan father. When the conflicts in Burundi worsened, the family went to Rwanda, where the genocide had just ended. Solange was about four at the time. During the journey, her parents got separated and she never saw her mother again. Her father passed away a couple of years later, and Solange was raised mostly by her grandmother. She lived in Rwanda for six years and then in Uganda for five before being resettled in the United States at the age of 15 with her grandmother, an uncle and his family. She had fewer than six years of education when she entered an American high school that did not have a strong academic reputation.

Academically, Solange did well in her first year of college. She completed 36 credit hours earning mostly As and Bs. She intended to follow a career in pharmacy, which she said had always been her dream. In the spring of her first year, however, she felt it would be selfish to go to graduate school when she needed to start helping her family financially as soon as possible. She switched her major to accounting and graduated in four years. Solange reported her major accomplishment:

> My major proud moment is when I ran the ILL [InterLibrary Loan] department, so, that was challenging, and I did it successfully. I ran the ILL department from the summer [...] until February. [...]. 'Cause I kind of faced my fear. I used to hate talking on the phone, 'cause I used to get frustrated when people can't understand what I'm saying. And so, [...] I learned how to talk on the phone, how to be professional, [...] how to write professional emails [...] about like [...], a problem someone has, like a customer. So I just learned so much work experience [...] I learned how to supervise and delegate and leadership skills [...] It was stressful, but it was – I think it was worth it. (Exit Interview)

Solange had been a student worker at the ILL section since she was a sophomore. After her supervisor left, she was given the opportunity to be responsible for the ILL until a new hire was made. Thus, she left her other job as a budget specialist in the office of the vice-president to work exclusively for the library. She typically put in 20–25 hours a week, supervising four student workers. She told me excitedly: 'Work is great. I love work'.

Solange's choice of major accomplishment is similar to the other participants' in that they all stemmed from participation in non-academic communities. In general, their accomplishments derived mostly from work, leadership (e.g. starting the Muslim club), public recognition (e.g. resident assistant of the year, Multicultural and International Student Leadership Award) and sports.

Discussion

As shown earlier, students reported major areas of growth that supported the analytic themes of maturity, independence, self-esteem and self-confidence. It is somewhat remarkable that none of them chose to discuss academic growth during their college years. Clearly, they did grow and learn from their academic studies, which was evident when some of them asked whether their answer should be in relation to academic issues. However, when given free reign, they all chose to gear their answers toward personal growth. This is noteworthy, considering that college can affect students in many other ways including career and moral and intellectual development (Mayhew *et al.*, 2016).

Participants were then asked to explain what had helped them grow in the areas they had reported. Except for Tabasum, all attributed most of their growth to residential life and their student work experiences. Both types of experiences stem from engagement in non-academic communities of practice, albeit in an academic context. Regarding the residential campus experience, Arezo, for example, explained, 'I'm more independent. [...] Freshman year I was like I can never think of living alone. [...] Living here [...] with a roommate [...] is different than like living at home with parents' (Exit Interview). As for the student work experience, for example, Yar Zar attributes becoming 'more mature in making decisions [to] my job experience really, being an RA [resident assistant], you know, yes, you are a leader [...] if you have to write them up, you do, you're their friend at the same time you're doing your job' (Exit Interview). Likewise, Solange explained that working at the library boosted her self-confidence.

The effect of college on students' self-concept and self-esteem has been discussed by Pascarella and Terenzini (2005), who conclude that, in general, going to college promotes psychosocial (e.g. self-concept, self-esteem) changes in students. They found that, even though there is a statistically significant and positive effect of college on students' self-esteem, these effects are small and possibly indirect; that is, such changes cannot necessarily be attributed to attending college *per se*. The findings of the current study, however, suggest that, for these six participants, attending college and participating in co-curricular or non-academic communities of practice had a strong and positive impact on their personal growth.

Further, the absence of references to academically related areas of growth in participants' exit interviews should not be taken to indicate that there were none during their college years. All participants acknowledged that they had become better readers and writers than in their first year. At the same time, most mentioned that they felt they still read more slowly than their US-born peers and still had language, mostly grammar, issues in their writing. As Stermac *et al.* (2012) found, the still-developing English proficiency of immigrants often creates difficulty in academic performance. The 'insistence on the gold standard of native-likeness' (Ortega & Byrnes, 2008: 283) is difficult to escape, especially in an academic context, where learning is reified mostly through grades and, as Wenger (1998) claims, the way one's experience is reified by others may affect one's identity. Although these students completed courses successfully, their GPAs in their final semester ranged from 2.4 to 2.8. In other words, as Tabasum put it, they 'did okay with [the] academic part' (Exit Interview) but did not excel in terms of grades, which may have hindered their perceptions of themselves as full participants in the academic community of practice.

As stated above, non-academic communities of practice, which promoted most of the participants' self-perceived growth, also played a key role in participants' major accomplishments in college. Even Tabasum, who attributed most of her growth to knowledge gained in academic courses, chose accomplishments that resulted from engagement in non-academic communities. As a counterpoint, Fuentes (2012) reports a case study of a linguistic minority college student who devoted time and energy exclusively to academic endeavors and, as a result, became tired and overwhelmed, with strong feelings of alienation. The student did, however, graduate with a GPA that she needed to be admitted to graduate school, a fact that she perceived as outweighing her losses on a social and personal level. Participants in my study, in contrast, talked about feeling legitimized by the non-academic communities of practice to which they belonged. As Wenger (1998) explains, members of a community share a repertoire of practice such as routines, words and ways of doing things, which gives coherence to the community. Yar Zar and Solange, for example, illustrated their legitimate membership in their communities of practice when they referred to learning and being able to use specific routines and ways of doing things at work. Yar Zar mentioned that, as a residential assistant, he can separate friendship from professionalism when he needs to report a friend to college authorities. Solange described how she went from hating to talk on the phone to learning how to talk on the phone, acting professionally and being able to write professional emails.

In addition, as mentioned above, Wenger (1998) claims that reification plays an important role in how we perceive ourselves. Reification, simply put, transforms practice into a symbol. If, on the one hand, academic performance was reified in participants' decent but not excellent grades, their engagement in extracurricular communities of practice was reified in more prestigious ways such as receiving awards, completing a race and being promoted to a job that involved supervising others. It therefore may not be surprising that these participants mentioned growth and accomplishments deriving from those experiences. Participation in these out-of-the-classroom communities of practice enabled them to develop a sense of belonging in college and to construct a positive identity beyond the classroom. As Tinto (1993) stated, membership in such supportive communities is related to student persistence in college.

It is also remarkable that these students would engage in so many different communities of practice beyond their required academic work, considering the educational gaps they had when they started college. Participants generally worked from 15 to 20 hours per week during semesters, a practice that is associated with a greater risk of attrition (Mayhew *et al.*, 2016). Yet, they found time for sports, clubs and service. It appears to have been engagement in these non-academic communities of practice that, somewhat counterintuitively, made college experience successful for these students, likely supporting their persistence to 'survive these four years when odds were against [them]', as Yar Zar put it.

Conclusion

In my interviews with these students, it became evident that college had a much stronger effect on the participants than simply the conferral of a degree or the development of academic abilities. The conversations about major areas of growth and accomplishments allowed participants to showcase their best selves, the moments they were proudest of and the memories they will carry with them. To hear them speak excitedly of their success at work or their engagement in extracurricular activities makes one wonder what their college experience would have been like if college life had been restricted to academic courses. For these refugee-background students, participation in communities beyond the classroom enabled them to (re)construct their identities and enhance their sense of self, belonging and accomplishment. As mentioned, research discusses students who choose to focus exclusively on academic endeavors despite feelings of alienation. While it is important to take student agency into account, the development of a sense of belonging should also be considered, since belonging has been found to affect persistence in college and, ultimately, degree completion (Strayhorn, 2012).

Of course, memberships in different communities may overlap to a greater or lesser degree, and some memberships may be more or less supportive than others (James, 2007). The experience of the refugee-background students in this study shows that participation in extracurricular communities enabled them to construct identities that had a more positive impact on their sense of self than participation in core, required academic communities. Perhaps the positive identities they constructed outside the classroom supported their more modestly achieving identities inside the classroom, resulting in an overall successful college trajectory, with all six participants graduating within four and a half years.

This study has important implications for mentors and advisors working with refugee-background students in college. In trying to help students focus on academics, mentors and advisors might initially steer these students away from extracurricular activities. The findings from this study indicate, however, that participation in non-academic, extracurricular activities may be more than just 'extra'. Engagement in these communities of practice may promote a strong and positive sense of self, contributing to a positive identity – even when academic performance does not meet students' hopes and expectations. Mentors and advisors can help students design a higher education 'landscape of practice' (Wenger-Trayner & Wenger-Trayner, 2015) which may afford participation in a variety of communities of practice that could ultimately lead students to gain much more from college besides a degree.

Note

(1) Institutional and participant names are pseudonyms.

References

Barton, D. and Tusting, K. (2005) Introduction. In D. Barton and K. Tusting (eds) *Beyond Communities of Practice: Language, Power and Social Context* (pp. 1–13). New York: Cambridge University Press.

Creswell, J.W. (2003) *Research Design: Qualitative, Quantitative, and Mixed Methods Approaches* (2nd edn). Thousand Oaks, CA: Sage.

Dryden-Peterson, S. and Giles, W. (2010) Introduction: Higher education for refugees. *Refuge* 27 (2), 3–9.

Duff, P.A. (2001) Language, literacy, content, and (pop) culture: Challenges for ESL students in mainstream courses. *Canadian Modern Language Review* 58 (1), 103–132.

Duff, P.A. (2008) *Case Study Research in Applied Linguistics*. New York: Lawrence Erlbaum.

Fenton-O'Creevy, M., Dimitriadis, Y. and Scobie, G. (2015) Failure and resilience at boundaries: The emotional process of identity work. In E. Wenger-Trayner, M. Fenton-O'Creevy, S. Hutchinson, C. Kubiak and B. Wenger-Trayner (eds) *Learning in*

Landscapes of Practice: Boundaries, Identity, and Knowledgeability in Practice-Based Learning (pp. 33–42). New York: Routledge.
Fuentes, R. (2012) Benefits and costs of exercising agency: A case study of an English learner navigating a four-year university. In Y. Kanno and L. Harklau (eds) *Linguistic Minority Students Go to College: Preparation, Access, and Persistence* (pp. 220–237). New York: Routledge.
Harklau, L. (2008) Developing qualitative longitudinal case studies of advanced language learners. In L. Ortega and H. Byrnes (eds) *The Longitudinal Study of Advanced L2 Capacities* (pp. 22–35). New York: Routledge.
Hausmann, L., Schofield, J. and Woods, R. (2007) Sense of belonging as a predictor of intentions to persist among African American and White first-year college students. *Research in Higher Education* 48 (7), 803–839.
Hirano, E. (2014) Refugees in first-year college: Academic writing challenges and resources. *Journal of Second Language Writing* 23 (1), 37–52.
Hirano, E. (2015) 'I read, I don't understand': Refugees coping with academic reading. *ELT Journal* 69 (2), 178–187.
Hodgkinson-Williams, C., Slay, H. and Siebörger, I. (2008) Developing communities of practice within and outside higher education institutions. *British Journal of Educational Technology* 39 (3), 433–442.
Hurtado, S. and Carter, D.F. (1997) Effects of college transition and perception of the campus racial climate on Latino college students' sense of belonging. *Sociology of Education* 70 (4), 324–345.
Hynes, T. (2003) The issue of 'trust' or 'mistrust' in research with refugees: Choices, caveats and considerations for researchers. *Working Paper No. 98*. Geneva: Evaluation and Policy Analysis Unit, United Nations High Commission for Refugees.
James, N. (2007) The learning trajectories of 'old-timers': Academic identities and communities of practice in higher education. In J. Hughes, N. Jewson and L. Unwin (eds) *Communities of Practice: Critical Perspectives* (pp. 131–143). New York: Routledge.
Keddie, A. (2012) Pursuing justice for refugee students: Addressing issues of cultural (mis)recognition. *International Journal of Inclusive Education* 16 (12), 1295–1310.
Lave, J. and Wenger, E. (1991) *Situated Learning: Legitimate Peripheral Participation*. Cambridge: Cambridge University Press.
Lea, M.R. (2005) 'Communities of practice' in higher education: Useful heuristic or educational model? In D. Barton and K. Tusting (eds) *Beyond Communities of Practice: Language, Power and Social Context* (pp. 180–197). New York: Cambridge University Press.
Mackey, A. and Gass, S. (2005) *Second Language Research: Methodology and Design*. Mahwah, NJ: Lawrence Erlbaum.
Mayhew, M.J., Rockenbach, A.N., Bowman, N.A., Seifert, T.A., Wolniak, G.C., Pascarella, E.T. and Terenzini, P.T. (2016) *How College Affects Students (Vol. 3): 21st Century Evidence that Higher Education Works*. San Francisco, CA: Jossey-Bass.
McBrien, J.L. (2005) Discrimination and academic motivation in adolescent refugee girls. PhD doctoral dissertation, Emory University,
Merriam, S.B. (1998) *Qualitative Research and Case Study Applications in Education*. San Francisco: Jossey-Bass.
Mwangi, C.A.G. (2016) Exploring sense of belonging among black international students at an HBCU. *Journal of International Students* 6 (4), 1015–1037.
Ngo, B., Bigelow, M. and Lee, S.J. (2014) Introduction to the special issue: What does it mean to do ethical and engaged research with immigrant communities? *Diaspora, Indigenous, and Minority Education* 8 (1), 1–6.

Ortega, L. and Byrnes, H. (2008) Theorizing advancedness, setting up the longitudinal research agenda. In L. Ortega and H. Byrnes (eds) *The Longitudinal Study of Advanced L2 Capacities* (pp. 281–300). New York: Routledge.

Pascarella, E.T. and Terenzini, P.T. (2005) *How College Affects Students: A Third Decade of Research*. San Francisco, CA: Jossey-Bass.

Stake, R.E. (2000) Case studies. In N.K. Denzin and Y.S. Lincoln (eds) *The Sage Handbook of Qualitative Research* (2nd edn; pp. 435–453). London: Sage.

Stermac, L., Elgie, S., Clarke, A. and Dunlap, H. (2012) Academic experience of war-zone students in Canada. *Journal of Youth Studies* 15 (3), 311–328.

Strayhorn, T.L. (2012) *College Students' Sense of Belonging: A Key to Educational Success*. New York: Routledge.

Taylor, S.J. and Bogdan, R. (1998) *Introduction to Qualitative Research Methods: A Guidebook and Resource*. New York: John Wiley.

Tinto, V. (1993) *Leaving College: Rethinking the Causes and Cures of Student Attrition* (2nd edn). Chicago, IL: University of Chicago Press.

Vásquez, C. (2007) Comments from the classroom: A case study of a generation-1.5 student in a university IEP and beyond. *The Canadian Modern Language Review* 63 (3), 345–370.

Wenger, E. (1998) *Communities of Practice: Learning, Meaning, and Identity*. Cambridge: Cambridge University Press.

Wenger-Trayner, E. and Wenger-Trayner, B. (2015) Learning in a landscape of practice: A framework. In E. Wenger-Trayner, M. Fenton-O'Creevy, S. Hutchinson, C. Kubiak and B. Wenger-Trayner (eds) *Learning in Landscapes of Practice: Boundaries, Identity, and Knowledgeability in Practice-Based Learning* (pp. 13–29). New York: Routledge.

15 Conception Versus Reality: The Impact of Migration Experiences on Children's Educational Participation

Beatrix Bukus

> *This chapter contributes from an educational science perspective to a better understanding of the 'voluntary' vs. 'forced' migration divide and its relevance for educational participation. The context of this research is Leipzig, Germany, and the data examined is part of a qualitative study on biographies of school-age children involved in multiple and multidirectional migration during their obligatory schooling years. Participants came from two groups: (1) those who moved on from their first country of settlement due to the economic crisis and (2) those who were in flight and reached Germany through transit way stations. My analysis has shown that the plans that families have with regard to their target location and the way that they think about their migration process prior to departure are as impactful on educational participation as the reason/motive for the initial departure from the location of origin. Drawing on the comparison of four biographies in particular, this chapter suggests that the rigid distinction between voluntary and forced migration may prevent us from capturing the diversity of student experiences.*

The field of study dedicated to *involuntary migrants* is an interdisciplinary one. The various disciplines involved (e.g. political science, sociology, anthropology, human geography and education) approach the complexity of these human experiences from their own methodological traditions and disciplinary perspectives. Although any form of involuntary migration can only be understood as multifaceted, the discussion of this experience from the viewpoint of different disciplines can lead to more accurate conceptualizations of the phenomenon. As part of this endeavor, this chapter contributes from an educational science perspective to a better understanding of the voluntary – forced or voluntary – involuntary migration divide and its relevance for the educational participation of school-age children and young persons.

The term 'involuntary migrants' or 'forced migrants' refers to persons who migrate not as a result of their free will/choice but rather, due to those circumstances in the location of origin which do not allow individuals to meet basic physiological and safety needs (e.g. displaced persons, asylum seekers and refugees), or without their informed consent (e.g. trafficked persons). The definition of these terms is highly contested and politically loaded, yet decisive for the determination of inclusion and exclusion mechanisms (Zetter, 2007). Furthermore, the meaning of these terms varies according to the historical, geographical, academic and linguistic context. Additionally, the traditional dichotomies of migration (e.g. voluntary vs. forced, economic vs. forced, internal vs. international, temporary vs. permanent) are challenged by current trends of movement across the globe (Bailey & Boyle, 2004; Engbersen *et al.*, 2013; King, 2002).

Within both scholarly and public research in the German education system, there is a wide range of sources on the education of first, second and consequent generations of economic migrants. However, research on the education of asylum seekers and refugee-background children and adolescents is scarce (Behrensen & Westphal, 2009). In the few sources available, a clear distinction is made between the 'voluntary' and 'forced/involuntary' categorization. This situation results from the special status of asylum seekers and refugees within the national and international legal system, which has resulted in distinct treatment of these populations within education research. In contrast to earlier scholarship in the United States, where asylum seeker and refugee-background students often remained undistinguished from other immigrant students (McBrien, 2005), the German literature has always handled this group as distinct. However, in both contexts, a systematic comparison of these groups with regard to educational needs, resources and challenges is still desirable (Pinson *et al.*, 2010; Rutter & Jones, 1998).

This chapter presents preliminary findings from an analysis of biographical data of school-age children who were involved in multiple and multidirectional migration during their obligatory schooling years. This form of migration was found in the Leipzig (Germany) context among two groups: those who move on from their first country of settlement due to the economic crisis and those who are in flight and reach Germany through transit way stations. However, in attempting to code the biographies according to the voluntary/involuntary dichotomy, I discovered that such a simplistic *a priori* categorization would hinder me from recognizing the complexities of the data. My analysis of the individual migration and educational trajectories complicated the typical narrative, which focuses primarily on the motive and the circumstances for departure from the location of origin. The goal of this chapter is to highlight additional, equally important aspects of the migration experience that impact the educational participation and social integration of school-age children and adolescents. I use these findings to argue that from an educational research standpoint, the rigid distinction between voluntary and forced migration needs to be reconsidered with regard to its capacity to capture the diversity of student experiences and to serve as a basis for educational policy.

Literature Review

The chapter draws on data collected between 2014 and 2015 in a city in the state of Saxony in Germany. Due to the geographical and historical context of the research questions and the data, as well as to the fact that education scholarship is usually centered on specific nations, rather than themes or regions, I draw mainly on the German academic scholarship on the migration–education nexus (Adick, 2005), but make connections to findings in other contexts where appropriate.

Only in recent years has educational research into migration in Germany (e.g. Fürstenau, 2004; Niedrig, 2005; Rakhkochkine, 2010; Siouti, 2012) and other European contexts (e.g. Cozma & Popa, 2010; Kawecki et al., 2012; Laoire et al., 2011) started to explore the diverse forms of migration (e.g. circular, return, return due to deportation, multiple and multidirectional migration) among school-age children. Current research is shifting from an exclusive focus on one-time and unidirectional economic migration in order to broaden the concept of migration and account for the diversity of experiences of school-age children. Research on the situation of asylum seeker and refugee-background children in Germany is, because of the reasons mentioned in the introduction, limited to a few studies (e.g. Krappmann et al., 2009; Neumann et al., 2003; Seukwa, 2006; for an overview, see Behrensen & Westphal, 2009). However, the influx of asylum seekers in 2015 and 2016 has triggered new research on involuntary and mixed-cause forms of migration, some of which has not yet been published. In the available sources, study participants are usually *a priori* categorized as asylum seekers or refugees on the basis of their motive for departure, without any further discussion of this categorization and its effect on the data analysis. In contrast to this approach, I argue in this chapter that it is worthwhile to question this categorization and look into the individual migration and educational trajectories in order to reveal what other aspects, beyond the motive for departure, shape participants' experiences.

Key Terms and Methodology

This chapter draws on preliminary findings from a larger study focused on the period of time between when school-age children leave their countries of origin and the first months after their arrival to Leipzig. The main questions for this research project were:

(1) How do school-age children characterize the reasons for and the circumstances of their migration – particularly when it is multiple and multidirectional?
(2) How do they characterize their participation in formal, informal and non-formal education (Morrice, 2012; Overwien, 2013; Rauschenbach, 2008) during their multiple and multidirectional migration? 'Participation' includes:
- the pupil's access to and attendance in educational programs;
- the pupil's motivation for and experiences with learning the language of instruction;
- the pupil's attitude and motivation toward participation in formal education and in the life of the school and the local community;
- the concrete challenges that the pupil faced at the way stations along his or her educational trajectory, including the current way station of Leipzig.
(3) What do participants perceive to be the effects of multiple and multidirectional migration on their lives and educational participation?

Multiple and multidirectional migration is experienced in the Leipzig context by two distinct groups of school-age children: firstly, among those who were part of war-induced family migration and arrived to the German city after passing through several transit locations; and secondly, among those whose caregivers settled as part of labor migration in one European Union (EU) country, but involuntarily relocated to another European country, due to the economic hardship following the world economic crisis of 2008. After identifying this distinction among the participants' experiences, I formulated the following sub-question, which is the focus of this chapter: Besides the motive for migration and the circumstances at the location of origin, what other aspects have an influence on educational participation?

In this research project, I collected biographical data and educational histories for 13 participants through problem-centered semi-structured interviews (Witzel & Reiter, 2012) and ego-centered network drawings (Hollstein & Pfeffer, 2010). The participants' ages ranged from 11 to 18. All of the participants (referred to with pseudonyms) had migrated to Germany with their parents or other caregivers. By the time of the interviews, all participants had attended public school from between 4 and 16 months. They were recruited according to the criterion that the pupil had undertaken at least two international border crossings during his or her obligatory schooling years. To recruit participants, I coordinated with teachers of German as a second language who taught newcomer classes at public schools in the state of Saxony. The participants collectively spoke seven languages, and an interpreter was provided as an option for each interviewee; six students chose to speak in German and/or English. Both parental and student consent forms and information sheets were translated into the pupils' preferred languages. The participation was voluntary and the ethical aspects of the research were reviewed by a university research committee. To best exemplify the findings within the scope of this chapter, four participants' biographies were selected.

Data were analyzed inductively, using codes (see Table 15.1) that emerged from the data (Kelle & Kluge, 2010). To more closely examine the factors influencing educational participation, I focused on the relocation processes involved for both forced migrants and those involved in work-related family migration. This resulted in a set of subcodes, which shed new light on the data (see Table 15.1 [2.a–2.f]).

Figure 15.1 presents the respective migration routes of the four participants discussed in this chapter. Each shape represents a separate country where the participants resided, including the location of origin and all way stations; however, temporal aspects of the relocations and

Table 15.1 Coding tree

Migration	(1) Reason for moving **(2) Relocation process** (3) Participation in moving (4) Arrival to a new place/first experiences at new place (5) Comparison of place one and two (6) Difficult and easy aspects of life at new place and new school (7) Duration of stay at way station (8) Camp	**(2.a) Current location is clearly defined before departing from location of origin** **(2.b) The stay at the locations between location of origin and current location planned as temporary** **(2.c) The location(s) between location of origin and current location are foreseen and planned** **(2.d) The relocation was organized by legal means or by illegal means** **(2.e) The family/caregivers have connections at the destination** **(2.f) Duration of stay at the temporary location(s)**
Education at the way stations	Enrollment into the new school Language of instruction Class methods Learning strategies Coping strategies Subjects and scripts Transition to regular class Marks and certificates Repetition of class level Language learning Problems at school	
Life at locations	Life at way station Free time at the way station Contact with other people Peers and friends Language use	
Evaluation of the involvement in multiple and multidirectional migration	Evaluation of moving twice Plans for the future	

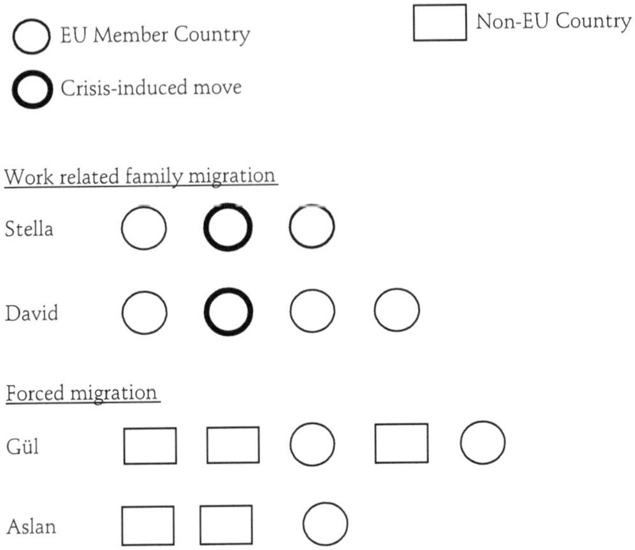

246 Part 2: Access and Equity

○ EU Member Country   ☐ Non-EU Country
⬤ Crisis-induced move

Work related family migration

Stella   ○ ⬤ ○

David   ○ ⬤ ○ ○

Forced migration

Gül   ☐ ☐ ○ ☐ ○

Aslan   ☐ ☐ ○

Figure 15.1 Migration route of participants

stays are not included. It is important to note that even this figure implies a divide between forced migrants and those involved in work-related family migration.

Findings

My analysis showed that the time and experiences between departure from the location of origin and arrival at the latest way station (Leipzig, in this case) has an influence on how pupils tackle the challenges of education. I argue that the perception of and reactions to the challenges in Germany appear to be dependent on the ways in which families perceived the planned migration route prior to departure and how they view the current and the previous way stations. Thus, there are two key factors impacting the educational participation of pupils: The first is whether the family has made a clear-cut decision about the final country of settlement (here, Germany) prior to leaving the country of origin. The second is whether the family considers the time spent between the location of origin and the current location of settlement as only a transit phase, which influences the attitudes and behaviors of school-age children in regard to language learning and engagement in formal education. Given that this conceptualization of transit as temporary is mainly – but not exclusively – to be found among those who left their location of origin due to war, it is easy see how this factor might be confused with that of the original motive for migration.

The four biographies chosen from among the larger participant sample were selected to exemplify the findings. Two pupils were involved in the economic migration of their families and did not conceptualize the way station(s) prior to the one in Germany as the location(s) of permanent settlement, meaning also that they did not have Germany as their target country in mind prior to departing from home. The other two pupils, who were involved in forced migration, had their transit locations in mind as a temporary location, whereas Germany was the intended destination. I show two biographies each to illustrate that the pupils' participation in formal schooling at the second or subsequent stage seems to be influenced by a number of factors. In the cases of the families and pupils involved in EU internal labor migration, they considered their first country of settlement as the main target. Consequently, if their subsequent way stations became targets, this was the result of a less voluntary move, due to the economic crisis.

In the first case, my goal is to illustrate a migration experience in which the first country of settlement was the intended target country for long-term settlement. The family's subsequent move to Germany was unintended when they first left their location of origin. This way of thinking impacted how the participant (Stella) and her family perceived the subsequent move, resulting from the economic crisis, and how Stella experienced both learning a new language and participating in formal education in the new context.

> Stella was 15 years old at the time of the interview. She was born in a small town in Serbia, but lived in Sofia, in Bulgaria. She attended kindergarten and primary school in Sofia, where the language of instruction was Bulgarian. She completed fourth grade there, but in the second half of the school year her parents moved to Palma de Mallorca, Spain, because her father, who was highly qualified, found a new job. Stella joined them at the end of that summer. She matriculated into the sixth grade because placement was determined according to the year of birth; thus she skipped fifth grade and repeated seventh grade. Stella was enrolled in a regular class where she studied all subjects, rather than taking separate Spanish language courses. She learned the new language with the help of language learning software, with great enthusiasm and hard work. Although the change from one school system to the next prevented her from having continuity in her educational biography (missing a grade level, repetition), she considered herself successfully incorporated into her new context by the end of her third year there. She reports finding academic success and having an active life outside school with her peers.
>
> Stella's family lived for about four years in Palma before the father decided in the midst of the economic crisis to search for a new job in

Leipzig, with the help of a German colleague. Stella experienced the relocation to Germany very negatively, which she expressed by constantly contrasting her time in Leipzig to her ideal years in Spain. She began her German schooling in the eighth grade, rather than repeating a year. At the time of the interview, Stella had been living in Leipzig for one year and seven months. For the first half of the school year, she attended a German as a second language class. In the second school year, she was fully incorporated into the regular class; however, she reported a lack of good peer relationships. She also faced academic challenges due to a gap in background knowledge for physics and chemistry resulting from the fact that the German curriculum introduces these subjects earlier than that of Spain. In comparison to Stella's time in Spain, where she spent considerable time studying independently, in Leipzig she skipped many classes and had no sense that she could succeed. In speaking about her future plans, she mentioned Germany as being a temporary way station in her life.

Stella's case shows how important it is to examine individual migration routes in order to identify experiences that might affect students' educational and social participation at the current way station. She discusses a successful educational and social experience at a location which was perceived as a long-term settlement location (Spain); in contrast, she speaks about her current location (Germany) as one of necessity, where she is aware of the challenges she must overcome to integrate successfully, yet she lacks the motivation to do so. In sum, her level of motivation is deeply colored by how the migration trajectory unfolded and how the current location was not planned at the time of departure from the location of origin.

The next case of internal European migration belongs to David. In contrast to Stella's family, David's parents were unskilled laborers who left their home country seeking better work opportunities.

David was 16 years old at the time of the interview. He was born in Romania, where he attended the first three grades in his home village in a public school, but did not complete the third grade. His family left to go to Spain to look for a job when he was nine years old. His parents did not find work for a year so they maintained a transitory lifestyle in Spain and decided that David should not attend school until their job conditions were certain. He did not have contact with local people and therefore did not learn Spanish. He spent his days with his mother at home or in parks and watched Romanian television. After it became clear to his parents that they would not find a job in Spain, the family moved to the city of Béziers, France, where relatives were living. David, who was 10 years old at this time, was enrolled in a local public school in Grade 5. For the first few months, he attended a French language class. He completed Grades 5 through 8 and learned French. The most important thing for David was that in France he was surrounded by many friends and relatives, mainly Romanians.

After four years, when David's parents lost their jobs, they moved to Germany. At the time of their arrival there, Romanian citizens did not yet have the right to work; therefore, David's parents found occasional, inconsistent work. David attended German classes at a high school and by the time of the interview was incorporated into the regular classes of a public school in the German town. David believes that the relocations had a negative impact on his schooling. He thinks that with every move he has lost something and that his way stations are separate blocks in his life. He wanted to stay in France because he had developed a high level of competence in French and wanted to complete school and become successful. He speaks about the time in France as a good time when he was content with both his academic performance and his life outside of school. After his parents moved to Leipzig, he lost all this and was supposed to start over again. He also had to leave family members behind. After rebuilding his life in France, David did not want to take on the challenge a second time. David is completely resigned, having given up on learning German; he often skips school. In the future, he wishes to return to France.

David's family's decisions to move are driven by work opportunities; because of this, he experienced the first and the third way stations as transitory. These first two cases have in common that both pupils initially considered the locations prior to moving to Germany (i.e. Spain and France, respectively) to be places of permanent residency. David's case illustrates that although the conceptualization of a way station as temporary is found mostly among those involved in involuntary migration, it can also be present for economic migrants. These two cases support my argument that the simplistic divide between voluntary and forced migrant pupils hinders a full picture of the experiences that shape the pupils' educational needs at the current way station. The families of Stella and David think about their migration as one relocation between the location of origin and the location where the family would build a permanent life for themselves. Their economic migration was therefore characterized by a process of multiple and multidirectional migration. Both students are resigned after experiencing that the efforts put into their integration in Spain and in France have not paid off in Germany.

The next two cases, in contrast, illustrate a conception of the migration trajectory as one with multiple moves and transit phases between the location of origin and the clearly defined target. Specifically, the cases of Aslan and Gül depict a migration plan with Germany as the target country, with way stations along the route. Their interviews demonstrate the impact of this type of migration experience on the youth's educational participation.

> Aslan was born in Damascus, Syria, into an Arabic-speaking family. He completed the first three grades of primary school in the public school system. Because of the war, his grandparents relocated to Istanbul, Turkey, to gather information and make contacts. Subsequently, at age nine, he moved to Istanbul with his parents and sister and spent a year there. Aslan attended fourth grade in a mainstream school of a Turkish district mainly inhabited by Syrian asylum seekers and displaced persons. His parents considered the Turkish formal school system an opportunity for continuity in Aslan's educational career. He spent most of his free time with Arabic-speaking pupils in programs organized by the local mosque.
>
> Aslan's family has contacts in the target city in Germany and organized their migration route legally. After the school year, the family moved to Leipzig to stay with family members who had been living there for over a decade. Aslan had been living in Leipzig for nine months at the time of the interview. He was learning German outside of school from a German native-speaker family member. He reported being aware that he would live in Leipzig long term, and he reported high motivation to learn German and succeed in the formal education system. Three months after arrival, Aslan matriculated into a Leipzig public middle school at Grade 5. He was 11 years old at the time of the interview. Aslan found the time in Istanbul challenging but enriching. He thinks that it would have been easier to arrive from Syria directly to Leipzig and not to go through difficulties in Turkey. He conceptualizes the relocation as a one-time event which was disrupted by a transit year.

In contrast to the cases of Stella and David, Germany was planned as the target destination for Aslan, and the pupil therefore focused on successful participation in the formal schooling and context. Even though there was a short-term incorporation into the educational system of the transit country, the pupil remained motivated and engaged at the target location. The case of Aslan points to those factors identified above as influential. Aslan's family had contacts at the way stations, did not get involved in the asylum system and anticipated spending time in the transit location, which allows this case to be positioned differently on the voluntary and forced migration continuum from a case where the family lacks these resources. In this respect, the case of Aslan contrasts with the final case – Gül – presented next.

> Gül was born in Aleppo, Syria, and lived in the city with her parents until she was 14. Because of the war, the family left Aleppo to go to the father's relatives in Afrin, Syria. Gül lived there for about two months. It

was clear to her that her family would go to Germany because her mother learned about it through the internet and she decided to flee to Germany with the whole family. Based on this decision, Gül moved to Aksaray, Turkey, where her brother immediately found a job as a nurse. She lived with her sister and brother in a flat, separate from her parents. She did not attend school in the four months she lived in Aksaray. Gül's family did not have contacts in Turkey or Germany and organized their travel through illegal means.

Next, Gül ended up with her parents and sister in Bucharest, Romania, living in an asylum center. The way station in Romania was neither planned nor foreseen by the family. As the asylum system in Bucharest did not allow access to public schooling, Gül did not participate in formal education for a year. During that year, her family lived in isolation at the asylum center. The family then returned to Aksaray, Turkey, and her parents eventually returned to Aleppo and sold their flat.

Gül's parents now had Germany as the target location, which led to a new attempt to reach it. Around this time, however, Gül became separated from her parents and travelled for a couple of days with smugglers to Germany along with her sister. She was moved to various locations within Germany and after many months she arrived in Leipzig, where the family was reunited. Between the time the family left Aleppo and was reunified, approximately two years had passed. In this time, Gül did not participate in formal education. After starting school in Leipzig, she considered it a new start and was enthusiastic. She was matriculated to Grade 7 and in the following school year was integrated into a regular eighth-grade class.

Gül's case further supports my argument that we cannot thoroughly evaluate or predict a pupil's educational participation based solely on the forced–voluntary migration dichotomy. Furthermore, it is important to examine how the experiences along the migration route also affect that pupil's educational participation. Gül and Aslan's cases show that despite educational gaps due to the transit phase, their motivation and enthusiasm to tackle the challenges in Germany persisted, which provided a good basis for succeeding in acquiring a certificate from high school. In contrast, Stella and David, whose families did not plan to move on from the first migration location, experienced a loss of motivation to participate in school, which had a negative impact on their academic success.

Discussion

This chapter has demonstrated the importance of studying the life and migration trajectories of individuals in order to complicate existing dichotomies, such as that between forced and voluntary (economic) migrants. While it is necessary to consider refugee and asylum seeker pupils as distinct from voluntary immigration populations, this study suggests that academic research and the pedagogical practice in schools should adopt a more nuanced approach, taking into account all of the ways in which school-age children are involved in migration. The simplistic categorization according to the motive for migration does not shed light on the complexity of experiences along the migration trajectory, which might influence the level of success with social and educational integration. The findings in this case study shed light on the role that a family's perception about the migration trajectory plays in the educational participation of the children, which is arguably as impactful as the primary reason(s) for departure from the location of origin. These aspects draw attention to the importance of considering each individual's entire migration and educational trajectory, rather than simply categorizing children based on only one specific aspect. Future research should explore how the other aspects mentioned by the pupils might affect their educational career and how these relate to the aspects of motivation for departure.

One of the limitations of this study is the small sample size, which is not sufficient to challenge the implications of the forced–voluntary dichotomy. However, these findings point to the need for complicating the overall migration narrative in future research. The findings also suggest that educators and school administrators should consider the potential impacts of diverse migration experiences on pupils' educational participation when making decisions related to curriculum development, intake assessments and the school enrollment processes of newcomers. The findings suggest a need for better cooperation among various national educational systems to ensure that educators can access information and potentially coordinate curricular content offered at the different grade levels. It would also be useful if students involved in migration had access to detailed information about the content in each subject they have covered during their school attendance at a particular location. At the level of the European Union, this might be possible through an online database that teachers could access and edit. Greater transparency about curricular content could result in a more tailored intake procedure that takes into account not only the official documents provided by the student, but also his or her migration, education and language background, including an assessment of existing content knowledge in the different subjects. In this way, the risks introduced by temporary integration and multiple migration might be counterbalanced.

With regard to everyday interactions with students, my findings suggest that taking students' experiences at the previous way stations into account might help teachers to better understand the motivation of their students in learning a new language of instruction and embracing (or resisting) the new social and educational environment. In many cases, lack of motivation results in student withdrawal, which may be addressed through conversations and relationship building between the student and the teacher. I truly believe that until the aforementioned suggestions at the systemic level are put in place, the level of student and teacher interaction remains the most hopeful terrain for making use of my findings.

Notes

(1) The precise definition of the category 'school age' varies from one educational and legal framework to the next and thus a coherent definition proves challenging. This chapter uses the term 'school-age' according to the legislative framework of the state of Saxony in Germany, which means all persons in the age group 6–18.
(2) The state of Saxony in Germany follows a three-step model of educational integration for newcomer pupils who arrive to public school institutions without the level of German language skills necessary for successful integration into the regular subject classes. In the first phase, termed here as 'German as a second language' or DaZ (Deutsch als Zweitsprache), the students exclusively attend German language classes. In the second phase, they also attend regular subject classes, while in the third phase, they are fully integrated and have only one language class per week. For more information, see https://www.schule.sachsen.de/lpdb/web/downloads/deutsch_als_zweitsprache_2009.pdf?v2.

References

Adick, C. (2005) Transnationalisierung als Herausforderung für die International und Interkulturell Vergleichende Erziehungswissenschaft [Transnationalisation as challenge for the international and intercultural comparative education]. *Tertium Comparationis* 11 (2), 243–269.
Bailey, A. and Boyle, P. (2004) Untying and retying family migration in the new Europe. *Journal of Ethnic & Migration Studies* 30 (2), 229–241.
Behrensen, B. and Westphal, M. (2009) Junge Flüchtlinge. Ein blinder Fleck in der Migrations- und Bildungsforschung [Young refugees. A blind spot in the migration and education research]. In L. Krappmann, A. Lob-Hüdepohl, A. Bohmeyer and S. Kurzke-Maasmeier (eds) *Bildung für junge Flüchtlinge. Ein Menschenrecht* [*Education for Young Refugees. A Human Right*] (pp. 45–58). Bielefeld: W. Bertelsmann.
Cozma, T. and Popa, N.L. (2010) Children of Romanian circular migrants. An overview of current educational research, policies and practices. *Scientific Annals of Alexandru Ioan Cuza University of Iasi. Educational Sciences Series* [*Analele Stiintifice ale Universitatii Alexandru Ioan Cuza din Iasi. Seria Stiinte ale Educatiei*] XIV, 303–314.
Engbersen, G., Leerkes, A., Grabowska-Lusinska, I., Snel, E. and Burgers, J. (2013) On the differential attachments of migrants from central and eastern Europe: A typology of labour migration. *Journal of Ethnic & Migration Studies* 39 (6), 959–981.
Fürstenau, S. (2004) *Mehrsprachigkeit als Kapital im transnationalen Raum: Perspektiven portugiesischsprachiger Jugendlicher beim Übergang von der Schule in die Arbeitswelt* [*Multilingualism as Capital in Transnational Social Space. Perspectives of Portuguese Speaking Youth at Their Transition from School to Work*]. Münster/München: Waxmann.
Hollstein, B. and Pfeffer, J. (2010) Netzwerkkarten als Instrument zur Erhebung egozentrierter Netzwerke [Network drawings as tools to collect ego-centred networks]. See https://www.researchgate.net/profile/Juergen_Pfeffer/publication/

265195974_Netzwerkkarten_als_Instrument_zur_Erhebung_egozentrierter_Netzwerke/links/5751e21a08ae10d93370e4e4.pdf.

Kawecki, I., Kwatera, A., Trusz, S. and Majerek, B. (2012) The social and educational situation of circular migrants' children in Poland. *Annales Universitatis Paedagogicae Cracoviensis. Studia Sociologica* [*Yearbook of the Pedagogical University of Cracow, Social Studies*] IV (2), 147–161.

Kelle, U. and Kluge, S. (2010) *Vom Einzelfall zum Typus. Fallvergleich und Fallkontrastierung in der Qualitativen Sozialforschung* [*From a Case to a Type. Case Comparison and Case Contrasting in the Qualitative Social Research*]. Wiesbaden: Vs Verlag für Sozialwissenschaften.

King, R. (2002) Towards a new map of European migration. *International Journal of Population Geography* 8 (2), 89–106.

Krappmann, L., Lob-Hüdepohl, A., Bohmeyer, A. and Kurzke-Maasmeier, S. (eds) (2009) *Bildung für junge Flüchtlinge – ein Menschenrecht: Erfahrungen, Grundlagen und Perspektiven* [*Education for Young Refugees – a Human Right: Experiences, Basics and Perspectives*]. Bielefeld: Bertelsmann.

Laoire, C.N., Carpena-Méndez, F. and Tyrrell, N. (2011) *Childhood and Migration in Europe: Portraits of Mobility, Identity and Belonging in Contemporary Ireland*. Farnham: Ashgate Publishing.

McBrien, J.L. (2005) Educational needs and barriers for refugee students in the United States: A review of the literature. *Review of Educational Research* 75 (3), 329–364.

Morrice, L. (2012) Learning and refugees: Recognizing the darker side of transformative learning. *Adult Education Quarterly* 63 (2), 251–271.

Neumann, U., Niedrig, H., Schroeder, J. and Seukwa, L.H. (2003) *Lernen am Rande der Gesellschaft : Bildungsinstitutionen im Spiegel von Flüchtlingsbiografien* [*Learning at the Periphery of the Society: Educational Institutions through the Lens of Refugee Biographies*]. Münster: Waxmann.

Niedrig, H. (2005) Der Bildungsraum junger Flüchtlinge [The education space of young refugees]. In F. Hamburger, B. Tarek and H. Merle (eds) *Migration und Bildung: über das Verhältnis von Anerkennung und Zumutung in der Einwanderungsgesellschaft* [*Migration and Education: About the Relationship between Recognition and Impertinence in the Immigration Society*] (pp. 257–278). Wiesbaden: VS Verlag für Sozialwissenschaften.

Overwien, B. (2013) Informelles Lernen – Ein Begriff aus dem internationalen Kontext etabliert sich in Deutschland [Informal learning – A term from the international context gets established in Germany]. In S. Hornberg (ed.) *Erziehung und Bildung in der Weltgesellschaft. Festschrift für Christel Adick* [*Education in the World Society. Festschrift for Christel Adick*] (pp. 97–112). Münster: Waxmann.

Pinson, H., Arnot, M. and Candappa, M. (eds) (2010) *Education, Asylum and the Non-Citizen Child: The Politics of Compassion and Belonging*. New York: Palgrave Macmillan.

Rakhkochkine, A. (2010) Bildungssituation der Kinder zirkulärer Migranten [Education of circular migrants]. *Tertium Comparationis* 16 (2), 230–248.

Rauschenbach, T. (2008) Bildung im Kindes- und Jugendalter. Über Zusammenhänge zwischen formellen und informellen Bildungsprozessen [Education in childhood and youth. Relation between formal and informal education]. In C. Grunert and H-J. von Wensierski (eds) *Jugend und Bildung: Modernisierungsprozesse und Strukturwandel von Erziehung und Bildung am Beginn des 21. Jahrhunderts . Festschrift für Heinz-Hermann Krüger zum 60. Geburtstag* [*Youth and Education: Modernisation and Structural Changes in Education at the Beginning of the 21st Century. Festschrift for Heinz-Hermann Krüger*] (pp. 17–34). Opladen: Budrich.

Rutter, J. and Jones, C. (1998) *Refugee Education: Mapping the Field*. Stoke on Trent: Trentham Books.

Seukwa, L. (2006) *Der Habitus der Überlebenskunst: zum Verhältnis von Kompetenz und Migration im Spiegel von Flüchtlingsbiographien* [*The Ingrained Art of Survival: The Nexus between Competence and Migration as Reflected in Refugee Biographies*]. New York: Waxmann.

Siouti, I. (2012) *Transnationale Biographien. Eine biographieanalytische Studie über Transmigrationsprozesse bei der Nachfolgegeneration griechischer Arbeitsmigranten* [*Transnational Biographies. A Biographical Study about the Transnational Migration of Second Generation Greeks*]. Bielefeld: transcript Verlag.

Witzel, A. and Reiter, H. (2012) *The Problem-Centred Interview*. London: Sage.

Zetter, R. (2007) More labels, fewer refugees: Remaking the refugee label in an era of globalization. *Journal of Refugee Studies* 20 (2), 172–192.

16 Afterword

Martha Bigelow

This international volume could not be more timely, given the high numbers of displaced people worldwide and the fact that so many schools and teachers are new to the experience of teaching refugee-background students. This beautiful collection of work exemplifies how research can be done in ways that work in conjunction with the desires that many former refugees have to remake their lives in a new land, on their own terms. The chapters in this volume lead me to the following comments and questions about education for refugees and refugee-background students.

It is fascinating to read studies from so many different countries – Australia, Canada, Germany, Norway, Scotland, Sweden and the United States – discussing refugees from a wide range of countries of origin, including but not limited to Bhutan, Burma, Cambodia, Guatemala, Iraq, Somali and the Sudan. This scope of the volume also illuminates that while educators are localizing solutions to particular contexts and groups, there can also be reinventing of the wheel on a worldwide basis, which points to the need for cross-border collaboration among educators, an idea modestly suggested by Bukus for the European Union. I would ask for even broader access to curricular solutions and programmatic innovations across contexts. We need to make the education of refugee-background students a worldwide endeavor and collaboration. This collection of work makes inroads into answering a number of essential questions:

How are refugee-background students unique? It is clear that the path from danger and disaster to classrooms in a new country may share similarities with the experiences of others who cross borders under duress. But these chapters illustrate how and why it is useful and important to explore how refugee-background students may be unique, despite vast diversity between and within groups. Their perspectives may diverge from other (im)migrants who cross borders under different sociopolitical or economic circumstances. Additionally, many countries have specific laws and regulations that apply to refugees, but not to other (im)migrants. And we know that relatively few refugees are able to obtain an official refugee status compared to the millions worldwide who are displaced. The chapters in this volume show us that people with refugee backgrounds have predictably enormous differences within and across national and ethnic groups – in their stance not only toward education and language learning but also toward cultural adaptation as they may be trying to negotiate ways of sustaining cultural, religious, linguistic and other practices in a new place. Sometimes, refugee-background newcomers suddenly, and possibly jarringly, feel minoritized in multiple and intersecting ways. For example, were they the religious, ethnic or racial majority in their place of origin and then upon arrival become minoritized or stigmatized in these same ways under new societal rules or assumptions? And how does this change across regions and cultures within their new countries of resettlement? While this phenomenon of racialization occurs among other (im)migrants, it can be very different for refugee-background migrants when the host society perceives them differently than, for example, (im)migrants who cross borders without official documents (Portes & Zhou, 1993). In other words, this volume helps us to see how people who have a refugee background may be both similar and different from other border crossers, and illuminates that many refugees cross multiple borders before they arrive at their final place of resettlement (for example, see the chapter by Bukus on this issue).

What do educators of refugee-background students need to know in order to be effective with refugee-background students? This volume abundantly shows that educators need a particular and complex set of skills for teaching students who have been refugees. One of the key dispositions or commitments that teachers must have is to recognize students' strengths. For example, Montero's chapter on Rohingya self-healing through narrative shows a teaching approach as well as the need for educators to be prepared to cope with stories of trauma. Dahl, Krulatz and Torgersen's chapter documenting refugee-background students' resistance and agency with regard to which languages they perceive as necessary is an excellent example of the need for educators to uncover what refugee-background students want and need to learn and to adjust their curriculum accordingly. Pucino's chapter on strategies for coping with racist or xenophobic interactions in the United States is instructive for educators in most educational contexts these days because, unfortunately, so many refugees need to be prepared to confront hostility.

What teaching approaches work with refugee-background students? The contributors to this volume are clearly grounded in a sense of what good pedagogy should include. Readers interested in developing literacy, including initial print literacy, should consult Nakutnyy and Sterzuk's chapter as well as Omerbašić's chapter on digital landscapes of knowing. The point of departure for these authors is clearly assets oriented in how they conceptualize literacy, how they develop literacy among their students and how they both value out-of-school literacy practices. It is so important to particularize this work in the many different cultural groups from which refugee-background learners come because the answer is never exactly the same – often because out-of-school literacy assets are different for different groups.

What epistemologies are needed to do ethical research with people who have been refugees? The epistemologies and theoretical frameworks in this collection are current and carefully applied to the questions at hand. For instance, literacy is not conceptualized as only a functional or only a de/encoding cognitive process, but rather as a set of processes that occur in social contexts (see Nakutnyy and Sterzuk). We see the power of youth participatory action research in Papa's chapter, while Browder's study focusing on Chin students shows that large quantitative analyses can also help us uncover academic and English learning progress among students with limited or interrupted formal education. Ethnography is strongly present in this volume: I appreciated the chapter by Crandall, for example, because of the way he represented the voices of Ali, Shafac, Ade and Najm, as they share their stories of education pre-resettlement as well as their critiques of their education in the United States. Park and Valdez put linguistic ethnography to good use when they explore the translanguaging practices of Nepali-Bhutanese adults, which also illustrates the high-leverage pedagogy that translanguaging can be for refugee-background students. Other chapters are excellent examples of how to do qualitative inquiry via interviews through, for example, careful content analysis in the chapter by Dahl, Krulatz and Torgensen and abundant use and analysis of participants' voices in the chapter by Kahn. Pucino applies Bronfenbrenner's ecological theory to her qualitative study of Iraqi-background refugees, which reminds us of the layers of experiences and ideologies influencing students' lives.

This volume also shows that educational institutions are not necessarily set up for all refugee-background students to be successful. I join the authors in asserting that this situation should be the problem of schools and teachers, not of the refugee-background students. For example, Holmkvist, Sullivan and Westum illustrate how important it is for teachers to understand the role of trauma in the teaching and learning process. Their study documents that it is essential for teachers to understand as much as possible about post-traumatic stress disorder given the prevalence of this condition among refugee-background individuals. This is an issue that should be taken up in in-service and pre-service teacher education. Korntheuer, Gag, Anderson and Schroeder highlight other structural obstacles – namely, how students who have been refugees can be systematically excluded from vocational education in Germany. In addition, Khan's research shows how refugee-background youth in Scotland can succeed, despite serious structural barriers to education. These chapters illustrate how crucial it is for educators to be vigilant about the ways in which refugee-background students' needs may not be served in educational institutions. We see that most schooling experiences were not designed intentionally for this population, so it is our responsibility to flex systems and institutions in their best interest, as defined by the students.

Ultimately, all of the chapters in this volume stand *with* refugee-background individuals and families in their efforts to learn new languages, adapt to new contexts and assert their own representations of personhood on their own terms. Readers can settle into this volume knowing that the representations of the experiences of people who have been refugees – their voices, their desires and their best interests – are at the heart of the work. In this respect, this volume is an advocacy statement for quality education for refugee-background students that builds on what they already know and fully recognizes what they may have experienced *en route* to classrooms in unfamiliar countries and cultures. I feel deep gratitude to the authors and the editors of this collection for their work in nuancing the diversity among people who have refugee backgrounds, noticing and documenting their assets and explaining so carefully the many facets of adjustment they experience in the resettlement process.

Reference

Portes, A. and Zhou, M. (1993) The new second-generation: Segmented assimilation and its variants. *Annals of the American Academy of Political and Social Sciences* 530, 74–96.

Index

Academic Language and Literacy Diagnostic (ALLD), 29
action research, 9, 96, 159, 162, 258
activity theory, 6, 34
adult learners
    deficit perspective, 3, 84
    educational goals, 107–19
    older, 7, 49–63, 153, 258
    research gaps, 1, 34
    trauma, 10, 177–88
Afghanistan, 111, 216, 228, 231–2
agency
    and citizenship policy, 146, 149–56
    and discrimination, 212, 219–21
    and language learning, 153–6, 257
    and literacy, 87
    perceptions of refugees, 3, 5, 9, 210, 237–8
    student goals, 113
apprenticeship programs see vocational education
Arabic, 42, 82, 84–5, 87–90, 180, 214, 250
asset-based perspectives, 4, 7, 51, 62, 67–8, 128, 141, 168, 182, 188, 257
Australia, 4, 8, 11, 84, 125–8, 132, 141

Benadiri, 36, 42
Bhutan see also Nepali-Bhutanese students, 53–4
bilingualism, 51–3, 160–1, 166, 168, 173–4
Bourdieu, P., 127, 162
Brexit, 144–6, 154–6
Bronfenbrenner, U., 10, 208, 211–12, 219–20, 258
Bulgaria, 247
Burma, see also Myanmar, 17–18, 20–2, 26, 66–9, 74, 94, 96–102, 106, 228
Burmese language, 66, 71–2, 74, 76, 78, 98
Burundi, 151, 234

Cambodian students, 9, 159–74
Canada, 4, 7, 82, 85–9, 94–7, 99–101, 106
capital
    aspirational, 165–6, 173
    cultural, 9, 35, 147, 162

    familial, 165, 173–4
    linguistic, 35, 127–8, 168–9, 173–4
    navigational, 159, 170, 173–4
    resistant, 165, 170–4
    social, 5, 9, 127–8, 169–70, 173–4
    spiritual, 174
    symbolic, 126–7, 139–40
case study
    historical context, 44
    instrumental, 95–6
    qualitative, 35, 82, 128, 229
    two-case, 196
Chin
    refugee status, 20–1
    students with limited or interrupted formal education (SLIFE), 6, 17–18, 22–6, 258
citizenship
    British policy, 144–56
    denial of, 96, 102
    education, 8–9, 108–9, 144–56
    and institutional discrimination, 195–6
    language requirements, 146–7
    status, 2, 11
code-switching, 51, 60–1, 77–8
coding of data, 55, 85, 111, 149, 164, 180–1, 183, 213, 229, 242, 245
collaborative vocabulary building, 54–7
college see higher education
communities of practice, 10, 225–6, 231, 233, 235–8
community cultural wealth, 159–65, 169, 172–3
Critical Race Theory (CRT), 160–2, 169
critical sociocultural theory, 66, 68–9
crosslinguistic awareness, 49, 52, 55–62
Cruickshank, K., 84
cultural competence, 93
culturally relevant pedagogy, 68, 82, 90
culturally sustaining pedagogy, 52, 68–9, 77–9, 95, 257–8
Cultural Practices of Literacy Study (CPLS), 83
curriculum
    citizenship, 8–9, 146–8, 151–2, 156

culturally sensitive, 199
hidden, 8, 107, 118–19
and literacy practices, 6, 67, 77, 83, 89
media critique, 221
student input, 118, 156, 257
student transitions, 136–7
theme-based, 45
translanguaging in, 51–63
transparency, 252
and trauma, 93–4, 102
writing, 7, 44–6

Dari, 111, 180
deficit orientation see deficit perspective
deficit perspective
  disruption of, 66, 68–9, 74, 79, 128, 160
  and literacy practices, 83–4
  and translanguaging, 49, 62
  and perceptions of refugees, 3, 5, 154–5, 210
Devanagari, 54
digital landscapes of knowing, 7, 66–79, 257
digital language experience approach (D-LEA), 94–5, 97, 102
discourse
  academic, 29, 168, 173, 200
  deficit, 69, 75, 78, 160–2
  macro-level, 210, 212, 219–21
  media, 10, 218–19, 221
  political, 208–11
  of power, 100
discrimination
  institutional, 10, 193, 195–7, 199–205, 209–10
  structural, 193, 195–7, 200–1, 204
  student experiences, 208, 210–21
  systemic, 191, 195, 199
  teachers, 114
domains of transition, 130–40
drawings, student-generated, 9, 58–60, 62, 76, 78, 84, 125, 128–38, 244

ecological theory of development, 10, 210–14, 216, 219–21, 258
English as an Additional Language (EAL) see English for Speakers of Other Languages (ESOL)
English language see also English for Speakers of Other Languages (ESOL)
  and citizenship education, 146–7
  and discrimination, 214, 216, 220

and employment, 149–50, 156
as lingua franca, 149–50
literacy development, 88–9, 94–6, 102
perceived importance of, 107–12, 115–19, 152, 155–6, 168
phonetics, 61
proficiency, 8, 23–9, 57, 108–12, 147, 163, 232, 236
for self-advocacy, 151, 154
and students with limited or interrupted formal education (SLIFE), 17–18, 20–9
English Language Learners (ELLs) see English Learners (EL)
English Learners (EL), 6, 9, 17–18, 20–29, 34, 36, 43, 57–8, 62, 102, 220
English as a Second Language (ESL) see English for Speakers of Other Languages (ESOL)
English for Speakers of Other Languages (ESOL)
  and citizenship education, 147–55
  and first language use, 49–50, 52, 168
  high school classes, 18, 21–3, 35–9
  literacy development, 88–9, 94–6, 102
  placement testing, 24, 54
  transition out of, 8, 94, 125–40
  and translanguaging, 50, 52–3, 60
  and writing experiences, 37–9, 45
ethnography
  case studies, 33–47, 125, 128–30
  critical approach to, 35, 161
  linguistic, 258
  of literacy practices, 70, 83–4
Europe, 1–2, 42, 107, 110, 114, 248
European Union, 8, 11, 144, 146, 244, 252, 256

Facebook, 43–6, 70–2, 75–6
field notes, 49, 55, 70, 128, 164, 229
focus groups, 177–8, 180–1, 183, 186–7, 196
France, 248–9
funds of knowledge, 5, 7, 45, 50–3, 55, 60, 62, 68, 126, 128, 140, 162

García, O., 51–2, 57
German language, 193–4, 196, 200, 244–5, 248–50
Germany, 4, 10, 191–205, 241–51, 258
grounded theory, 229–30
Guatemalan students, 9, 159–74

Harklau, L., 136–7
hidden curriculum, 8, 107, 118–19
higher education
    access, 108–10, 113, 193, 225–6
    aspirations, 166
    benefits for refugee-background students, 10, 225–38
    challenges for refugee-background students, 225–6, 229, 231, 236
    personal growth, 230–8
    writing, 41
high school see secondary education
home languages
    classroom use, 49–55, 61–3, 67
    legitimizing, 52
    literacy in, 4, 6, 18–19, 22–9, 50, 62, 78, 113
Home Language Survey, 18–19

identity
    enactment, 72, 77–9
    development, 140, 225–7, 231, 236–8
    national, 9
    personal history, 46
information-sharing networks, 7, 85–90
institutional discrimination see discrimination
integration
    and citizenship policy, 144–56
    community, 8, 89, 108, 115, 118–19, 186
    educational, 9, 82, 90, 192, 198, 203, 243, 252–3
    and language learning, 109–10, 115, 118–19, 149–50, 153–6
interpreters, 53, 115, 187–8, 244
interrupted schooling see also students with limited or interrupted formal education (SLIFE), 6, 19, 23–8, 127, 247–51
interviews
    qualitative, 130, 148, 219
    multimodal, 9, 52, 70, 72
    semi-structured, 36–7, 70, 85, 110–11, 180, 196, 212, 229, 244
Iraqi students, 10, 208–21, 258
Islamophobia, 208–212, 215–20

Kakuma refugee camp, 36–7, 39–41
Karen
    ethnic group 7–8, 69, 71, 126–8, 129, 132–3
    language see also Po Karen, 66, 71–2, 74, 78
    students 126–8, 133–6
Khmer, 163, 167–8, 171–4
K'iche', 163, 165–6, 168–9

language ideology, 117
legal status, 160, 192, 198, 200–4, 250–1
literacy
    artifacts, 85
    contexts of, 6, 68
    development, 83–4, 88–9, 94–6, 102
    emergent, 24, 26, 82–3, 94–5, 98, 127
    L1 (first language), 4, 6, 18–19, 22–9, 50, 62, 78, 82, 113
    mediators, 7, 84, 87–8, 90
    multimodal, 52, 66, 70–4, 78–9, 84, 129
    out-of-school practices, 33–4, 67, 69–70, 77–9, 85, 87, 257
    as a sociocultural practice, 34, 82, 258
    Western conceptions of, 50
literary analysis, 33, 38–40
Lorenzatti, M., 84

mainstream education
    first language use, 168
    transition to, 8, 94, 125–41
    writing instruction, 34–9, 44
Malaysia, 20–1
Maryland, 19, 21
meaning-making
    collaborative, 57, 74
    and literacy practices, 6, 82–90
    and translanguaging pedagogy, 49–50, 55–8, 62
mental health see also post-traumatic stress disorder (PTSD), 92–4, 99, 102, 150, 155, 180, 182
mentoring, 203–5, 238
mentor texts, 39, 95
metalinguistic awareness, 49, 52, 55–62
microsystem, 210, 212–16, 218, 220–21
migration
    involuntary/forced migration, 11, 19, 83, 86, 160, 180, 196, 202, 218, 241–9, 251–2
    multidirectional, 244, 249
    multiple, 11, 241–5, 249, 252, 257
    voluntary, 11, 241–6, 249–52
missing schooling see also students with limited or interrupted formal education (SLIFE), 23–7, 247

motivation, 114, 116–17, 204–5, 211–12, 244, 248, 251–3
multilingualism
   as asset, 52–3, 71–4, 77–8, 160
   and digital texts, 7, 66–7, 73–4
multimodal texts, 7, 9, 52, 70–2, 78–9, 129
Muslims
   British citizenship, 147–8
   Burmese, 69, 74, 76
   discrimination against, 10, 148, 208–212, 214–20, 257
   Myanmar, see also Burma, 17–18, 20–2, 26, 66, 68–9, 74, 94, 96–102, 106, 228

narrative analysis, 8, 92, 95–101, 106
Native Language Literacy Assessment (NLLA), 29
native speaker myth, 63
naturalization see citizenship
Nepal, 53–4
Nepali-Bhutanese students, 49, 51–63, 258
Nepali language, 49, 53–4, 56–8; 60–2
New Literacy Studies, 82, 84
Norway, 4, 8, 107–19
Norwegian, 8, 108–13, 115–16
numeracy, 59–60, 94

oracy, 83, 87
out-of-school
   literacy practices, 33–4, 67, 69–70, 77–9, 85, 87, 257
   lives, 83–4
   writing, 45–6

personal history, 44, 46–7, 71, 148
photovoice, 9, 159–74
Po Karen, 66, 69, 70, 71
police, 171–2
positionality of researchers, 5, 36–7, 53, 69, 112, 148, 163, 214, 230
post-traumatic stress disorder (PTSD) see also mental health
   and language learning, 179–80, 183–6
   pedagogical responses to, 183–7
   teacher perceptions of, 9, 178, 181–7, 258
prosocial behavior, 92, 94, 98–102
proximal process, 212, 216–18, 220

qualitative meta-analysis, 197
Qur'an, 40–1, 84

reification, 236–7
resettlement
   challenges, 66–8, 71–2, 74, 83, 209, 220, 225, 229, 257
   and integration see integration
   and language learning, 50–4, 109–11
   qualifications for, 2–3
   and students with limited or interrupted formal education (SLIFE), 18–21, 27–9
resilience, 3, 5, 7, 83, 94, 99–100, 180–3, 186, 188, 205, 219
Rohingya, 7–8, 92, 94–102, 257
Romania, 248–9, 251
Rwanda, 151–2, 228, 234

Scotland see also United Kingdom, 4, 9, 147–8, 153, 155, 258
secondary education
   access to, 193–5, 198–200, 204
   discrimination, 212–21
   educational background, 20–1
   English language learning, 18, 21–3, 35–9, 114–16
   transition to mainstream, 8, 94–5, 125–41
   writing, 33–47
segregation, 199–200
sheltered instruction, 126–30, 137, 139
social media, 43–6, 70–3, 75–6
social networks, 67, 84–7, 89, 154–5, 169–70, 174
Somali Bantu, 36–40, 42, 46
Somali students, 6–7, 33–47, 149, 153
South Sudan, 82, 85–7
Spain, 247–9
Spanish, 163, 165, 168–9, 171, 173
standardized testing, 7, 33, 37–40, 160, 213, 227
statistical analysis, 24–7
Street, B., 84
structural discrimination see discrimination
structural narrative analysis, 92, 97–8, 106
student-centered instruction, 10, 50–2, 139, 173
students with limited or interrupted formal education (SLIFE)
   as co-researchers, 160, 163
   and higher education, 225, 231–3
   identification of, 6, 17, 19, 23–8
   implications for schools, 28–9, 95

and language learning, 6, 18–23, 25–9, 62, 127, 258
as writers, 33–4
survey, 110–11, 121–22
Sweden, 4, 177–88
Swedish language, 178, 180, 182–4, 186–7
symbolic politics, 144–6, 151
Syria, 250–1

teachers
biases, 84, 113–14, 210
bilingual, 154, 173, 168
perceptions of, 38, 42–5, 49, 88, 137–9
roles of, 34, 40–2, 44–6, 110, 133, 218, 257
and translanguaging pedagogy, 50–4, 57–63, 173
and trauma, 94–7, 102, 177–88
views on language learning, 113–17
tertiary education see higher education
Thailand, 20, 66, 71, 74
transit countries, 242, 244, 246–7, 249–51
translanguaging
and meaning-making, 49–50, 55–8, 62
pedagogy, 7, 49–63, 173, 258
and writing, 56, 58–61
translocal knowledge, 7, 66–7, 69–71, 77, 79
trauma
and altruism, 99–100
classroom impacts, 9, 93, 258
and English education, 150, 155
narratives, 94–6, 101
self-healing, 7–8, 93–4, 98–9, 101–2
and spirituality, 101
trauma-informed teaching, 9, 93, 186–7

unaccompanied minors, 1, 161, 197–8
United Kingdom, 4, 9, 109, 144–56
United Nations Convention on Refugees, 20
United Nations High Commissioner for Refugees (UNHCR), 2–3, 100, 106
United States
Chin refugees, 18, 20–6
higher education, 226
language learning, 50, 109–10, 214
refugee resettlement in, 4, 38–39, 42, 46, 53–4, 67, 69–71, 208–11
Universal Design for Learning (UDL), 10, 184–5

vocational education, 10, 113–15, 141, 191–205, 258

Williams, C., 51
writing
activity genre research, 33–4
authentic opportunities for, 38–41, 44–5, 95, 97
collaborative/community, 45–6
college level, 41
legitimate audiences, 7, 45–6, 97
lives, 6–7, 34, 45
process, 33, 45, 55, 58
and translanguaging, 56, 58–61

Yosso, T.J., 162, 164–5, 170